OUR SECRETS ARE THE SAME

OUR SECRETS ARE THE SAME

The enduring friendship at the heart of Simple Minds

JIM KERR & CHARLIE BURCHILL

WITH GRAEME THOMSON

CONSTABLE

CONSTABLE

First published in Great Britain in 2025 by Constable

1 3 5 7 9 10 8 6 4 2

A CIP catalogue record for this book
is available from the British Library.

ISBN: 978-1-40872-089-9 (hardback)
ISBN: 978-1-40872-088-2 (trade paperback)

Typeset in Palatino and Filosofia by SX Composing DTP, Rayleigh, Essex

Printed and bound in Great Britain by Clays Ltd, Elcograf S.p.A.

Papers used by Constable are from well-managed forests
and other responsible sources.

MIX
Paper | Supporting
responsible forestry
FSC® C104740

Constable
An imprint of
Little, Brown Book Group
Carmelite House
50 Victoria Embankment
London EC4Y 0DZ

The authorised representative
in the EEA is
Hachette Ireland
8 Castlecourt Centre, Dublin 15,
D15 XTP3, Ireland
(email: info@hbgi.ie)

An Hachette UK Company
www.hachette.co.uk

www.littlebrown.co.uk

This book is dedicated to all who have opened their hearts and minds to the sound and songs of Simple Minds.
– Charlie Burchill & Jim Kerr

Contents

Preface: Let Glasgow Shake

Easter 1977.

It is eleven o'clock on a Sunday morning. Charlie Burchill and I are standing outside a converted bungalow across the road from our not-much-missed alma mater, Holyrood Secondary School, in Glasgow's Southside.

Seventeen and ready for something. Anything.

Inside is John Milarky, who has apparently forgotten that we have arranged to come and discuss putting a band together.

After much banging and yelling at the door, eventually John opens up. He is wearing a pair of jeans and nothing else. Rake thin. Bare feet. He has left his girlfriend in bed upstairs. In my memory, her high heels and underwear are scattered around the living room. In more innocent times, this guy used to be the principal altar boy. It's an impressive transformation.

John goes straight into it: 'I've only got a couple of songs, but it's gonna be a bit like this.'

We expect him to play us a cassette of his songs – but no. We are getting a performance. One we will never forget.

John is quite camp. He certainly smokes camp, blowing the smoke theatrically out of the side of his mouth. He lights a cigarette, puffs nonchalantly into the air and picks up his Les Paul – it is a real Les Paul, not a copy. The guitar strap is a piece of frayed rope. He slings it over his bare torso and plugs into a Vox amp. There is no microphone stand. The flex is taped up the wall and then across the ceiling, from where the mic hangs down, somewhat menacingly, at head height.

Charlie and I are in punk heaven.

1

I think, He looks a bit like Richard Hell.

I think, He could be our John the Baptist.

John plays a song called 'Pablo Picasso'. He plays it as though his life depends on it. He is snarling and spitting, slashing at the Les Paul. It is one of the greatest, bravest performances I will ever witness.

Sunday morning. Suburban Glasgow. Old grannies and kids are coming back from Mass.

And the fucking windows are shaking.

John asks if we are in.

My God, yes – we are in.

Intro Music

'Our Secrets Are the Same'
(Kerr/Burchill)
Side A
(Vocal Mix)

Kerr/

Charlie Burchill. 'Charles', always, to his mother.

Best friend. *Bon vivant*. Sore loser. World's Worst Shopper. Super polite. Terminally indecisive. Tenacious. Tough. Loyal. Competitive. Killer smile. Infectious laugh. Voracious reader. Mystery man. Great, great guitar player. Slow to anger but, oh boy, when he finally blows . . .

My internal movie projector contains so many enduring images of Charlie.

Perhaps surprisingly, I don't immediately think about us being on stage together in Simple Minds at Live Aid, or the Nelson Mandela Birthday Tribute concert. I'm not picturing the O2 or Madison Square Garden.

Instead, the images begin at the point when I first laid eyes on him at eight years old. A chubby king of the castle, playing happily in the sandpit.

I see Charlie walking home from school. He is wearing a blue overcoat, cherished LPs by Alice Cooper and the Doors under his arm.

I think about our landscape moments. Life in widescreen. Hitchhiking around Europe. Me and him on the side of the road in the rain. Sleeping in the shadow of Teatro Romano in Verona. Travelling the autobahn, happy as birds, not knowing where we would rest that night or where we would be the next morning.

I think about our fear and loathing moments: the acid and the TV evangelist. Me and him in a queue to catch the cheapest flight possible from Delhi to Kathmandu over one of the most precarious mountain ranges in the world. Having a laugh at an old guy in airline uniform, pushing bags and cases around. *Ha, ha! He looks like he's about to drop dead any minute* – then we see him climb into the cockpit . . .

Reading poetry by the Yamuna River.

Lugging a bag full of books through the Australian outback.

In Moscow, determined to find the bench in the Patriarch's Ponds park where the opening scene of Mikhail Bulgakov's *The Master and Margarita* is set.

Hiking through the desert in Jordan, heading for the Dead Sea.

So many shared moments. And then the COVID pandemic. What we came to call 'The Plague of Lighthouse Keepers'. In the bestilled world of Sicily, where we both now call home, it was back to fundamentals: just me and him looking at each other. 'What are we doing?' 'I don't know!' But Charlie had the tools of his trade in hand, and as long as he had those, and there were peanuts in the minibar in the room next door, and still a few bottles of whisky in the cellar, I knew we were going to be all right.

* * *

Since the age of fourteen there has been no world for me without Charlie Burchill. We first met when we were eight. By our early teens we were fast friends. From that point our bond has taken many forms: singer and guitarist (and the rest) in Simple Minds; intrepid travel buddies; co-delinquents; night trippers; songwriting partners; neighbours all over the world – and still, more than half a century later, the best of friends.

Together we have embarked upon what for many of our generation would seem the ultimate adventure: forming a rock band from ground zero and forcing the altimeter up, up, up, until we touched the most elevated levels of success. For almost half a century, with Simple Minds we have navigated the sudden pressure drops, the changing currents and headwinds of fortune, good and bad.

What did we discover? We concluded that life is not so much about finding yourself as creating yourself along the way. We found that there is no pre-written script; the world opens up to those who open up to it. That you can indeed transcend whatever circumstances in which you were born.

Charlie and I, it transpired, were committed existentialists before we had any clue what it meant; free agents determining our development through acts of the will, always in the process of making or creating who we are as our lives unfold.

In the seventies, I spent the last years of our schooldays in Toryglen, in the Southside of Glasgow, in a waking dream. I would powerfully imagine that it might be possible for me to successfully spend my life working within music. By then, rock music had become an overriding passion. Dreaming about it would never be enough. At some point I had to rise up and forcefully turn my fantasy into reality. Sure, the world needs dreamers, but it also needs doers.

For us both, Simple Minds became a call to action. It was our means of making something from nothing. In the desire to create a new reality for ourselves, we each had distinct attributes. No question, Charlie and I needed each other. We challenged our apparent destiny, the narrow path that society (still) lays out in front of working-class kids like us.

Instead, we sought a challenge based on the notion of building something original, redefining for us what 'work' means, embracing the unknown with heart and soul.

The band we formed became our crusade. If we are permitted the conceit of a legacy, perhaps ours is to illustrate the value of dedicating your life to a cause, to take a mighty swing at an almost impossible target, to conjure up a world of ideas and pursue them all with utter commitment.

Simple Minds are known worldwide as a group. For Charlie and me, however, after a certain amount of time it became a way of being. In the sense that everything else that has occurred in our lives has been filtered through the prism of our roles in Simple Minds. The band is created in our image, yes, but it also shapes how we live. Music became our way of navigating the world: our compass, our propellor. Eventually music became our passport to all manner of experiences that were once unimaginable.

We remain locked in a friendship which merges intellect, spirit, dreams and passion. Fun, too. Somehow there is a fluidity there. Our relationship is solid but it has never been rigid. When the storms roll in, as they inevitably do from time to time, we have learned that we will bend but never break.

Time passes. Life changes. People come and go in the same way that branches fall off a tree. When stasis kicks in, deadwood occurs. Meanwhile, the roots and essence of our relationship stay strong as new experiences, new adventures, new ways of being come through.

Almost from day one, Charlie and I have relied on an unspoken dialogue. It's a legacy of the people who brought us up, and of the fact that socially, geographically and demographically we are so close: the same school, the same religion, the same working-class attitudes. We don't discuss these values; we're not even proud of them, as such. They're just there.

There are rare times when misunderstandings arise or we are not on the same page, but underpinning everything is a clear shorthand. It's not a mafiosi code, exactly – or is it? Charlie will never talk about Simple Minds in an arrogant way, or in a way that's too self-aware. But he will very quickly say, 'We can't do that, we're Simple Minds.' Perhaps all gangs and all tribes do that, but he holds fast to it.

Who is Charlie Burchill?

To lean on a stock phrase, I know him like the back of my hand. On stage, I look around and he is right there, always; exactly where I expect him to be. Where I need him to be. I know him better than I know anyone, including my own family. When it comes to certain codes, we don't even have to speak. Charlie will only need to move a muscle on his face, or I will see a glint in the eye, and I will know exactly what he's thinking (and I usually know *why* he's thinking it, too: *Oh God, here we go!*).

And yet no matter how profound that connection, you can never know anyone in totality. Because here's the thing: how well do I *really* know the back of my hand? Do I actually know how it works? Do I really understand what's going on under there?

Charlie is the deepest guy I have ever met. There's a lot of mystery involved with him, which keeps the relationship fresh and vital. In my view, it's not so much that he doesn't allow others to access all his many parts, more that he himself won't open up to them.

Like his father, Charlie is incredibly polite to everybody he meets. He would never sit in a taxi without asking the driver their life story. (This sometimes drives me crazy.) He will acknowledge people and treat them exceptionally well. With our crew, he knows the names of everyone's kids. He makes it his business. Why? Because he wants them to feel at ease and acknowledged, and because he likes them and appreciates their work. But I know that if I were to sit with the bus driver, they would find out more about me in half an hour than they would find out about Charlie by chatting with him for five years.

He doesn't reveal. He retains. Part of his politeness means that he would think that telling you about himself was too indulgent, or that he was bothering you with his worries. I'm much more verbal. If I have a problem, it's a puzzle. I think out loud, working my way through it. Charlie doesn't think out loud. He puts his head down and plugs in.

I have never met anyone more tenacious. Charlie is a hedgehog. He simply bores into a challenge, ceaselessly. Me? I'm more of a fox; sometimes a scaredy cat. I'll analyse risk and reward, adopting and dropping strategies along the way. But Charlie is ever willing to dig deeper. Working through the night. No thoughts of ever giving up. Rarely blinking.

Many times, I have owed my livelihood to those character traits. There was a period when I thought the game was up with Simple Minds. Charlie's attitude, unspoken, was, *This is going to continue, because I'm not even going to entertain the idea that it won't.*

On the surface he is a sweet, smiling guy – but he will not relent. He will wait it out. He has a different calculation of time from me, and I've learned that he is right. It took me a long while to accept that patience is vitally important in terms of survival; in the game that we're in, yes, but also in the game of life. Charlie's willingness to wait things out is remarkable.

The writing on the wall? He doesn't give it the time of day.

'Our Secrets Are the Same'
(Burchill/Kerr)
Side B
(Guitar Mix)

Burchill/

Jim Kerr.

Staunch friend. Extreme enthusiast. Born optimist. Obsessive. Dreamer and romantic. Tough cookie. Big brother. 'Monk'. Strategist. Early to rise (and to bed). Charmer. Chancer. Cheerleader. Storyteller. Loyal. Loner. Leader.

Jim and I grew up in the same street in Toryglen. Almost sixty years later we still live in the same street. In Taormina, Sicily, my house is one minute's walk from his.

We've travelled so far and yet, when it comes to our relationship with one another, essentially we have always been in the same place.

* * *

Jim and I have interacted in the same way since our schooldays. No fawning, no backslapping. Precious few hugs. We laugh a lot. We are mutually curious. The flow of ideas in both directions remains strong. We share book recommendations, songs, films. I am always making music. Jim is always reading, writing, listening to podcasts. Absorbing stimuli. And it shows. He puts an immense amount of thought into everything. He doesn't have a television; whenever he wants to watch the football, he comes to mine.

The fundamentals were established decades ago. He is the big brother in his family; I am the youngest in mine. It doesn't tell the whole story, but it tells a good part of it. I think back to our teenage hitchhiking trips around Europe,

9

before we even started Simple Minds. At times when we were travelling, we would come to a junction: 'Right, what are we going to do?' Jim would always have some strategy. In some ways, I suppose, I have always been happy to put my trust in him and follow.

I always sensed huge potential in Jim. I felt it even when we were very young. I recognised that he had The Thing. And if you don't have The Thing, you don't have anything. When we began forming bands, Jim didn't play anything and initially he didn't want to be the singer. But somehow already he was the glue that held everything together.

Many great musicians and fine people have made lasting and significant contributions to the group, but I maintain that Simple Minds would never have happened on any level without him. To say that we would never have had the success we have had is on the one hand transparently obvious, because as the singer and lyricist and focal point he brings so much to it — but it goes beyond that.

It is Jim who has choreographed Simple Minds from the start. He still does. He provides an overview. He creates a context for anything we do. And he has a way of making you feel like what you are doing is important and special. Jim's optimism isn't simply optimism for the sake of it. His enthusiasm is utterly natural and heartfelt, and it has always guided our band.

You can have endless reserves of talent; if you don't have a Jim, you're nowhere. I wanted to play guitar. I had some aptitude and aspirations, and I would have done something with them, no question, but I would never have possessed the drive and the focus required to create — and sustain — a group, an idea, like Simple Minds under my own steam. For that, believe me: you need a Jim.

The flip side is that he is capable of driving me to the end of my tether. Jim routinely gets up at 5 a.m. I don't. I may in fact not be all that long in bed at that hour. Walking through an airport at 7.30 in the morning the day after a seven-month tour has ended, he will say: 'So you'd better start writing for a new album.' It goes on and on: *We need to do this, then we need to do that.* I sigh. 'We've just this second finished a tour, Jim! Can you give us a break for a minute?' Two days later he's still pushing. It's relentless. A little obsessive, even. Over the years it has proved to be a powerfully necessary trait, but at times I think, *I'm going to drug him. I'm going to put something in his drink.* It was perhaps too much for some former band members.

We don't talk about what makes it work. We never have. It's never seemed necessary. Jim and I have always operated under the auspices of an unwritten manifesto. It isn't anything as tangible as a codified set of rules, but we have established through a tacit understanding that there are things that our band can and can't do – in terms of music, naturally, but also in terms of how we handle ourselves.

We are very different in many respects. As in any good long-term relationship, parts of the other person remain a mystery. The obvious factor within the context of Simple Minds is that Jim doesn't play an instrument, and I don't write words. It means we still have the capacity to surprise each other. Jim's lyrics come from a place I could never hope to access; he has a special way of expressing emotion.

On the other hand, if I play Jim the same three chords three times in half an hour, he hears three new songs. Every time, he will see different pictures. I value that. As a musician, there is a point where you have to be very careful about how you use the knowledge and the skills you pick up as you become more accomplished. Part of you always strives to remain a child and keep seeing wonder in the simple things. Jim has that quality. I can be playing absent-mindedly on the keyboard, and he'll say, 'That's dynamite!' I'll say, 'It's C to G.

As basic as it gets.' But he is already seeing the pictures. I'm still surprised that Jim gets surprised by things.

It's good to know that even now we have a lot still to discover about each other.

1

Connection

We are born alone. We die alone. And in between we spend our lives looking for something. Connection. That's all we want. Every once in a while, we might find it in a true friend.

– Christopher Walken

November 1967. The first big sliding-doors moment.

I am eight years old and we are moving from our tenement flat in Govanhill to a new housing scheme in Toryglen.

As the removal van containing all the Kerrs' worldly possessions pulls up outside perhaps the tallest building I have ever seen, I am told to go out and play with my younger brother Paul. The street is partly a building site. The future is still under construction.

It is a Saturday. No school for us. Within minutes we come across a gaggle of similarly aged boys playing on top of what appears to be a castle made from builders' materials. I recognise one of them: a friend that I'd gone to school with in Govanhill called Choccy Bradley. His family has also moved to Toryglen. Choccy is playing with another boy who is sitting at the summit of this tower of stone and sand. King of the castle. 'Can we play?' I ask. 'Yeah,' says Choccy, and gestures to the boy. 'This is Charlie.'

I won't forget the first sight of him. Beatific. That smile. Charlie. Charlie Bubble. There aren't many overweight kids in Glasgow in 1967; Charlie is practically spherical. Charlie Bubble. The Bub, or Bubble, for short. For some of us, that will always be his nickname. Decades later old school friends will ask: 'How's the Bub?'

I discover that Charlie now lives in the same street as me. What I can't possibly know at the age of eight is that he will become my best friend, songwriting partner and co-conspirator in the great adventure that our lives become.

Sliding doors.

What would have happened had fate not got inside my mum's head?

Kerr/

My life is filled with several great episodes of coincidence. Sliding-doors moments. Sometimes literally. I met both my ex-wives at elevators; the first when I was coming out, the second while I was waiting to go in.

Arguably the most profound instance was my family's decision to move to Toryglen in 1967. In the early sixties, they were knocking down our building in Kidston Street. It wasn't personal. They were knocking down buildings all over the Gorbals, where my parents had grown up and were still living at the time of my arrival.

Just as Londoners are all too keen to declare themselves cockneys, Glaswegians love to say that they hail from the Gorbals. It oozes authenticity. A taste of the Mean Streets. I was born in Rottenrow maternity hospital on 9 July 1959, but the first night I spent at home was in Kidston Street, where Mum and Dad had a one-bedroom flat. Charlie was born only fifteen minutes away, yet it was far enough to make a difference. I was christened in St Francis Church in the heart of the Gorbals; Charlie was christened in St Bonaventure's in the Oatlands. I win. It's possible that I still jibe him about this.

After leaving Kidston Street, our little family moved a mile up the road to another one-bedroom tenement in Carfin Street in Govanhill, where we stayed for three years. I clearly remember my brother Paul being born there. Privacy was at a premium; I was all of three-and-a-half and privy to so much. Many of my mother's numerous sisters were there to keep me amused. Later, I remember being sent to Mr Rodgers's shop at the bottom of the street. Three-and-a-half, mind you. I was given the note and told to hold the money tight. I toddled off proudly to buy rolls for everyone and Mr Rodgers gifted me a small box of Cadbury's Milk Tray chocolates because he knew that Paul had arrived.

I had a brother and it was great. Until now, it had all been about me; suddenly it wasn't. I don't remember feeling any jealousy. What I do remember hearing almost immediately was, 'You're the big brother now, and it's your job to look after your wee brother.' At an early age that was profoundly instilled in me.

In time, after Paul arrived, we made the move to Toryglen. The area was a twenty-minute walk from Govanhill through a wasteland of old chemical factories and garages called the Malls Mire. It's a nature reserve now; it certainly wasn't back then. In strictly geographical terms, it was hardly a great leap into the unknown. And yet the Malls Mire felt like our equator. We were crossing from the Old World to the New World. We were leaving behind the tenements, widely regarded as Dickensian slums, and heading into the future.

This is where the hand of fate played its first card. Sliding doors.

My dad had saved up before my parents had married and as a result they owned their first flat. They took on a mortgage, which was quite unusual then. I remember my dad telling me later that his mother wasn't happy at all when he took on a mortgage because it was debt, and debt was bad news. There was also, I think, an element of, *Who do you think you are?* But he was undeterred, and Mum and Dad had their own flat in the Gorbals and then Govanhill.

When it was time to relocate again, Mum decided at the very last minute that she didn't want to move her family into the tenement that my father had already arranged to buy in the north side of Glasgow. Instead, she insisted that we should set our sights on a flat situated within one of Glasgow's first ever council-run tower blocks in Toryglen.

My mum had her aspirations and dreams. Dad had his own. He thought, *We don't need a council house. I can do it.* But she went on a charm offensive, and when Mum went on a charm offensive it was extremely hard to resist. She was attractive looking and very good at disarming people. My mum was from a family of twelve siblings – mostly girls. She had a lot of sisters. She was a machinist from the age of fifteen and later worked in Greggs bakery for most of her life. She was a typical Glasgow factory girl. She loved her work, loved that life. She had a very positive personality. When we started the band she said to me, 'You're going to really make it!' That was a very Mum thing to say. She also said, 'All good bands have a good beat.' There's a lot of truth in it. It was always interesting to get her take on things.

Initially she had been told that all the new flats in Toryglen had gone, but she managed to persuade not only my dad but the council that space should be found for the Kerrs. The tower blocks in Prospecthill Circus were some of the first high rises in Glasgow, perhaps even Britain. To my mother, this was New York. It felt that way to me, too; like stepping from the pages of *Oor Wullie* and rollerblading into *Batman*. This was the modern world: central heating, indoor toilets, baths, elevators.

My mum loved the sheer *newness* of it. I was talking on one occasion to Jimmy Iovine, who produced Simple Minds' album *Once Upon a Time*. I made reference to his Italian lineage. American-Italians are typically extremely proud of their roots, and I said to Jimmy, 'Come over soon and visit me in Italy.' He said, 'No. I don't like Italy. I don't like old stuff. I like new.' I think that applies to a lot of immigrants. It's easy to romanticise the old stuff. My mum liked new.

Had she not pushed for that flat, who knows what might have happened? For a start, I might never have met Charlie.

It wasn't a Hollywood-style meet-cute at the sandpit. He was there and then he was gone. All the Catholic kids who had moved to Toryglen from the Gorbals and Govanhill went to St Brigid's primary school. Except Charlie. His mum worked in Polmadie, so he continued attending school at St Bonaventure's. He travelled there and back with her every day. I think she thought it was better not to uproot him and put him in a new environment. As such, the only times I would really see Charlie in our primary-school days would be in the street after school.

By the age of nine and ten it was all about football. I played. Charlie didn't. However, he used to be friends with a boy called Jimmy, who was the goalkeeper in the St Brigid's school team, which I played in. He was a highly potent mix of not-very-good and extremely emotional. As the goals flew in over his shoulder, Jimmy would either burst out crying or go completely berserk; often he did both at the same time.

It would be incorrect to say that Charlie was a team mascot, but he tagged along with Jimmy for the games and it was always a joy to see him. Everybody loved Charlie. For a little round kid, he had a wonderfully deep laugh – he still does. It was also very loud, which made it even funnier. When poor Jimmy lost the plot, Charlie would piss himself laughing. We all enjoyed that. Then we would ask Charlie if he would try to get our goalie to calm down so that the game could carry on.

Those are my most vivid memories of Charlie until we both started at Holyrood secondary school. He was one of the kids on our street who everyone liked. There wasn't much direct contact. We all ran with our packs. Charlie ran with the kids at the other end of the Circus. I ran with the tower-block mob.

Burchill/

I was seven when our family moved to Toryglen. The summer of 1967. The same year Celtic won the European Cup.

I was born on 27 November 1959, in an area of south Glasgow called the Oatlands. By a strange coincidence, our road was called Toryglen Street. Five of us in a two-room, top-floor tenement: Mum, Dad, me and my two brothers, Jamie and John, four and eight years older respectively. From the top floor we could look over into Rosebery Park and watch the amateur football games. The front room doubled as a bedroom. So did the kitchen. Outside toilet.

To my mum and dad, it was Beverly Hills.

Like the Kerrs, my parents were originally from the Gorbals. The photographer Oscar Marzaroli later became renowned for his stark images documenting life in and around the tenements in the Gorbals during this time. The buildings and general environment were in notoriously poor condition. Much later, the Glasgow *Evening Times* published a supplement featuring some of Marzaroli's greatest pictures. My dad kept it for years because, I think, it provided a visual document of how far he had travelled. Simple Minds have a song called 'Concrete and Cherry Blossom'. It's about where Jim and I grew up, but it is also a metaphor for finding beauty even in the most unexpected places. About trying to be optimistic and grabbing life. My dad was so proud of moving from the Gorbals slums to those two rooms in the Oatlands. It was a big step up for my parents.

I had a very happy childhood, and I retain very strong and fond memories of our first home. It is in many respects a vanished world. I had a strange experience quite recently while travelling by taxi in Glasgow. We were idling at a traffic light. I knew roughly where we were but all I could see was a flyover. The scene was at once instantly familiar and completely disorientating. I asked the taxi driver where this was. He said, 'This used to be Toryglen Street.' I pointed. 'The house I was born in was just over there.' It was very strange. It's all gone. I had an urge to go back and have a look – but it's a motorway.

We lived very happily in the top-floor tenement flat, but the move to Toryglen was another step up. From Beverly Hills to paradise. Suddenly we had central heating instead of the coal fire. Three bedrooms. No one slept in the kitchen. Like thousands of others in our communities, my parents had put themselves on the waiting list for the new development. We knew a lot of families who moved to Toryglen as the city cleared out areas such as the Gorbals, Govanhill and the Oatlands. It was a time of regeneration in Glasgow. The scheme in Toryglen predated the building of Scotland's new towns, but there was already a concerted effort to move families into new builds and out of the tenements, with the intention of redeveloping these crumbling urban areas. As it turns out, often they didn't regenerate them at all, or not until many years later.

We felt very lucky to move. For us, Toryglen really was a paradise. New Glasgow. The only negative that quickly became apparent to me, perhaps not so much to Jim, was sectarianism. The blight of Old Glasgow – though that stain lingers even today.

It was the first time I had come across the Catholic/Protestant divide in the city. In the Gorbals and the Oatlands the demographic was predominantly Catholic. In Toryglen it was a mix. The balcony floor we moved into consisted of sixteen houses. A few doors down from us lived a Protestant family. They wouldn't talk to any of my family because we were Catholics; we would walk past their house and be blanked. My grandmother stayed with us for a time after my grandfather died. She was an O'Rourke, a feisty battleaxe who didn't take this kind of nonsense lightly. Subsequently, there were a few run-ins with the neighbour nearby.

It may have been the first time I had come across any of this, but my parents were used to it, because in Glasgow it was ingrained and it has been well documented how bad it was. But I found it strange.

That aside, Toryglen was a fantastic place to grow up. We had been living in the maisonettes for a few months when Jim and his family moved into the tower block on the same street. I don't remember the meeting at the sandcastle. In fact, I don't remember Jim at all during the initial period after he moved to Toryglen.

My first clear memory of meeting him is on a bus on the way back from school football games: me laughing and Jim picking up on it. Everybody loved the way I laughed. I remember him in particular. Out of everybody, he seemed the most obviously intelligent. At the age of nine or ten, I have no idea how or why that realisation came across, but it was very apparent to me as we sat on the bus. It was quite a peculiar moment of recognition.

After that, although we didn't have much contact, I would see Jim regularly and always think, *Wow, he is very different from anybody else.* The way he looked, the way he dressed. Nine years old. Even then it was obvious to me.

2

Cowboys and Astronauts

I have loved the stars too fondly
to be fearful of the night.

– Sarah Williams, 'The Old Astronomer to His Pupil'

I end up living on the eleventh floor of the high flats, a state of being which just so happens in some near-future time will feature in the opening line of David Bowie's 'Queen Bitch'. When I later get into Bowie, the song seems to sing directly to me. Though, admittedly, there aren't many cruisers in Toryglen in 1967.

My father says to me: 'You can see the whole world from up here!' – and, truly, it feels as though you can. At night, it is a picture window on the city, a panorama of lights, sights and sounds. Not so much a sanctuary as an eyrie. It feels wondrous. Perfect for a dreamer like me, as the clouds go drifting past my head. I spend a lot of time as a kid staring up at night. Lifetimes later, in Sicily, I will also spend a lot of time on the terrace, staring up at the darkened sky.

It is amazing the things you might see.

On the eleventh floor, not only do I feel I can see the whole world, but I have a sense that it is full of possibilities. There are things going on. The parameters are widescreen. The railway line to London runs close by us at the Circus. At night, especially, with the window cracked open, I can hear the trains passing by. The sound fuels my imagination; the idea of people going places, and people coming back from places. Where are they going? What are they going for? There is something deeply comforting about the sound of those trains, and the echoes of men working on the line late at night. You realise you aren't the only person awake in the world. You realise there are other lives being lived.

Kerr/

In 1967, the gods were smiling on two of our lifelong loves: football and music. By the time Charlie and I had moved to Toryglen, Celtic had won the European Cup, the first ever British club to do so. The Beatles released *Sgt Pepper's Lonely Hearts Club Band* two days later. Early on, for both of us, football was perhaps the more dominant of the two passions. Music soon surpassed it, but there are many evenings still where I will go over to Charlie's place in Taormina and we will watch games together.

Celtic winning the European Cup was a huge moment for the city. Or half of it, at least. During the time in which we were coming of age, it was a toss-up between Glasgow and Naples as the biggest dumps in Europe. They were seen as ravaged, post-war places. Collapsed cities. The shipyards were going, the factories were going, our homes were being knocked to the ground. Sitting around the kitchen table, I would hear men talking about Glasgow being finished.

As children, we didn't quite understand what it all meant, but I'm sure I understood the subtext: we had been dealt a losing hand. Celtic becoming champions of Europe proved that to be far from true. We weren't the worst, we were the best. Talking to Charlie years later, I know he felt the same. Hang on a minute: you can come from here and *win*.

At the start of the Simple Minds documentary *Everything Is Possible*, there is a quote from the broadcaster Muriel Gray. Over the usual footage of dilapidated buildings, scrappy kids and urban wasteland, she makes a lovely comment: *Out of the darkness, flowers can grow.*

Those flowers are too often erased from the picture whenever our generation's experience of growing up in Glasgow is depicted. The optimism. The sense of possibility. I have very strong memories not only of events in my childhood, but atmospheres. It's easy to resort to clichés and see those years through rose-tinted glasses, but I felt love all around me – in my family, in the community, and among the friends we had. It wasn't until I was somewhat older that I started hearing about Glasgow's reputation. No Mean City? It didn't feel mean to me. We played in the streets and I don't remember any danger, unless it was from a mad dog. There were plenty of those.

Charlie and I didn't simply crawl out from under the wreckage of collapsing buildings. We were space-age kids. My father's generation dreamed of getting cowboy outfits. We dreamed of getting astronaut suits. Today, I listened again to the first song that ever captured my imagination. 'Telstar' by the Tornados. It is the strangest record. Wildly futuristic. I regard it as the prototype for Simple Minds' 'Theme for Great Cities'. Telstar was one of the first ever satellites to send out the images and live feeds that connect our world in sound and vision. It was launched into space shortly after Charlie and I were born. The numerous modes of global communication that now connect us all? They started there.

Our childhoods, therefore, are a kind of dichotomy. We were playing football on long-neglected Second World War bombsites as the Americans landed on the moon. Growing up in a monochrome Glasgow grinding slowly towards the end of its post-industrial glory, it's true that around us many people's dreams came crashing down as the factories and shipyards and steelworks began, one by one, to close. At the same time, our own escapist dreams were starting to take shape even before we knew what they were.

We were coming out of a proud city struggling with its identity, but there was also a rush to the future, a rush to rebuild, a rush to live. It's important to remind ourselves how positive these gleaming tower blocks were in our eyes. At the time, they were regarded as potent symbols of incredible progress. In moving to Toryglen, we were a part of it. We were walking between worlds. In the first decade of our lives, particularly, we were on the cusp of all of that. Two worlds in collision. Before we knew it, we were teenagers rebelling against Glasgow's poverty of aspiration amid dire socio-economic conditions.

3
Two Brothers

Help your brother's boat across, and your own
will reach the shore.

– Hindu proverb

*I am with my brother Paul at the quayside in Glasgow, waiting for
the night boat. We are going on our first family holiday – to Bray,
to the south of Dublin. I am four or five years old, and it is the first
time I have ever seen a suitcase, that universal symbol of transience
that will become such an integral part of my life. We must have
borrowed this one from a neighbour.*

*The boat will sail across to Northern Ireland, then down to Dun
Laoghaire, just outside Dublin. I will soon discover that there are
cows crammed inside the lower deck. It is very probably the first
time I have seen cows, too.*

*I have one hand on the giant suitcase, the other holding on to my
struggling brother's arm. The knuckles on my tiny fist are white as
he tries to break away. Because that's what Paul is like. He is at the
zombie toddler stage, just about walking, and already he can't be
pinned down. Unlike me. I only have to be told once.*

*It is our first journey away from Glasgow. Yet in a sense we are
going back home. From a century before I was born, Catholic Irish
have settled 'wherever muscle and strength is in demand'. On the
west coast of Scotland that means opportunities for employment in
coal mining, dock work and labouring of all stripes.*

*My Irish immigrant grandfather, Patrick Reighill, found employ-
ment working in the coalmines of Lanarkshire. On the other side*

of my family, my grandmother, Mary Mullen, was raised among the Irish community on Clydeside. Against that background, and although my brothers and I are raised as Scots, Glasgow born and bred, we are submerged in Irish culture. The local priests are Irish. My teachers are often Irish. My uncle is Irish. My cousins learn traditional Irish dancing. People sing Irish folk songs in our house on a Saturday night. I am Scottish, but now and ever after I will identify myself as being from Irish 'immigrant stock'.

The trip to Bray, therefore, is a homecoming of sorts. A confusing and exciting one. I am upset onboard that night because of the sleeping arrangements on the boat. Men and women are given separate quarters and I am away from my mum. We are told to behave. If we do, as soon as we get to Dublin we will get a knickerbocker glory.

The spell cast by our first ever family vacation will linger. Years later, I will still be able to picture the promenade at Bray and it will stir fond memories of outdoor music, marching bands, orchestras, puppets and variety shows. And an unforgettable knickerbocker glory for being a good big brother.

Kerr/

I was always the big brother. Charlie is different. Charlie is the wee brother – and very much loved for being so.

Because we're both very aware of the numerous ways in which he and I are similar, it has become more and more interesting to me to think of the differences between us. The really significant factor, in terms of psychology, is when you're the eldest sibling in the family, as I am, and when you're the baby of the family, as Charlie is. Not that Charlie is by any means the 'baby' in Simple Minds – and in fact, within his own family, he quickly outgrew his older brothers, and not simply because of the profile that Simple Minds gave him. Charlie is very much a creature of intellect. The truth is, he outgrew most people we knew.

And yet that sense of family hierarchy is deeply instilled in our natures. Going through life, I have realised how much the roles thrust upon us end up shaping our personalities and actions. In my case, the instinct is to look out for people. They, in turn, look to me for answers. Sometimes it feels as though it really is all on my shoulders.

Somewhere in my attic I have that sepia-toned Polaroid photo of me and Paul on the Broomielaw dockside in Glasgow in 1964. It's a good picture. It says something. There is some quality in the photograph that captures the sense of responsibility I felt, from a very young age, of having to take care of someone other than myself: 'You're the big brother. Hold on to him.'

My youngest brother Mark was born in Toryglen in 1970, when I was ten. When I went out to play in the streets with my friends, we had to take him with us. My dad worked as a builder and my mum worked part time. As I understood it, the bargain was: 'Be good. Help out. If I can do this job, we can go to Blackpool. Or we might get a colour TV.'

Mark and I were laughing recently about this. I would take him out in the pushchair, which would inevitably very quickly become a goal post. With him still in it. We used to play football in a grassy park in front of a dilapidated factory. On one occasion, someone disclosed that there was lead on the factory roof. Back then, if you could 'liberate' the lead, the big boys would help you take it to the 'scrappy', the local scrap-metal dealer, and you could make some money.

Everybody started climbing up on the roof. We forgot about Mark. He was left in the pushchair while we were up there. Within a few minutes we could hear the squad-car sirens circling and we all ran away. We had still forgotten about Mark. The police turned up to discover a ransacked roof and a baby boy left alone in the park. Even in Toryglen, he was beyond suspicion. After finding out who Mark belonged to, they took him to our front door. Far from being grateful, I believe the police ended up getting an earful from my mum: 'Haven't you lot got better things to do!?' I got a hard time later that night when I went home, but even then, Mark was still dragged along and tagged along whenever I went out to play. *You're the big brother. You need to look after him.*

I knew my role. I had known it ever since Paul arrived and I still know it today. When we go on tour, I'm the oldest, though I'm only a few months Charlie's senior. I'm older than anyone in the crew, in our management office, among our agents. At festivals, we'll often be the oldest band on the bill. None of the other original Simple Minds members were big brothers. Rather than any desire to be the 'boss', I think that fact instilled the idea that I had, and have, to be the one offering an overview; to make sure things are right, for good or bad. That's just how it has always been.

But I'm not Superman. I don't have all the answers all the time.

There was a day in the late 2000s when the whole world seemed to collapse all at once.

I was going through to Edinburgh from Glasgow to see our long-serving accountant, Sandra Dods. She had called an urgent meeting. En route, I received a call to say that there was no cure for Mum. Her cancer was terminal. Then I had to go straight in to see Sandra. It was the only time in my life that a tax charge hadn't been accounted for. It was owed by me personally. They wanted it, and they wanted it now. I didn't have it. I had started a hotel business in Taormina and the first few years were rough. We were learning – and losing money hand over fist. The bank in Sicily was getting anxious. The accountants were getting anxious. And now I was getting anxious.

But by far the biggest worry was Mum. I remember travelling back on the train and thinking, *What a mistake I've made. With Mum getting ill, I should be able to give all my attention to her.* As it happened, Mum was around for another couple of years but, nevertheless, it was a dark day. At the same time, I had to make major decisions in a matter of hours about the business. And I realised that there was no one to talk to about how to get through it.

In a period of crisis, even now Sandra might ask Charlie, 'What are you going to do?' And Charlie will reply, 'Jim will come up with something.' That's the downside of being seen as the person who sorts things out. Sometimes my partner Yumie says, just a little too flippantly, 'You'll sort it out, you always know what to do.' I'll say, 'I *don't* know what to do! I *can't* sort it out!' It can be very frustrating in that moment. People see you as Superman while you're thinking, *I do not have a clue what to do.*

With the benefit of hindsight, the best advice is: don't do anything. Try to get some sleep, if you can. Get up the next day and take a long walk. It's amazing how something at the back of your mind somehow finds its way to the forefront – and suddenly there's an idea.

Burchill/

In my family, I am an archetypal youngest sibling. I suspect I must have been quite the afterthought, and as a result I had the luxury of being pampered. Mum and Dad doted on me.

My brothers, Jamie and John, being four and eight years older, opened my eyes in different ways. When I was eleven, John took me with him around Europe for three weeks. We slept in the car, we slept at friends' houses, we slept in the NAAFI bases in Germany because we had a neighbour who worked there. I remember later saying to my dad, 'What were you thinking?! I was eleven and he was only nineteen!' But I was lucky. It planted a seed. By the time I was in my teens I had already been around Europe, and the idea of travelling was firmly ingrained.

In terms of music, at home there were two different camps. In Toryglen, John had his own room and his own record player. He was a blues and Motown guy. Loved B. B. King.

It was Jamie who really fired up my love of music. He and I shared a room, our two beds facing each other with a stereo in the middle. At first we only had two albums: *LA Woman* by the Doors and *Killer* by Alice Cooper. I loved the Doors. Robby Krieger doesn't get nearly enough praise. He is one of my all-time favourites. A brilliant guitar player, truly out there, folding jazz inside blues with a weird psychedelic twist.

Then it was *The Man Who Sold the World* by David Bowie. That was the big Bowie album for us; not *Ziggy Stardust* or *Hunky Dory*. In time, Bob Dylan became an obsession. One of my best friends at school was a Canadian called Anthony Daly. He was a tough guy, but he had his sensitive moments. Along with his brother, we went together regularly to the ice skating. Anthony was a huge Bob Dylan fan, and Jamie and I became huge Dylan fans, too. We loved Joni Mitchell and Loudon Wainwright III, but especially Dylan. I had all the bootlegs. I could do my *Mastermind* specialist subject on the guy, which might seem unusual considering the music we went on to make in Simple Minds. But I never wanted to write like Dylan. He was all about the lyrics and I couldn't do that. Plus, he had so many songs inspired by Celtic tunes and old folk melodies. A long way from Robby Krieger.

On our bedroom wall, we had a poster of Keith Emerson sticking a knife into his Hammond organ. One night Jamie came in tripping on acid. Woah! That didn't end well. Jamie was great. At that age, four years is a significant gap between siblings, but there was never any problem. He took me to all my earliest gigs, including my very first: Led Zeppelin at Green's Playhouse. *Houses of the Holy* tour. Jamie got me in.

When I first started playing guitar, Jamie and I learned together. I was desperate to play, even before I began listening to music seriously. I've no idea why or where the impulse came from. We weren't a musical family – with one exception. In the thirties and early forties my grandmother's sister Mary O'Rourke and her brother Joe had a music hall act called

Master Joe Petersen (The Phenomenal Boy Singer). Mary sang boy soprano. She dressed up as a boy. They were truly dire, but Mary became very famous as Master Joe and made dozens of recordings for Rex Records. My dad had gone to see the act when he was little, and he would tell me all about them.

My ambitions were a little more contemporary. I badly wanted to play guitar but couldn't afford one. We had a toy version. I played it until the strings broke and then just kept on playing it. My mum was a heavy smoker and eventually she got me my first guitar by saving up her Embassy cigarette coupons. It was called a Nymph and it was terrible. Jamie got a Yamaha and the two of us began learning together. After a time, Jamie fell away but I continued. In the afterglow of the Led Zeppelin concert, I went to McCormack's guitar shop in Bath Street, Glasgow. I had a fancy for a Les Paul like Jimmy Page. Jamie always says that as soon as I got a real guitar, I was off and running. I had been priming myself for such a long time. Now, there was no stopping me.

Jamie now lives in Wales. He's still great. Recently he got kicked out of a Simple Minds show in Cardiff for being a little overzealous. He battled his way right down to the front and started shouting at me to get my attention. Security weren't impressed. They told him he had to calm down. He wasn't having it. He likes a drink, Jamie, but he's a gentle guy. Finally, they had no choice but to huckle him out of the venue, because he was not for moving. They chucked him out like a bag of coal. Afterwards the band said to me, 'Did you see that mad guy down the front getting carted out?' I said, 'Oh, that was my brother, Jamie.' He was almost seventy at the time. He just wanted to say hello.

My brothers shaped my tastes and looked out for me. My parents indulged me. Classic youngest sibling. Whereas Jim, with his personality, could only ever have been the eldest within his family. From early on, Jim had quite a demanding role. His dad had a drink problem when he was younger.

If you are the eldest son in a relationship like that, you grow up much more quickly and build certain defences.

Somewhere inside, he has an immense self-confidence. It can be a problem. I have seen it waver – but not often, and not a lot. I've only seen Jim cry twice in his life, and one of those occasions was when his mother died. I don't know if it is entirely natural to be like that, although we both perhaps have a block on that score. We tend not to get overly emotional, coming from our background. In Jim's case, I think a lot of it is rooted in having always been perceived as the one who has to hold things together. In the past I would think, *I hope you have a safety valve and can release some vulnerability.* As we've grown older, it's good that he and I can go on walks and talk to each other a little more openly about our emotional lives.

Jim carries a lot of responsibilities for many, many people. So do I – but Jim more so. As much as it is part of his DNA to be the figure who is always there for everyone, there are limits to what any one person can take on. I worry sometimes about who looks out for him. I hope I do. It's not always easy, because he is exceptionally good at leading the way. He loves rallying the troops to the cause. Even when I first got a guitar, he was telling everybody that I was the best guitar player around. That's the managerial side of Jim, but it is also the big brother speaking.

Kerr/

I have another brother.

Pre-Toryglen, one day at our flat in Carfin Street in Govanhill there was a commotion. On the floor above us lived Shug and Mary Donnelly and their son Joe. My parents liked them. Shug was a builder, like my dad. Really friendly guy. Joe also had a grandmother who lived nearby, his mum's mother, who he often stayed with.

On this morning, Shug called in at our flat. I could tell something was going on. Especially when I was told to go into the other room. Once the conversation was over and Shug had left, Mum sat me down: 'Right! Joe is going to be coming to ours for breakfast every day now. He'll be coming down this morning and going to school with you.' Fantastic. No questions asked.

It was very unusual in those days for married couples to split up. Almost unheard of. We didn't know anyone who had. Subsequently, I found out that Joe's mum had left to 'stay with his auntie', which was *really* unusual. Mum was going to help Shug with Joe. He still slept upstairs in the flat where he lived with his dad, but he'd come downstairs in the morning to our house, we would get dressed at the fire and have tea and toast, and then we'd go to school.

It created another brother for me. Joe was born in February 1959; I was born in July the same year. We were the same age and in the same class. Unlike Paul, I wasn't responsible for him. We were best friends but competitive, whether the task was climbing buildings, playing football or fighting.

Three years later, when our family was readying to move to Toryglen, Joe became very upset at the thought of us leaving. My mum spoke to Shug. She told him Joe could come and live with us. He could come back and stay with his dad at the weekends. She didn't make a big show of it, but what an incredible act of love by my mother. Joe moved with us to the tower block in Toryglen and stayed until he was fourteen or fifteen. At that point, his gran moved nearby and Joe lived with her, but we were still just along the road.

Joe is associated with one of my proudest memories. When I reached the age of twelve, I could no longer get into the school football team. It was a dagger blow to the heart. The final twist of the knife was the fact that not only could Joe get in, but he was already good enough to play for the under-fifteens. Football was such a big deal in our lives then. On this memorable day, Joe was playing in a local cup final and we all went to cheer him on. He scored the winner. It wasn't merely the winner, it was the most amazing goal I had ever seen. I get emotional even now writing about it. It was one of the proudest days of my life and I couldn't even get on the bench. For years afterwards, Joe would rib me about it. But the pride I felt was a brother's pride.

As music took a grip, like the rest of us Joe started messing around with guitars. He was in our first band, Biba Rom. He was into it. He had the same dreams. What made Joe different was that he got a serious girlfriend before any of us. When Joanne moved to London for work, Joe followed her. When punk came, he wasn't in Glasgow to be shaken up by it the way we were shaken up. He had a life of his own by then.

Later, Joe picked up music again. He played bass in a band called the Silencers alongside Martin Hanlin, another close schoolfriend. They were a good group. In terms of main-stream success, they missed out by a whisker. We booked the Silencers to support Simple Minds in 1989 on the *Street Fighting Years* tour. They went down well every night, but in the aftermath of one of their support slots I found them all sitting on flight cases looking dejected. I was just about to go on stage. The intro music was starting.

'What's the matter?'

'You don't really get much opening up, do you?'

'You go down a storm every night, what are you moaning about?'

Then Joe, unfortunately for him, said: 'You get a bigger cheer when you take off your damn jacket.'

I smiled. '*Do I?* Watch this!'

I went on stage and somehow made the act of removing my jacket last for two minutes. The audience bought into it and screamed themselves hoarse. I milked it to death as Joe and his band stood miserably watching from the side of the stage. I grinned and raised a thumb. At least it wasn't a finger. After years of jiving from Joe about my hopeless football skills and him being a winner, I had finally got my own back.

34

We still rib each other about the competition we had as kids. When it comes to the important stuff, no one can beat the success Joe has made of his life. He is still with Joanne. It's an amazing love story. He has a family. In his professional pursuits he has done very well. He's had such a happy life, this kid who turned up at the door one day and caused a commotion in the house. I think of the amount of self-pity Joe could have exuded given those circumstances, but he didn't blink once. He attributes it to having good people around him when it mattered. And my goodness, what an amazing act of kindness by my mum and dad.

4

Through the Eyes of Love

If I chance to talk a little wild, forgive me;
I had it from my father.

– William Shakespeare, *Henry VIII*, Act 1 Scene IV

You must know that there is nothing higher,
or stronger, or sounder, or more useful afterwards in life,
than some good memory, especially a memory
from childhood, from the parental home.

– Fyodor Dostoevsky, *The Brothers Karamazov*

Early eighties. Simple Minds are headlining Tiffany's in Glasgow and my father is finally coming to see us play.

It's a big hometown gig. Friday night. Queues around the block. And he messes up. He goes to the pub after work and one thing leads to another. He is late home to meet my mum and arrives at Tiffany's by himself – half pissed, with all his work gear on. After the show, I don't see him backstage.

The next morning, I walk into our kitchen at Toryglen. I am still staying at home whenever I am back – which is more or less never. What's the point in wasting money on a flat? Mum is downstairs, working in Greggs. I can feel her annoyance at my father vibrating from eleven floors up. The man himself is in the kitchen looking very sheepish. Almost forlorn. He always makes breakfast on a Saturday, scrambled eggs and toast.

I nod at him.

He says, 'You boys are going to make it.'

I think, OK, this will be interesting. The guy's not exactly a world expert on the music industry and he's only just bothered to come to see us play. How will he quantify this statement?

He explains. There is a bar down one side of Tiffany's. At the end of the bar, they sell chips. My dad says that during our show he focused in on one fan who was going particularly crazy watching our set. He smiles. 'Everybody was losing it, but this guy was really losing it.'

My dad continued watching as the fan took his place at the end of the line to buy chips. The queue was a mile long and it took an age to get served. Eventually he got his food. My dad looks at me: 'Have you got a song called "Meri-Meri" or something?' He means 'The American'. I tell him the name of the song. He nods. 'Aye, well, you started into playing that one and this guy just threw all his chips away and ran straight down to the front.'

He looks up from his scrambled eggs.

'Anybody who can make someone throw away their chips is going to make it. Youse are going to be fucking huge.'

Kerr/

If we were playing a game of word association, 'Dad' would match with 'Hero'. That is my earliest sensory memory of my father: that he was the greatest guy on the planet. I wasn't alone in thinking that. He was incredibly popular. People really liked Jimmy Kerr. When you walked down the street with my dad, people would cross the road to speak with him. He was funny and warm and charismatic. All these words were used by his friends at his funeral.

He actually could charm the birds out of the trees. A Glaswegian Kes. As a boy, he was into 'fleeing the doos': flying the doves. He had a little birdhouse, and he went all over Glasgow collecting cuckoo eggs. There was a network of older guys doing the same thing. He got into a lot of trouble from his parents, because he was only ten or eleven, and he was off on his travels, off with the birds.

Later, once he was married and I was little, he would take me to these strange spots where his friends had their birdhouses. They were always hidden away down railway tracks or in creepy corners in the woods. Inside, there were hordes of these things, flapping around an inch above my head. My very present fear of birds is directly due to him. I still experience a horror whenever one of these creatures flaps its wings. Shooting the video for 'Sanctify Yourself' with that little white dove as my co-star took more courage than most people might realise.

Birds were a hobby. By trade, Dad was a builder. One of my very earliest memories is of his cement-splattered work boots, giant-sized to my toddler's eyes, spilling out of the cloakroom cupboard in our hallway. Looking back, the memory of those boots symbolised the most honest form of work. Though he wasn't a miner like his uncles and grandfather, physically my dad made similar demands on his body to bring home the weekly pay packet.

Not that my mother could ever find it within herself to detect any great nobility in those boots. She had a compli-cated relationship with them, and not simply because they occasionally left a dirty trail behind them on 'her' carpets that were still being paid off. Dad regarded those mucky boots as a badge of honour as he trudged off to work every morning; they were part of the proud uniform worn by a particular kind of man. In contrast, though Mum greatly valued him and what he brought home to our family, she seemed slightly embarrassed by the lack of social prestige in having a husband who was a labourer. I imagine at times she dreamed of what it might be like to be married to a man who instead wore 'a nice collar and tie' to work and provided the family with an equally nice bungalow situated in one of Glasgow's leafier suburbs. She didn't romanticise drudgery.

She aspired upwards. That's how we ended up in the high flats in the first place.

In our home in Toryglen, all the pictures on the wall were aspirational. Yuri Gagarin. Russian. First man in space. JFK. The Irish connection. You came from nothing and you could become president of the USA. Joe McBride. Local hero. Joe broke all the records for Celtic in the season they went on to win the European Cup, then broke his leg and didn't get to play in the final. Joe lived in our old street in Govanhill. He had a crew-cut like an astronaut. I thought Joe had a foreign name at first, because after being at the game on a Saturday, my dad would sit in his seat after twelve pints and shout: 'Joey-Burst-The-Net!' For ages, I thought the guy was Italian: Joey Bostanetta. I was lucky enough to meet Joe years later and he laughed hard when I told him the story.

The Pope's likeness was also on our wall. My mum's doing. Dad wasn't bothered. He wasn't interested in religion at all, whereas my mum was very much invested in us being good Catholic boys. Dad made it clear that we had to do what our mother told us, but out of the side of his mouth he would whisper, 'What a load of baloney . . .'

Dad worked on the sites during the week and on a Sunday morning we had to go to chapel with Mum. Saturday afternoons he would be in the pub or at the football.

On a Saturday morning, he was ours.

He would cook breakfast and then we would go to the public baths, then next door to Govanhill Library. My dad always had his head in a book. I don't know who he was quoting, but I remember him saying: 'If you read, you will never be a slave in your mind.' When I signed the forms to join up at the library, he really went the distance to tell me how lucky I was. 'Unlike so many kids around the world you have access to this precious thing. *This is a golden ticket.*'

My upbringing was so working class I didn't even know that it was working class. Where we lived, it was just all one class. Dad was a proper Red, a diehard socialist, but he held no grudges. If he saw someone in a flash-looking car, he would nod and say, 'Some guy has done well for himself.' He didn't resent successful people. It was more that he believed everyone should have a route open to them to aspire upwards. At the same time, it was on your own head to take the time to educate yourself. When I had my first fancy pad I remember us both lying in the swimming pool. I liked to wind him up: 'Not such a Red *now*, are you?' 'Why not? Everyone should have a fucking swimming pool!'

He was very big on civil rights. He would listen to the speeches of Martin Luther King. There was always this mantra: *the poor Blacks*. I don't know how many times I heard that. Though we didn't have a huge amount, in the greater reckoning he understood *exactly* how lucky we were and made sure we knew it, too. He possessed an acute sense of righteousness that played a key part in my thinking years later, when Simple Minds came to be involved in calling for the release of Nelson Mandela.

For a few years, my father had a problem with alcohol. I never found out what was at the root of it. Midlife crisis? A bout of the blues? *What's it all about?* Who knows. But he was drinking too much. Still working, still functioning – but drinking hard. Unfortunately, he wasn't a good drinker. He wasn't violent, but he became antagonistic. He wasn't himself.

It was a tough period, and it coincided with my first couple of years in Simple Minds. Along with Charlie's parents and Brian McGee's mum and dad, Dad had given us money to make our first demos and to buy equipment. After that, he never seemed particularly interested. He didn't come to see us play and I didn't see much of him. There wasn't a lot of communication taking place. I think he may have been a little ashamed. Through those years, there was understandably some difficulty between him and my mum. They were still living under the same roof, but I didn't get the impression that they were as close as they had once been. His chip-based epiphany in Tiffany's occurred during this time.

Eventually he went to a single Alcoholics Anonymous meeting – and never drank again. After that, my father became very proud of our band. I particularly remember one Saturday morning after another show in Glasgow. He had been a good boy this time. He was in the kitchen and I handed him a bag. Inside was our first ever gold disc. I only saw my father cry twice in his life. He cried then.

Once Simple Minds took off, Dad became my travelling companion. We had a lot of adventures. He came on the road with us many, many times. I knew that he would get a real kick out of some of the opportunities that being around the band presented. If we were playing in Cologne, he would spend the whole day in the cathedral – not praying, but looking at how they built it, pestering them to pull the original designs and drawings out of storage. He was that kind of guy. One of our most memorable trips was to Russia. I've got great pictures of him in Red Square. We went to the Gambia. He hung out with Dylan at Live Aid. Right until the end, he was coming out on tour with us. In my house in Perthshire, there's a photo of Dad in Nashville on Willie Nelson's bus. The pair of them spent two hours together. Willie was having so much fun he almost missed his show.

My dad could hold a meaningful conversation with any-body, be it a top politician or a binman. Wherever I went with him, all around the world, that was always apparent. Charlie loved him. My kids loved him. My partner Yumie loved him. Chrissie Hynde adored him. Everyone loved Jimmy Kerr. He was a terrific guy.

We are given our fundamental values in the home. My mother certainly played a significant role in shaping the kind of person I have become. My father is where my intellectual curiosity comes from. He was always worth listening to.

41

He was always interesting. There would always be a point to him telling you something: 'Listen to this, Jim. It's important.' I'm glad I did.

Burchill/

I didn't know Jimmy Kerr particularly well when Jim and I were kids, but to say he was a larger-than-life character in our area would be a massive understatement. Everybody knew him. He was smart, charismatic, irreverent, hilarious.

Jim's parents were friendly with my parents, John and Ellen. Even from afar, I always felt that they were somehow different from other people around us. It's hard to put a finger on why. There was something very direct and straight about them. Jim's mum Irene was a beautiful-looking woman. Lovely, hospitable. Very bright and social.

In time, Jimmy Kerr became a huge part of the Simple Minds story. We travelled all over the world with him, and not only on tour. He and I became close. He became a second father to me.

It's amusing for me to see that Jim has inherited so many of his dad's traits. There's a fellow in Taormina who sells fish. Jim and I go down to see him and the guy always seems to be talking about how much time he spends keeping fit – and yet he's got this great big belly. After a while of listening to him go on about his gym regime, Jim will just grab his tummy and give it a good old shake. That's a total Jimmy move. It's almost breach of copyright. I tell Jim, 'That's just like being with your dad.'

My father was a less gregarious character than Jimmy Kerr. Jim has compared him a few times to Paul Buchanan from the Blue Nile. He looked quite like Paul, and he had a similar manner. Quiet, quite diffident. There was a real sweetness about him. He was a dynamite guy. A gentleman. He worked on the railways. When he was younger, he used to drive a tram in Glasgow, then he worked for Red Star organising the parcels on the trains. He did that all his life, working different nightshifts: ten until six; six until two.

He was open-minded about everything and everyone. No weirdness, no prejudice. He was quite religious, but he didn't have a bigoted bone in his body. He went to church and when we were little all three children also had to go. At a certain point me and my older brother orchestrated a revolt. We told him we weren't into 'this bullshit'. 'Fine, no problem.' After that none of us went to church.

Considering the quite conservative social backgrounds in which they had all been raised, it is all the more remarkable that both our sets of parents not only allowed Jim and I to pursue our dreams – they encouraged us. They never once said, *Get a job*, or, *You're kidding yourselves.* The very opposite.

It wasn't so much that they believed in what we were projecting. They didn't understand a thing about the band and deep down I'm sure they didn't believe that any of our outlandish dreams had a hope of coming true. It was more that they were nice people who wouldn't get on our case like a lot of other people's parents would. They said, or at least implied through their actions, *Do what you want to do.* In other words, they believed in us and wanted us to be happy. A great gift from any parent.

They would come to some Simple Minds Glasgow shows, but only occasionally. Early on, Jim's mum was more present than his dad. In later years, Jimmy came to a lot. My parents came only rarely. They weren't paying particularly close attention to what we were doing. When it came to music, my dad used to talk very fondly about Perry Como.

It was a blessing that they were able to see the band come to fruition and achieve success. On one memorable occasion they came to see Simple Minds play Wembley Stadium. As a bonus they got to meet the great Irish comedian Dave Allen. We had bumped into Dave on a plane the day before. We told him who we were, that we were playing Wembley, and invited him to come – and he did, much to our delight and surprise. Backstage there were all our mums and dads – and Dave Allen. They were very excited about that.

Kerr/

I was in Charlie's house a lot. At home he was always 'Charles'. The place was spotless.

His family were typical good people who lived on the street where we grew up. His dad was, genuinely, the politest man I have ever met. I can still picture him coming back home, especially on summer nights, in his dark blue railway jacket. Always whistling. A happy and very clean-cut guy. Rake thin, chiselled features. Slightly long hair swept back. He was the kind of man who would go to the pub on a Saturday night for one pint. Quiet, decent, friendly. Super polite. A proper gentleman. Just like his youngest son.

Charlie's dad was quite tall. His mum was wee. Ellen had a smoker's voice, a Velcro rasp. Her best pal was her ma, Charlie's gran. Ellen wouldn't have been much older than my mum, but she seemed somehow to come from a different generation. She was wonderful. Super friendly, always welcoming: *Come on in, come on in . . .* She worked in the bookies in Toryglen, next to my mum in Greggs. A cigarette permanently in her mouth.

There was always something going on in Charlie's house. I remember a time when his grandad was staying there. Sadly, he was in the early stages of dementia, although we didn't really know then what that was. One day he was sitting downstairs in his pyjamas, and we had been given strict instructions: 'Boys, look after him.' Charlie and I had promptly gone upstairs and started listening to the Doors, getting right into it. After a while we went down for a cup of tea. I looked around: 'Where's your grandad?' The door was open. 'Oh shit!' We went outside and noticed a commotion up the road at the football pitch. The boys were getting upset with the old lad in his pyjamas trying to join in the game.

Our parents lived relatively modest lives. When we started getting some success with Simple Minds, there was no source of reference for them. This was completely unknown territory. None of us had known anyone that had ever made a record, never mind being on the radio and television. That didn't happen to people like us. Football could happen. It almost happened for my brother Paul, who was a gifted player and had trials with Liverpool and Aston Villa. Everyone in Toryglen knew somebody who played for a club – but *this*? You had as much chance of being an astronaut or winning the Grand Prix. It was a totally new world.

When we got our first record deal, we were paid a decent advance and we took all our parents to dinner at the Ubiquitous Chip in the West End of Glasgow. A very classy establishment. I think it may have been the first time that all the band members' parents had met, although my family knew the Burchills and the McGees. We had never been in a restaurant where each of us was given three forks and three knives. Evidently, neither had our parents. It was meant to be a celebration, but it fell flat. It wasn't right. It was too much. Nobody felt comfortable.

I look back now and recognise that the experiences we had in Simple Minds must have blown the minds of our parents. My mum told me a funny story when Charlie and I had come back home after touring *Sons and Fascination* in America in 1981. While we were away, she had met Charlie's mum in the street. Ellen was the kind of person who would begin a conversation halfway through it. She said: '*That Charles*! He's away in America with your Jim, and he hasn't got his keys. We can't go out of the house because we don't know when he's coming back. If he comes back and he can't get in, he'll go off his nut!'

It wasn't: *Isn't it great?! Simple Minds are on their first US tour.* It was: 'He's away to America with Jim and he hasnae got his bloody keys – so we cannae go out!' Our parents would never have thought to phone our management office to check the tour itinerary or even have known what the phone number was. What we were doing very probably overwhelmed them, but they didn't want to appear overwhelmed. They tried to take it in their stride, but I'm sure most of that world didn't make the slightest lick of sense to them. I vividly remember the look of shock and confusion on Ellen's face when Charlie brought her back a 'live' pineapple from London. 'What's *that*?!' I don't think any of our parents would have seen a real pineapple before. They belonged in tins. The concept of touring America wasn't even on their radar. I don't think they ever sat down and listened to the records. They would hear songs on the radio and people playing them in the local area, but the music was unrelatable to them.

In time, they became more accustomed to the stature of the band and the spoils of success. There is a lovely photograph taken when we played Wembley Stadium on the *Street Fighting Years* tour, of Charlie's mum and dad, my parents and Mick MacNeil's parents sitting in the royal box eating fish and chips. Our friend Billy Sloan had gone out to get them a fish supper from the local takeaway. Forget the Ubiquitous Chip. This was a far more fitting celebration for the people to whom we owe so much.

5

La Bella Figura

Italy is a dream that keeps returning for the rest of your life.

– Anna Akhmatova

You may have the world if I may have Italy.

– Giuseppe Verdi

July 1973. My first trip abroad. I disembark from the plane at Rimini airport and realise the world is, in fact, in colour. Wow! **Porca Puttana!** *From monochrome Glasgow to this saturated, cinematic intensity: the heat, the light, the smells, the flora and fauna. Overload. Welcome to the sensual world. Welcome to Italy. Welcome . . . home?*

There are around thirty of us on the school trip. All boys. This is a very unusual outing. First of all, I'm not at all sure how my mum and dad have managed to conjure up the money to send me. Secondly, our school trips are usually to less exotic locales. Being a Catholic school, Lourdes is a big favourite. But this time it is shimmering Italy.

A few weeks ago, I saw David Bowie at Green's Playhouse in Glasgow and I can't get it out of my mind. With my new job in the butcher's shop I have money for clothes. We are told to turn up in school uniform. I turn up in a double-breasted suit with platform boots that are too small for me. In my head, I am Ziggy. Ziggy with blistered feet. We haven't even left Glasgow yet and I am in trouble.

We take the train to London, then the bus to Luton Airport, where the nine o'clock news delivers a bombshell: David Bowie has retired from rock and roll. His final ever show was at Hammersmith Odeon. I am stunned to the soles of my pinched platform boots. Later, to our relief, we discover the news has been somewhat overhyped. It is an early lesson in rock and roll myth building.

On the first morning in Italy, as will become a lifelong habit, I get up earlier than anyone else. There is a famous promenade in Rimini and I walk all the way along it. At the very end I find a tiny record shop, which more than fifty years later will still be there. The window is a music-mad schoolboy's dream: dozens of 45s in picture sleeves, a concept that has not yet made it to Britain. They have 'The Jean Genie' adorned with an image of Bowie, and Genesis singles with amazing photographs of Peter Gabriel. It is the first morning of the trip, and before I have even eaten breakfast in the hotel, I have spent all my holiday money.

Luckily, Tony Donald is also here. Tony is a dab hand at milking the milk run. He is our rookie Rockefeller. Cash on tap. I ask Tony to bail me out. 'Not a problem, Jim.' It is an incredible two weeks. Everything happens. Just when I think things can't possibly get any better, a girls' school from Manchester checks in at the hostel next to us. I have just turned fourteen, and the world suddenly seems to have opened up to me. I have fallen in love with Italy.

Kerr/

In the words of Italophile British writer Roger Mitchell, 'Italy remains a simple country at heart. It exists principally to reward the eyes, to make blood, with a clear premium on what looks good. *La Bella Figura.*' The beautiful figure. The national identity is fuelled by panache and swagger and, Mitchell continues, the eternal and unshakeable certainty that Italians are 'very superior in all the important matters of existence', chief of which are football, food, wine, fashion, fast cars, churches, nature, art, beautiful women and handsome men.

Italians are passionate people. They run hot. Their enthusiasms can cut both ways. As with Simple Minds, there are deep-rooted rules of engagement. Ingrained codes of behaviour. Betray those and there can be hell to pay. No wonder Charlie and I ended up living here.

I would learn all this over the course of many years' engagement with the place, but the love I felt in Rimini was more or less instantaneous. Within days if not hours of disembarking from the flight, I swear I knew that later in life I would live in Italy.

I had already been smitten from afar. In the 1970 World Cup everybody I knew supported Brazil. Not me. I was rooting for Italia. The *Azzurri* eventually lost in the final, but I was absolutely captivated by them.

The seeds of my Italian fascination were perhaps sown even earlier. My grandad had visited Sicily with the Eighth Army during the Second World War. He travelled through the entire island. There are photos of 'the Kilties' in Taormina, which I only found out much later. When he was a couple of whiskies to the good, he would speak about Mount Etna and it fascinated me, as it still does today. He would rhapsodise that Italians were the greatest people on earth. The women were particularly lovely, he'd often add, to which my grandmother would respond: 'If they're so lovely, away back there, then!' I think he may have had a story here. A wee adventure.

Three years after Rimini, when me and Charlie went hitchhiking, we ended up in Verona. Italy again. A few years later still, it was one of the first countries to really take to Simple Minds outside of Britain. It remains a stronghold of support to this day.

You might say, *Ah, but who doesn't love Italy? Who doesn't love Tuscany and Venice and Rome?*

Yes, but Sicily . . . Sicily is another world again.

Simple Minds first came here in 1983. At the time very few gigs happened in Sicily. When Frank Zappa had come there had been a riot in Palermo. People warned us off. 'Oh, the Mafia will steal your equipment! You won't get paid!' We liked a challenge. We couldn't wait to come.

Our first gig was in Messina. We arrived from the mainland on the ferry. Coming over on the water and seeing Sicily materialise as the sun was rising is something I'll never forget as long as I live. It lit up something in me that has never died.

In Messina, the gig was held up for an hour and a half. The local character who operated the generator had asked my brother Paul, who at the time was our tour manager, for a donation to the local church. A 'contribution'. To which Paul replied, succinctly, 'You'll get fuck all.' The guy shrugged and responded with the Italian equivalent of, 'OK, I'm away for my dinner.' The clock ticked onward. The crowd was becoming restless. It was all getting quite angsty. Eventually an accommodation was reached, we went on and had the time of our lives. It was an outdoor show, in a basketball arena. We were playing right on the water. Across the Messina Strait I could see the lights burning on mainland Italy. I remember being on stage and thinking it was one of the most beautiful scenes I had ever witnessed.

The following day, en route from Messina to Catania to fly out of Sicily, one of the Italians in our party explained that they wanted to show me Taormina. We were taken to lunch at a restaurant high above the main town. It was the day of my twenty-fourth birthday; it was also the birthday of Simple Minds' lighting designer, Steve Pollard. I have a feeling someone else within our party had a birthday on the same day we visited Taormina. It was also the end of a very successful run of Italian dates. As such, a general mood of buoyancy and celebration was in the air. At lunch, someone brought out a cake with candles while below us the town erupted in a festival of light, colour and sound. It happened to be the feast day of the patron saint of Taormina, San Pancrazio. There were fireworks, marching bands and crowds carrying statues through the town. I later learned such a spectacle is a regular sight throughout the summer months, as Italian couples marry in the many churches that line the town's main artery, Corso Umberto.

I was entranced by it all. I made myself a promise: *As soon as possible, I am coming back here on holiday* – and I did. I met a girl in Rome and six months later we drove all the way down through Naples to Sicily. She seemed to know all these shady figures.

Italy, I realised, was mysterious, magical and great fun.

Burchill/

In common with Jim, I've had a strong connection to Italy for the longest time. And like Jim, there was also a woman involved.

Throughout most of the decade when Simple Minds were becoming a global success story, I had an Italian girlfriend, Gabriella. We met in 1980 and stayed together for nine years, on and off.

Gabriella was an air hostess, but she was also an artist. She played saxophone. It is, in fact, her fault that my efforts at playing sax feature on some of the earliest Simple Minds records. I liken them to a cat being strangled. I started learning saxophone with her and we would often play together. Jim's brother Paul would call us Pigbag. I don't think it was a compliment.

On one occasion we were staying in a hotel in Milan. We had been listening to *Off White* by James White and the Blacks, a very avant-garde New York brass outfit. We loved their album and were attempting to play together in that style. After a while the concierge in the hotel came up to our room and knocked, quite firmly, on the door. He said, 'Sir, please, please, can you stop playing now? *Please.* Maestro Solti is trying to sleep in the room below.' Can you imagine! Georg Solti, the legendary conductor, was trying to get some shut eye in Milan only to be confronted with our experimental sax skronks crashing through the ceiling.

During that period, I was living out of a suitcase. When we had any time off the road, which wasn't often, I based myself between Scotland and Italy. Gabriella was from Turin but lived in Rome, and I spent a lot of time there. I was back and forth; Romin' in the Gloaming. I always felt very comfortable in Italy. Over the years I spent long periods in different parts of the country, but the north was my patch. Perhaps my and Jim's visit to Verona on our teenage hitchhiking trip had been an omen.

When I was married, throughout the nineties my family was based in Dublin. After my divorce, in the early 2000s, we sold up in Ireland and I had to work out where I was going to live. I had a close friend in Rome who had an apartment that was available, and I quickly took it and moved back there. It was familiar and by then I could speak the language reasonably well. I took all my equipment, and I started writing and working in the city.

Later, after I met my partner Win Hong, who is Dutch, I lived with her in Holland. But Italy was always calling. Jim and I had been toying with the idea for years of both living here permanently. He came to Taormina in the early 2000s, and I finally bought a house here in 2023.

It is hard to put it into words. There is something almost narcotically enticing about Sicily. It gives me the best of both worlds. Sicily is culturally distinct; it has its own flavour – and yet it's still Italy. And for a long time, Italy has felt like home.

Kerr/

Sicily is a genuinely cosmic place to live. It throws up the question, just as Mount Etna throws up clouds of volcanic tephra: *who are we?* Because this is where it all started. Sicily was one of the great centres of Greek civilisation. The waters I'm looking at right now are the same waters that are written about in the *Odyssey*. This is one of the spots where philosophy and intellectual thought began. This is where Archimedes worked it out. Eureka? You betcha! This is where East meets West meets Africa. There is a richness here that I can feel in the air. Some days I can practically touch it, as I walk the hills of this three-pointed island with a huge, active volcano at its centre.

It is an amazingly rich place. Primordial. It holds special powers. The apartment I'm writing in today is just across the road from the hotel I built in Taormina. I only visit the hotel perhaps once a week, but I see holidaymakers coming and going in the street, and I talk to them. On the day they arrive, on a flight from Birmingham or Manchester or Dortmund, they look a little tired and beaten up. I see them three days later and they're transformed. Lit up. There is a richness here that feeds the spirit.

Every person finds their connections in different ways and in different places. I have felt energised in New York, in Glasgow, in the Highlands. But I find it most often in Sicily. You can't discount the sun, which seeps into the culture. Sicilians are warm. People here still hang out of windows to talk to you. Alongside the weather, landscape, food, cultural ambience and history, not for a minute forgetting people I have met and the friendships forged along the way, one of the main reasons I value my life in Taormina so much these days is the notion that it intrinsically helps me in my goal of living in good health, mentally and physically, for as long as possible.

I remember when I finally committed to coming here to live. Another eureka moment. I thought, *You have made art your life, should you not also make your life art? If you are fortunate enough to have the wherewithal: should you not strive to make your life art?* In both my case and Charlie's, I believe we've achieved that in deciding to live here.

I am a born enthusiast. That's what motivates me to push to make things happen. Enthusiasm. From the Greek word *entheos*: to be filled with love, or God, from within. You love something to the extent of picking up the guitar or finding yourself at the side of the road with your thumb out. You love something enough to stick with it through hell, high water and dozens of ex-band members. And you love something enough to the extent of saying, *Not only am I moving here, but I am going to build a hotel here even though everyone says I am crazy; that it's the worst place to invest in and I don't know anything about it.* All of which was true! I did it anyway. Because *not* to do it was going to make me angsty, restless and antisocial. I hope my enthusiasm shines through all the things I have done, but living in Sicily might just be the most profound and rewarding manifestation of it. It turns life into art.

I have put down roots in the place I always imagined I would. Chrissie Hynde would verify this. She used to say to me, 'Jim, you're going to end up as an old guy sitting in Italy growing tomatoes' – which has turned out to be not quite true. I grow olives, not tomatoes. But from the first day I set foot in Italy I had the desire to live here.

It wasn't a bad school trip, all told.

6
Inside/Out

Be a loner. That gives you time to wonder, to search for
the truth. Have holy curiosity. Make your life worth living.

– Albert Einstein

Back to reality.

The teacher is going around the class asking each of us to read a passage out loud from our school books.

As my time to read approaches, I sense what's coming.

The boy in front of me finishes.

It's my turn.

The teacher barely looks up:

'Jim? Don't bother.'

Kerr/

As exposing as it is to admit it, as a boy I craved attention. Recognition of some sort. That's not easy to come by when deep down you think there is nothing about you at all that could be described as being anything other than solidly average. Believe me, throughout my school years, at best I was no more than solidly average.

When I was young, I had a pronounced stammer; pronounced enough that it was always made fun of. I was never bullied, but whenever I came into a new set of social circumstances someone would inevitably comment on it. I hated it, of course, and at school I had a couple of ignorant teachers who made it harder. Whenever we were doing a class reading, they were so dismissive. They thought they were doing me a favour by passing me over. They weren't.

One teacher even took it upon herself to suggest that it might be better for me to go to a 'special' school, because then I wouldn't get bullied or picked on – despite the fact I didn't get bullied or picked on. My mum soon put that idea to bed. Yes, people would comment on my stammer, but they would also comment if someone had ginger hair or freckles or wore glasses. Those are the rules of engagement at school. They didn't take the mickey every day. Also, I was quite handy. I could deal with any trouble.

It was only when I went outside of my circle that I was bothered by it. From a young age, as opposed to throwing myself into that world every day, on occasion I decided to amuse myself. Whereas other kids would stay at home and draw or paint, I would retreat into my own world for an hour or two. My dad always told great stories and afterwards he would say, 'Now, *you* tell *me* a story.' I found that through this game of storytelling, this small act of creation and imagination, I could occupy myself for a long time.

I have come to understand that my connection with words had a lot to do with staying quiet. I stayed quiet because sometimes it was very frustrating trying to be understood. And I found that when I was quiet, thoughts drifted into my head. I didn't start to write from any intellectual impetus. I began as a little kid amusing himself on days when he didn't feel like playing with other kids or having to struggle to explain himself. Ever since, writing and playing creatively with words has given me a place I can slip into. A place that gives comfort and security. I had no idea what the merits of poetry were, but I realise now that I was already developing a poetic view on even the everyday things that surrounded me.

The stammer made me go inside myself. That became a very present part of my character. I have an introvert side, but

I'm not introverted. I am very sociable in certain scenarios, but perhaps not as socially active as people might imagine. On the road, I've missed out on so many 'legendary' nights and experiences by instead retreating to my room, not feeling the same need as just about everyone else in our group to join the fray. To this day, I spend many hours of the day on my own. Guess what? I love it. Perhaps more than that, I need it to function and I'm very protective of it. I feel very trapped and get angsty when it's not available. It's one of the reasons I love to get up early. I like to have the world to myself when my brain is fresh, and the day full of promise.

During the first part of the COVID pandemic, I ended up spending months completely on my own in my house near Loch Earn. It was a doddle. Absolutely no problem. If you can live in your own head, and you have a curiosity and a desire to learn and pull the essence out of the things you encounter, that kind of independence and self-sufficiency is a great resource to draw from. If you develop that when you're young, it is a very useful attribute.

I'm still a bit of an odd fish. The main town in Taormina is five minutes' walk from where I live. Each day, everyone congregates there to eat, shop, drink and chat. I go perhaps once a week and, if you met me on the street, you would meet a very sociable, outgoing person. But I'd rather head for the hills – and I do, every day. Goat bells and crickets for me. I love it. It's where I get my thinking done. I come back hours later full of ideas and plans and thoughts. There's so much to do, to read, to write, to think, to walk, to talk on the phone, to listen to music. None of that involves needing other people around.

I had been living in Taormina for twenty years by the time Charlie rocked up. He came to live here because he loved the place as much as me, but it was quite convenient that by the time he did he could use all my contacts to help him set up shop. Charlie talks to everybody. He knows every waiter and every chef. He'd only been here three months and already the town was ringing to the cries of, 'Charlie, Charlie!'

One day I was in town and felt peckish. It was half-past two. The restaurants tend to shut their kitchens after two, but I tried my luck at one place where I didn't know the maître d'. I said, 'I know it's late, but . . . any chance?' He put on a comically pained face. It wasn't looking good. Then I heard a voice from the back room shouting in Sicilian: 'Let him in, he's Charlie's pal!' *What?* I've been here for twenty years! It tells you a lot about him, but it also tells you a lot about me.

I like my own company, but by no means am I a loner – and neither am I lonely. I have some of the same traits as my dad, who was a popular man. As a kid, if I wasn't going out, most days people would come to the door asking for me. That hasn't changed. I'm in a very fortunate position that whenever I do want to socialise, there are people who seem happy to see me. And usually, I feel I bring something to the party because I have been thinking about things and have something to say.

I was never a wallflower. But in my stammering days, which lasted well into the early years of Simple Minds, I wouldn't have spoken to you until you had spoken to me. To go from that to throwing yourself into a rock band and, furthermore, to taking the front position, is quite an interesting journey. When you're jumping up and down and waving your arms around on stage, you are essentially saying: *I'm worth looking at. I'm worth listening to.* Perhaps subconsciously I recognised a means of getting the attention I always craved without having to say too much.

Burchill/

Jim and I are complete opposites, which is another reason we fit together like two jigsaw pieces.

I could never in a million years live like Jim and he could never live like me. He spends a lot of his time alone. I'm a

58

much more social creature. I know everyone in Taormina. He gets up at the crack of dawn and goes to bed early; I stay up until four o'clock in the morning. He doesn't drink; I love a drink. I can't sleep in the daytime; I get four hours' sleep at night. I have too much nervous energy. Always jumping around. Jim is completely different. I call him the Monk.

Recently I went back to Holland to see Win Hong. I'd left some things at Jim's house and when I came back to Taormina I called him. No answer. I walked up to his apartment. Every door was open. I was shouting, banging on the doors. Nothing. I went in and saw that my stuff was there, so I took it and left. Two hours later Jim noticed that he'd had a missed call from me and rang. I told him I'd just been at his apartment to pick up my things. '*Really?*' He had been sleeping there the entire time I was shouting and clattering about. The Monk.

Jim takes his time. He conserves energy. He thinks before he speaks. When an interviewer asks him a question, there is often quite a long pause before he answers. That may be partly a legacy of his stutter, even though Jim hasn't stammered for a very long time. People who don't know him well might sometimes take that pause in the wrong way. It can be intimidating, but it's not intended to be. It's just the way he is. He thinks a lot about his words. I have often tried to learn from it and I haven't learned a thing. Ask me a question and I dive in instantly.

You could talk to each of us for one minute and the ways in which we respond sum up so many of the differences between us.

7

Biba Rom-Com

I never studied anything.
I joined bands and made all my mistakes onstage.

– Ringo Starr

We have formed a band and we call it Biba Rom. Me, Charlie, Tony Donald, Brian McGee and Joe Donnelly. Not just a school band – it is even more tightly knit than that. We are all in the same class at Holyrood. It is quite something.

McGee has a drum kit, and we have been bashing around in his parents' basement. His dad knows someone at the Polmadie Railwayman's Social Club on Pollokshaws Road and we are booked to play at the Christmas party for the members' children and grandkids. Our brief is to play pop songs from the top thirty. Instead, we play 'Heroin' and 'Waiting for the Man' by the Velvet Underground. Our set proves prescient; heroin is in fact starting to creep into the Gorbals around this time. I like to think it is an educational party for the local youngsters.

We are all half-cut on cheap cider and blackcurrant. Snakebite. Otherwise known as Dutch courage. Charlie and I are dressed in satin bomber jackets. He may be wearing clogs, although he wouldn't thank me for pointing that out.

It is terrifying but exhilarating. At the end, we feel like 'made' men. A couple of our pals are 'roadying' for us. They say we were great. Our first review. And that's it. One gig. Over and out. For some reason we aren't motivated to go and find any more. Perhaps we feel we have peaked.

Burchill/

The first person I met when I started at Holyrood secondary school was Alan Brazil, who went on to become a very successful Scotland international footballer and then a radio broadcaster. We were placed together alphabetically. Brazil. Burchill. Despite the fact he was middle-class and a bit posh, we became good friends. We went ice skating together. We're still good friends, even if Alan's ice-skating days are long over.

Jim and I were also friends, but initially we weren't particularly close in secondary school. I remember exactly the moment it became a much faster bond. We were both walking around Toryglen with albums tucked under our arms and we started talking. I had *Killer* by Alice Cooper and the Doors' *Absolutely Live*. Jim had an album by Jobriath and Bruce Springsteen's *The Wild, the Innocent & the E Street Shuffle*. I asked if he wanted to swap albums. He did. I played them both when I got home and somehow got Jobriath confused with Bruce Springsteen. Then Jim introduced me to the Velvet Underground; I hadn't heard of them before, but Jim was already a fanatic. He even had a banana mural painted on his bedroom wall; a replica of the Andy Warhol designed cover for *The Velvet Underground and Nico*.

This time it was an instant connection. I had my own friends, but suddenly everything for me seemed to be channelled through Jim. He was the conduit. He brought people together. He made things happen.

We started a band: Biba Rom. The bass player was Jim's friend, Tony Donald. Tony had a bass, I had a guitar, and it seemed logical that we would go up to Tony's house and try to play some things.

This is really the origin story of our lives in Simple Minds: Tony and me getting together and trying to learn Velvet Underground songs. We were the ones making the music, but when Jim was around there was a complete shift in focus.

61

His role was slightly undefined, but it didn't seem to matter. He just needed to be there. He was organised and energetic, and it was evident from the word go that he was a leader. It wasn't just that he was a manager type. He was a born motivator and so encouraging of my early efforts as a musician. With everything I did, it was always, 'Amazing, amazing!' That enthusiasm was crucial for someone like me, who needed a push. From the get-go, he instilled a belief that we could be something. I would never have thought that of myself, but I now realise he believed it completely, even then. I truly think I would never have gone far in music had Jim not been the kind of person that he is.

Similarly, I always sensed huge potential in Jim, even when we were young. I had known years before, just from observing him on the bus, that he had some unique, indefinable quality. When we became closer it became even more evident. I thought, *This is the guy who will take us to where we want to be.* Even at that point he could pass for a rock star. He was cool. He looked amazing. He had a strong kind of charisma, and I was very drawn to it.

In terms of Biba Rom, it wasn't immediately apparent to some of us what he was going to do. There was talk about him playing keyboards. But it was obvious to me that he had to be the singer. It wasn't even a choice in the end; it just happened. Perhaps it is a paradox that somebody with a very heavy stammer could also be super-confident and end up front and centre of a rock band, but it didn't seem strange to me and the stammer was never an issue. It presented no barrier whatsoever to him communicating.

It was exciting. When you form a band, so much of it is about simply starting. There comes a point when there is nothing else for it but to do it. You gather a few like-minded people together and you say it out loud, like a magic spell: *we have started a band.* Out of nothing, suddenly, there is something tangible. In one sense, it's as easy as that. It's a mindset.

When you sit down with somebody to play together and see that it can work, it does something to your psyche. We were still fans. We were just trying to play the music that we loved. We would pick the simplest songs, like the Velvet Underground, because we could learn them easily. We only needed two or three chords. And yet it was a giant step. To go from being a fan of music to creating music, however crudely, is to cross a kind of Rubicon. The urge to do it, and the belief to start, was very significant for me. It marked the moment I realised that this was feasible. Until then, it was just a whole lot of dreaming about it. Jim woke me up.

Biba Rom played informally at friends' houses, but our only gig was at a kids' Christmas party. Over the years, I had forgotten about the venue. The social club isn't there any more. Simple Minds recorded recently in Gorbals Sound, a very good studio in Glasgow. It is owned by a friend of ours, who told us he was going to turn the back area into a radio station. He took us in to have a look – and there it was. The room where Jim and I played our first ever gig.

Biba Rom only performed once in public, but its roots proved auspicious. Four of the original five members of Simple Minds were in that band.

Kerr/

Charlie had changed a lot physically. The Bub days were over. He was a lithe, charismatic, good-looking little guy. Hell of a popular kid. Killer smile. Big on ice skating. Before pubs and clubs and the dancing, that's where the girls went and where you could hear music. Alan Brazil and Charlie were regulars at the ice rink. The idea of Alan on ice skates these days presents quite a challenging image, but I can confirm back then it happened quite frequently.

We were all starting to listen obsessively to music. *Properly* listen. Our tastes were developing. By then, T. Rex had arrived, Bowie had arrived, Roxy Music had arrived.

At school, people were starting to walk around with albums under their arms. These were like flares sent up into the air. As we entered our teens, here was a means of identifying who was part of your tribe and who wasn't.

Charlie and I started to talk a lot about music. We had some common ground, but we were coming from slightly different directions. He and his brother Jamie were much more into the singer-songwriter sensibility than me: Loudon Wainwright III, Van Morrison, Dylan. Jamie was very popular. By the time we were twelve he already had dyed hair, clogs and patchwork jeans, and was walking around Toryglen carrying a guitar in a case. Charlie and he shared a bedroom. To step over its threshold was to enter a shrine to music. I can still go there in my head: the records, the guitars, the posters on the wall of Jimi Hendrix, the Doors, Joni Mitchell. So many of our dreams – and early songs – started in that room.

Charlie, me and Tony Donald started to walk to and from school together. Around this time, not only were we buying records, but we were also going to our first live concerts. Charlie's was Led Zeppelin. Tony's was Alice Cooper. A couple of months later, I saw Genesis and Bowie. We'd walk to school the next day talking excitedly about it. 'What was it like, what was it like?' 'Oh my God, it was incredible!'

Tony was a very big part of it all. He was Simple Minds' original bassist and a great friend. We called him Big Skin. Skinny. Skin. Even my mum called him that. Tony always had money. He had a job delivering milk. The milkman had some indeterminate difficulties, which meant he often had trouble adding up; Tony proved highly adept at massaging the accounts. He bought lots of records. If we didn't have the cash, Tony would buy us concert tickets. He seemed older than his years, and certainly older than the rest of us acted. He already had quite an impressive collection of pornographic magazines, because he looked quite adult and had an arrangement with the chemist who sold them. Money, porn, concert tickets. The world revolved around Tony. Charlie and I were satellites.

Tony was the connection. He lived halfway between me and Charlie. He had noticed that Charlie had a guitar. At the same time, Tony had bought a bass. We would go up to Tony's house and the two of them would play. The choice of venue was a strategic one. Tony's mum was rightly famed for her biscuits and cakes.

Biba Rom was an extension of school, of friendship. Me, Tony, Charlie, Joe Donnelly and Brian McGee were all in the same class. McGee had got a drum kit and a place we could play. Joe purchased his first guitar in July 1975. I toyed with keyboards but eventually it became clear that I was going to sing. The year 2025 is the fiftieth anniversary of Biba Rom's only performance, which makes it half a century since the first ever time I sang on a stage.

Afterwards, we kept the rehearsals going. Then Joe started doing his own thing and, for Charlie and me, hitchhiking took over.

For a while, that was all we wanted to do. Travel.

8

Under the Influence

It's not where you take things from – It's where you take them to.

– Jean-Luc Godard

Charlie and I start going to the Citizens Theatre in the Gorbals. We are 'getting into' contemporary theatre, literature and arthouse film. There is a shared interest in pushing the boundaries of our cultural experiences that most of the other people around us don't seem to have.

What prompts this lofty notion? A teacher called Robertson looks at the way we are dressed and sees the artwork on the records we constantly carry around and suggests we should go to the Citizens. He says, 'They have an avant-garde style of doing Shakespeare' – and indeed they really do; these productions are experimental beyond any reference we can think of. It is the first time I have heard that lovely phrase: avant-garde. I might have seen it written down before, probably in a John Cage review in the NME. *I have no idea what it means, but I like the sound of it.*

One of the first plays we see is Antony and Cleopatra. *Cleopatra is played by a man, and a band performs Lou Reed's 'Walk on the Wild Side'. Fuck me. And the actors! Although the Citizens is in the heart of the Gorbals, and although it is very much a Scottish enterprise, it seems to us otherworldly; as though we have stumbled upon a secret portal to another way of being. It somehow upends our version of the city we live in. It is a shimmering oasis within a cultural desert.*

There is an effect that will in time come to be called the 'Scottish cringe' – the inferiority complex felt among some Scottish people and the consequent embarrassment at the more clichéd expressions of our culture. Before we have even heard the term, we are well aware (and wary) of it. The Citizens has no truck with the 'Scottish cringe'. It reframes our perception of Glasgow, of Scotland, of art and music.

And ourselves.

Kerr/

We became regulars at the Citizens. Much of the early Simple Minds feel – the clothes, the mood and my approach to performance – was very much influenced by some of the characters we had seen performing there. I saw a photograph quite recently of one of the first Simple Minds gigs, and it dawned on me that my get-up was like something from the Citz's production of *A Midsummer Night's Dream*.

It was a world that was opening up to us in tandem with the music we were listening to. We were getting our first taste of arthouse cinema, starting with *Easy Rider* and some of the early Jack Nicholson movies, and the odd European film.

Each of these influences reverberated with the others. Although much of it sailed straight over our heads, there was an allure that matched our curiosity. Why did Charlie and I seek out this stimulus when other people around us didn't, particularly when we often didn't have a clue what we were going to get? I can only attribute it to an inherent curiosity. U2 had something similar going on with Lypton Village, a kind of metaphysical creative community they formed while growing up in Dublin. We didn't have a name, but when I later found out about Lypton Village, I realised that around the same time Charlie and I were taking a parallel path.

Unlike Charlie, I didn't have a big brother to show me the ropes, but there were some 'elders' in my tower block who threw out clues if you were sharp enough to catch them.

One was a top dog type called Alan McKinstry. Big Al. Another was a guy called John Sweeney. I remember being in the elevator one day with John Sweeney. 'What's the book, John?' '*The Tibetan Book of the Dead*. You should read that. You'll like it. It's good.' Or Pat Margie. I got in the lift one day and Pat was standing there without a jacket on.

'Where are you off to, Pat?'

'Sweden.'

'Sweden?'

'Aye.'

'How are you getting there?'

'Hitching.'

'Where are you staying?'

'Hang on a minute . . .' And it's some nonsense, literally a scribble written on a fag pocket.

But there was something about that lift, that magic box between worlds. It thrummed with possibilities.

'What are you doing tonight?'

'Taking acid.'

'Where did you get it?'

'Milkman.'

In Toryglen in the mid-seventies, there's a milkman selling acid. I'd get music tips. Someone would say, 'You've got to check out Syd Barrett, man.' 'Listen to Kevin Ayers.' 'Stevie Wonder is a genius.' I'd think, *Stevie Wonder*?! The guy that sings 'Isn't She Lovely'? 'Naw, that isn't *proper* Stevie Wonder. *This* is Stevie Wonder.'

They were informal mentors to me. A friend from Toryglen called John Brough was one of the first of us to go to London. He was living in a flat in Camden and he sent a letter back saying, 'You've got to come down and see this *thing* called the Sex Pistols. They're playing along the road from me in a pub in Finsbury Park. You'd love it.' There was a guy called Norman MacLeod. Nod. He said: 'You want to come with me on Sunday?' 'Where are we going?' I was a bit wary. I wasn't ready for Sweden. 'To see Tangerine Dream. They're the original synthesiser guys.'

I shan't get into names, but what could have been my first sexual experience took place in the elevator. She was older. If you bought her sweeties, you could go up in the lift with her. You'd see someone you knew sprinting off to the shops. 'Where are you going?' 'I'm off to R. S. McColl.' They'd be back ten minutes later with some cola cubes and a spring in their step. I think that was my first such encounter.

The elevator was a trip. It may have been a steel box in a concrete tower block where all our mums and dads were living quotidian lives above and below, but there was something about it, and these characters, that felt transformative. In the elevator I had a passport to *The Tibetan Book of the Dead*, lessons on analogue synthesisers, and sexual initiations. Really, it was our version of the street corner. You'd go in as one person and come out as another, usually armed with some new discovery to investigate.

Burchill/

The Citizens Theatre became a great source of interest and inspiration for us. We would walk in — house lights up, curtains drawn — to see a naked bald guy covered in white powder, sitting on stage for twenty minutes before anything happened. Two thoughts occurred simultaneously: *What the fuck is this?* And: *Whatever it is, it's amazing.* We were trying to figure out what was going on but couldn't quite get it. That was part of the appeal. I remember seeing *The Government Inspector*. Gogol. It had such a weird, surreal atmosphere. Very violent and intimidating. Quite brilliant.

Some of the actors at the Citizens, like David Hayman and Gerard Kelly, went on to have stellar careers. It earned a great reputation. Daniel Day-Lewis worked there. Rupert Everett. It was ultra pretentious and way above our heads, but we went with it. Why not?

It fed into the spirit of early Simple Minds, not only in terms of the imagery around the band, but the music itself. A lot of our early work has a similarly weird atmosphere: oppressive, authoritarian, redolent of government scrutiny. It's why we ended up having such a big crush on Berlin: the wall, the spies, the secrets, it all held a definite allure back then. We would get on a train in Berlin and there would be three passport checks from different guards: the Russians, the East Germans and the West Germans. We'd play some club and it would be like a building site, but everybody who was anybody in Berlin would be there. Jim was drawing on that atmosphere, and so were the rest of the band. That's why *Empires and Dance* ended up sounding the way it does. I can trace a line from that almost directly back to the Citizens Theatre.

The Citz lit a spark of curiosity in me, which ignited a lifelong love of reading. On tour, we spent endless hours in vans, on buses, in planes. What are you going to do? I started realising there was a whole world in books that I could access. It wasn't an intellectual pursuit. I wasn't studying. To me they were just stories.

There are many novels that I have read one hundred times that I could happily pick up tomorrow and read again. Dickens is a favourite. After being introduced to his work at the Citizens, Gogol became a big writer for me. Kafka. From there, I fell hard for the Russians. Chekhov. Dostoevsky. Bulgakov: *The Master and Margarita* is a staple. I like a lot of old science fiction: Asimov and Ray Bradbury.

When Simple Minds were making the early albums, these writers became part of our musical vocabulary. By which I mean, a lot of the music was loosely inspired by the general mood created in books written by several experimental authors. Borges was one. *Labyrinth*. 'Veldt' came from a Bradbury short story. There were movies as well. *The Tin Drum*. European surrealism. It was a process of osmosis, somehow tying the atmosphere of a piece of art from another medium into a song. I'm not sure how that synergy works, but in our catalogue it happens quite a lot. You're trying to translate something – and because it's not really possible, you end up with this other feel, which can be equally interesting.

Whether it's literature, theatre, film or music, for me colour is always the thing.

Kerr/

While working in America during the early seventies, David Bowie travelled with a flight case on wheels that converted into a portable library containing shelves packed with dozens of his favourite books.

A decade later Simple Minds had no such luxury. I can still recall Charlie on tour, carrying around a substantial leather bag crammed full of nothing but books.

Of course, these were the days before laptops, pads, pods, Kindles and smartphones had come into existence. If you were 'a reader' – and we all were, but Charlie is the most voracious reader I've ever met – there was nothing else for it: you had to hump your books around with you everywhere. I can still clearly see Charlie with his bag of books by his side: on the bullet train in Japan; on the tour bus in the middle of the Australian outback; while sharing a room in a motel in Missouri; most vividly of all, backstage in a dilapidated theatre in Berlin.

These days Charlie has the occasional problem with a recurring back/shoulder ache for which he blames the heavy guitars he has strapped on for most of his working life. My own theory? The obvious culprit is that big bag of books he lovingly carted all over the world.

71

9
Street Fighting Years

Fighting is truly one of the amusements of the
tenements. Nearly all the young people join in,
if not as fighters themselves, as spectators
and cheering supporters.

– Alexander McArthur & H. Kingsley Long, *No Mean City*

I write 'Street Fighting Years' as a poem in a letter.

The letter is written to Alan Clark, the brother of one of me and Charlie's closest friends. Alan is also the best friend of my youngest brother Mark.

One night, Alan is on the wrong side of town at the wrong time. As he is leaving a party with his girlfriend, he is murdered.

We turn around and suddenly he is gone.

Burchill/

There were a lot of gang-related territories in our area of Glasgow.

There was the Circus, which operated in Prospecthill Circus, the part of Toryglen where Jim and I grew up.

There was the Toi, which operated in another part of Toryglen.

There was the Hill, in Govanhill, where Jim lived when he was very little.

There was the Cumbie, around Cumberland Street in the Gorbals.

The Hutchie, down the same way.

And many, many more.

Gang culture was very prevalent. My brother Jamie wasn't involved but he knew a lot of people in gangs, which generally meant I was OK.

At the time Jim and I started getting bands together we were too young to be embroiled in that world, but it was always in the ether. You became accustomed to fights and situations suddenly flaring up into violence. Jim went to the dancing. I went to the ice skating.

A friend of mine got murdered there.

Kerr/

Glasgow was territorial once we got into our teenage years. It wasn't quite the stuff of the fifties and sixties, the notorious razor-gang lore of my father's generation, but all around us there were bovver boys and hard nuts in Crombies. Charlie and I knew who to be wary of. I wasn't in a gang – my tower block was more interested in *The Tibetan Book of the Dead*, krautrock and dropping acid – but I became embroiled in a few scrapes. It was scary as all hell, but I found it fascinating how addictive the adrenaline rush felt when you had won your skirmish. I understood the appeal of wild youth in combat.

Charlie and I lived in Toryglen until deep into the *New Gold Dream* years. We would come back after having been on *Top of the Pops* and *Whistle Test* and see the gangsters still hanging around. To us, they were just guys we had grown up with.

Violence was a rite of passage. Alcohol was another. In Glasgow, it was an integral part of the hard-man culture. Just as you were expected to be able to look after yourself physically, you were expected to show you could 'take a drink'. Among our crowd, Tony was once again the kingpin. We were fifteen and looked it, but Tony knew a pub in Glassford Street where we could get served.

We sloped off there one night during the Glasgow fair. I had some money, and I had just bought my first made-to-measure suit. I was convinced it was a bit of a *Young Americans* number.

Tony negotiated our entry into the pub where we drank pints of cider chased with Pernod and blackcurrant. Soon the world was spinning. Afterwards, we walked to St Enoch Square and as usual Tony bought a chicken supper. On the number 12 bus home I fell asleep – or more likely passed out. I awoke to the sight of Tony staring straight ahead and the sensation that someone had poured a tin of chicken soup all over me. I looked at Tony. He shrugged and said in his distinctive nasal voice, 'I'm really sorry about that.' He obviously wasn't feeling too well, but still – my brand-new suit! And I had to walk in and show it to my mum.

Those were typical teenage capers. We were all trying to emulate what the bigger guys around us were up to. Desperate to grow up fast. When it came to clubs – or 'the dancing', as it was universally known then – our favoured destination was Clouds, which was actually Satellite City, where Simple Minds played our first ever gig. That was where the hot girls went. Being merely lukewarm boys, more often than not we were refused entry. 'Not tonight, fellas.'

I drank during the early years of being in bands in an attempt to ease my nerves. I was drunk for most of the shows we did as Johnny and the Self Abusers. Sheer, desperate Dutch courage. That continued into the early days of Simple Minds. And then I stopped. Alcohol didn't work for me. Perhaps it also had some connection to my father's drink problem.

During our later Simple Minds days, Mick MacNeil, Derek Forbes and Charlie were all enthusiastic drinkers. Mick is on record as saying one of the first things he did when he left the band was to go into recovery. At the time, I didn't know that alcohol was in any way a serious problem for him. They all drank, and they were all pains in the arse when they did. As a non-drinker, after half an hour in the bar I thought that about pretty much everyone. I didn't join them. I'd had my fill.

10
The University of Record Shops

Born to Sing: No Plan B

– Van Morrison album title

I land my first paying job at the age of thirteen. A butcher boy. A couple of hours each day after school. All day Saturday.

The role consists mostly of delivering the goods as well as cleaning up the back store after closing.

The latter task can be revolting. Years later, I will still break out in a sweat thinking about the amount of blood and guts I encounter, particularly during the weekly visits to the city abattoir to pick up the carcasses of various freshly slaughtered animals. I do this for three years.

And to think I will one day marry rock and roll's most militant vegetarian . . .

Still, I think, it beats being at school.

Kerr/

Charlie and I attended the University of Record Shops.

I officially left school aged sixteen, with no qualifications. I had in fact stopped attending a whole year earlier, exempting myself on the grounds that for me there would be little point in continuing to study Latin, and a whole lot more sense in studying Lou Reed.

I recently read that, for our generation in Glasgow, the children of families where both parents were manual workers had only a 3 per cent chance of going to university.

I had a much older cousin who went on to higher education. To me, it seemed a distant world. It was tacitly accepted that such things would be a bridge too far for most of the people I knew. Certainly, it was never discussed as an option where I was concerned.

Many of my friends were second- or third-generation Irish immigrants. They were often part of large families, where perhaps a solitary child would be singled out as 'the smart one' and therefore deemed worthy of aspirations to become a teacher, a doctor or a lawyer. A phrase I heard a lot was that somebody was 'talented': 'Oh, John plays the accordion. He's talented.' 'Mary can draw. She's *talented*.' The implication being that such talents, like universities, were strictly reserved for other people.

Not that my family didn't aspire on our behalf. My mum appreciated how hard it was to make a living from manual labour. She would say to me, 'You don't want that life, Jim. You want to get a nice job, run a nice car, wear a nice tie.' It was less to do with financial attainment and more about doing well for yourself. My parents wouldn't threaten me with the consequences of not getting top marks at school. They were the kind of people who liked to make their children feel valued. As long as the report card was reasonably positive, I was in the good books. But God forbid if a teacher had negative things to say about my behaviour. Favours would be withheld.

My record at school was unremarkable but mostly acceptable. The subjects that captured my interest are still the subjects that interest me today: English, History, Geography. But when it came to Mathematics, Science, Chemistry? No thanks. And as for Latin. In Toryglen? *Non Credo!*

None of it mattered. I was marking time. Towards the end of my school days, like Charlie, my head was lost in music. It was blindingly obvious where my future studies were going to lie. By then I could skip school without Mum and

Dad knowing and I would spend the whole time listening to albums or seeking them out, going through the bins in the record shops, noting the recording studios, marking the names of producers and engineers, registering the songwriting credits. I devoured the music papers.

These were my textbooks. My parents and my teachers would never have thought that I was studying. But I was, and I was a fast and enthusiastic learner.

I was never a shirker. Working as a butcher boy had its downsides, but it was nevertheless a valuable experience in many ways. The boss recognised my efforts on his behalf and made me feel as though I was doing something of value for the first time in my life. Far more so than being at school. My first pay packet was £5 and I have never again felt as wealthy or as proud as I did on that day. I felt I had been of some use in the world. I was even able to offer a small portion of it to my parents. It made me feel less of a boy and more of a man.

I had only two things on my mind when it came to spending my earnings: to add to my ever-growing record collection, and to buy concert tickets. With a fiver being regularly squirrelled away, I soon had fortune enough to indulge those twin passions. Concert tickets were regularly less than £1 for decent enough seats; new albums cost less than £2.

I bought my first ever concert ticket for David Bowie at the Green's Playhouse in Glasgow. May 1973. A matinee show beginning at 4.30? When school wasn't over until four?! What choice did boys like us have . . .

Fifty years later I can recall the sheer excitement of merely holding that ticket in my hand. Those nights changed my life. I was aware that it was happening at the time. I didn't think for one moment I could also be a rock star; that was an absurd notion. Nevertheless, the profound energy generated by the music, the crowd and the lights, the entirely overwhelming spectacle of those first live shows, spoke profoundly to me. It told me I needed to somehow be involved in that world.

But not quite yet. The working-class boys of Glasgow were expected to become tradesmen of one sort or another. After three years at the butcher's, and after officially leaving the school that was already a distant memory, I became an apprentice plumber. My working life had progressed directly from blood to shit.

My uncle Johnnie was a boss at John Lawrence Ltd, one of Glasgow's largest construction companies. He said he could arrange for me to serve an apprenticeship as a joiner or plumber in the firm. Being a craftsman, he assured me, would set me up for life. Plumbing was the better paid of the two options. So it was that I spent the next two years after leaving school working on various huge construction sites throughout the west of Scotland. Not for a second did I consider seriously that this would be a lifelong vocation; my head and heart were already lost to rock and roll. However, to fulfil that aim I needed a regular weekly wage. A third of it went straight to Mum to pay for 'upkeep'; it was important for my dignity that I could contribute to the costs of my bed and board. The rest of my wages went towards buying records, saving up for amplifiers and microphones, and funding the hitchhiking trips that we would embark on during holiday weeks.

Meanwhile, Charlie was initiated into the building industry through his brother Jamie, who already worked at the plumbing company William Crann & Son. Tony Donald served an apprenticeship as a bricklayer. Before moving to London, Joe Donnelly was also a plumber at John Lawrence Ltd. I know for certain that during these years we all felt more as though we had been condemned to prison sentences involving forced labour than engaging earnestly in the apprenticeship roles into which we had enrolled.

Giving up 'a trade', the lifelong sinecure to which every working-class boy at that time was supposed to aspire, was not the done thing. I copped a lot of flak from my grandfather, in particular, for eventually packing in plumbing. He simply couldn't make sense of it. My own father could barely comprehend it. They tried to sell it to me: 'If you've got a trade, you can go all around the world.' The irony.

It saddens me very much that the last time I saw my grandad alive, I crossed over to the other side of the street to avoid him. Understandably, he was giving me so much stick about my choices in life and the way I looked. I was completely punked-out, with pink hair and all the leather gear. God knows what he thought, but I know what I thought when I saw him: *I can't deal with this today. He'll be gunning for me.* And I never saw him again.

A trade wasn't for us. Our formal education was over.

It was music or bust.

Burchill/

Socially, I had a great time at school. In terms of academic achievement, it was more of a slog. I had a terrific English teacher. Mrs Forrester. Her lessons were always interesting. She would hand out a journal written by some Roman centurion and, to me, it read like a strange kind of poetry. Mrs Forrester would make it entertaining. She was engaged and would explain the language and the detail in ways that brought the words alive. Most people in our class didn't get it, but I did. Along with my experiences at the Citz, I can trace my love of reading back to her.

There were, however, no great academic accolades to show for my enthusiasm. Instead, I got a job as an apprentice plumber at William Crann when I was fifteen. The work seemed mostly to entail cleaning the gutters on tenement buildings, which meant hanging over the edge of a slippery slate roof without a safety rope or harness. Nothing between me and a 30-metre drop.

I told my father about this precarious arrangement one day and he immediately said, 'That's it. No way. You're not working there any more. You're stopping now.' That was a huge thing. To actively advocate against his son progressing in what was regarded as a decent trade was not something to be taken lightly. By that time, I was serious about the guitar, and my parents thought, *We need to let him do it, because we're not letting him do* that.

Jim and I both trained as plumbers. Later, we occasionally attempted to do some 'private' jobs as a side hustle to get some money. It was always a disaster. Jamie would have to step in to fix the mess we'd made in people's bathrooms.

Like many aspiring musicians, in the end we went on the dole. We already felt that we were dedicating ourselves to music and therefore that was what we had to do to support our vocation. We chose not to work. We were musicians. We were in a band. That was our job.

11

We Travel

I travel not to go anywhere, but to go.
I travel for travel's sake. The great thing is to move.

– Robert Louis Stevenson

It is the summer of 1976. We hear word from our Camden contact, John Brough, that a band called the Sex Pistols are setting the pubs and clubs of London alight. He is adamant that they are the future of music. John may be in possession of a crystal ball. I mention this to Charlie and some other friends. I also mention that our latest idol, Patti Smith, is playing in Paris very soon.

A plan forms: we are going to hitchhike to London to see the Sex Pistols and then head to Paris by train and boat to see Patti. We can get a temporary passport from the post office.

In the end we are distracted by events. We fail to see either Johnny Rotten or Patti, but the adventure evolves. It gains a momentum, a narrative, all of its own. We end up travelling through Europe for three weeks, some nights staying in youth hostels, some nights sleeping outside. Modernist Germany. Classical Italy. Not knowing what the next hour will bring holds a fantastic appeal. You just stick out your thumb and . . . Who knows what might happen?

At first, the weather gods are not playing ball. Here comes the flood. Within days the gang is whittled down to just Charlie and me. We become demotivated. Dispirited.

Standing 'drookit' by the roadsides, we urge the weather gods to show mercy. Lo and behold. Not long afterwards, the rains cease. We make our way through sunlit France, Germany and Switzerland.

We reach Verona in northern Italy, where we sleep rough under the arches of the magnificent Roman Teatro. A little over ten years later, Simple Minds will film our Street Fighting Years *concert film here.*

Not now, but later, I realise that it is during these weeks that the relationship between Charlie and me truly cements. Seemingly alone in the world, or at least on the continent, with precious little money, in not giving up it becomes apparent that we share a similar tenacity, as well as a very active sense of wanderlust and desire for adventure. Crucial qualities that we will rely on in the years to come.

We are both invested to the same degree.

Both interested.

Both into it.

Kerr/

For many of our peers, the world stopped at the bottom of the street. For us, it was where it started. Hitting the highway, crossing the country on a quest for meaning was an archetypal story, handed down to us through the pages of so many novels. As kids we heard about the adventures of Tom Sawyer and Huckleberry Finn. Later, as teens, we were seduced by the idea of Jack Kerouac and his cronies in *On the Road*. We realised you did not have to be American to follow suit.

We came of age at the tail end of the hippie scene, which is where the impulse to go hitchhiking came from. We were also inspired by characters like Pat in the Circus. 'Where are you off to tonight?' 'Sweden.' There was a sense that a kind of liberation lay waiting beyond the end of the road.

My dad had a wanderlust. When he was young him and his friend embarked on an impromptu trip to Manchester and had a wee adventure. But his generation couldn't simply drop out and head for Nepal. It wasn't done. Whereas mine and Charlie's roving mindset was being formed in the wake of the existentialists and the hippies and the notion of alternative lifestyles; turning your nose up at the tried and trusted ways of life – the drudgery of working for the man (as opposed to waiting for the man). Our hitchhiking adventures were part of that. Once we were on the road, we were at the mercy of fate: who knows what would happen? Who knows what it would lead to? Who knows what it could become; who *we* could become?

Sliding doors.

We started local. There was a period when Glasgow's main venues were either being refurbished or shut down, and there were quite a few gigs elsewhere. I remember Charlie and I hitchhiking through to Edinburgh to see Deaf School and Doctors of Madness. We went down to Newcastle – we didn't get in – to see Patti Smith; we never seemed to have much luck with Patti. Otherwise, we were blessed. We only ever had pleasant experiences. Even if we didn't get to the gig, there was something about not knowing what was around the corner that became addictive. The idea of doing something interesting arrived with us at the same time. Can we get the money together to do it? When can we do it? *Should* we?

Burchill/

I have very strong memories of our hitchhiking trips. We started off as a gang of seven or eight: me, Jim and a few guys from the same housing scheme, a couple of whom lived in Jim's block. Looking back, it was obvious that they weren't the types to last the distance or handle sleeping in a farmer's soggy barn in rural France. Very quickly, people were dropping by the wayside one by one.

When it came to the final leg, it was just Jim and me. It had dawned on us by then that we viewed the whole trip differently from everybody else. We regarded it as an epic adventure, with us as the central characters. We spun romantic notions around it. Most of the others had just come along for something to

84

do, but we really wanted to try and explore Europe, and get a sense of what was going on in the world. There was a lot of music involved – not playing it, talking about it.

We got all the way down to Italy. Across the road from the amphitheatre in Verona is the train station where we slept when we arrived there after midnight. It got weird. I was woken up in the wee small hours by a bizarre old guy with nail polish on. He looked like something out of a surreal theatre troupe. He was right in our faces. A nightmare carnival vision.

We returned home penniless – literally. I was walking through a service station with no money, hoping to find us a lift, when I found a fiver. The gods smiled on us: *OK, we'll make it.* When we got back to Glasgow we were broke, but we had something more valuable than money. It was another experience that made us really commit to the idea of having a band and being serious about music.

It became a key reference point, one more experience that Jim and I had done together that we could later look back on and use as fortification. You learn a lot about each other's character in that kind of environment. At that age, you don't *really* know one another very well until the bond is tested. A trip like that, where you have no money yet you're trying to progress and move forward, required all the traits that would help us get through the early days of being in a band: having a bit of tenacity, a bit of imagination, figuring out how to do things on the hoof. Trust. Belief.

Even now, Jim has ideas where my first reaction is: *How are we going to do that?* But my instinct is almost always, we *can* do it, or at least we can give it a try. That mentality was forged early on. It's so much easier, too, when there are two of you doing anything. You egg each other on. You can't really draw back and get fed up. Solo artists have it incredibly hard. I thank God I'm part of a creative duo within a band.

The hitchhiking trips were formative. Not just personally, but creatively. The experience filtered through into the music on the early Simple Minds records, which captured the feeling we had of an intense fascination for Europe.

I listened to lots of American artists when I was younger. By the time Jim and I had started the band – or perhaps more accurately, by the time we were *thinking* of ourselves as a band – our sensibility was almost completely European. It was krautrock, Kraftwerk, anything a bit more colourful and avant-garde. Certainly not Americana. The European aesthetic was forged during our hitchhiking trip: travelling into Italy at midnight, visiting all these historic, mysterious places that we had heard about but had no idea what they were really like. Beauty. Brutalism. We saw it, we smelled it, we lived it, and it made such a big impression on us.

It all came through on the early Simple Minds records. Those trips were somehow translated into the music we ended up making.

Kerr/

Even after Simple Minds became successful, Charlie and I would grasp any opportunity to go off on our own escapades. I'm thinking of the two of us standing at the Taj Mahal, watching the Yamuna River rush past on its journey to the Ganges. We had just read *Midnight's Children* by Salman Rushdie and craved a taste of that Indian experience. We hopped off the plane on the way back from Australia, if I remember correctly. Years later we went hiking through the desert into Jordan. I can still see us, floating in the Dead Sea. We stood together on the ocean floor while scuba diving in Fiji and, perhaps even more memorably, were warned to keep an eye open for sharks as we swam out on the Cape of Good Hope in South Africa, enthralled to know that we were thrashing around at the point where the world's two most powerful oceans meet.

We both fell in love with *The Master and Margarita*. It may well be my all-time favourite novel. Charlie read it before me and regularly raved about it. It took a few attempts before I caught hold of it, but once I had, I was completely invested in the world of that novel – to the extent that in the eighties Charlie and I travelled together to Moscow and sat on the very bench in Patriarch's Ponds where the opening chapter takes place. Later, we ended up at the desk where Bulgakov wrote the book, which is now a tiny museum.

Unimaginable stuff. We have the *Don Quixote* spirit, though which of us is the Don and which of us is Sancho Panza is eternally open to question. We have found ourselves in the most extraordinary places because we imagined it would be worthwhile going. The epitome of that curiosity is that we both ended up living in Sicily, where Greek civilisation was nurtured, halfway up a mountain with Africa across the water – where he and I still try to come up with words and riffs.

All these years later, Charlie and I still refer to that hitch-hiking trip. We say we're still on it. *Because who knows what might happen?*

12

The Young Ones

Punk is freedom. The freedom to create, freedom
to be successful, freedom to not be successful,
freedom to be who you are.

– Patti Smith

Easter 1977.

The Doune Castle, Shawlands, Glasgow.

Usually when a band plays its first gig the audience consists of three men, two friends and a reluctant dog.

Our first gig as Johnny and the Self Abusers is rammed.

There are still precious few punk bands in Glasgow. We have the distinction of being indigenous punks. The only punks in the village. We put up posters and tell our friends, and they tell their friends, and when we turn up to play people are already queueing around the block. The punks have come from everywhere. They have come just to be punks. We are merely a useful context.

It is free, which helps.

We are a mad band. Three singers, of which I am one. A couple of dancing girls. John Milarky has a yen for playing saxophone. We do our thing. I have a feeling that we are probably awful. We go down an absolute storm.

Straight away, we get to feel as though we are rock stars. Halfway through the gig, amid the chaos and the smoke and the din, Charlie and I look at each other. I know what he is thinking: Wouldn't it be great to do this – properly – for the rest of our lives?

Kerr/

After we had been hitchhiking, we became acutely aware of the size and variety of the world out there. That awareness engendered a sense of emancipation: you don't have to be stuck. You don't have to take that job on the building site. It gave us confidence to combat the kind of people – and there are always plenty of them, then and now – who say, 'Who the hell are *you* to get up on stage?' There was a lot of that know-your-place thinking within the context we grew up in.

We were starting to see pre-punk English pub-rock bands like Kilburn and the High Roads and Dr Feelgood coming up. Tony had got the first Ramones album. We loved Patti Smith's *Horses*. Something was in the ether. At the same time, we were starting to fall out of love with a lot of our earlier influences. Roxy Music weren't really our band any more. Steve Harley felt like old hat. There was something else in the wind. We were desperate to discover what it was.

By the time we came back from that European trip, or so it seemed, the Damned and the Sex Pistols had released singles. Punk had arrived. More important than the music was the ethos. You could start a band, or a fanzine, or a fashion label, or make documentaries. Before that, the feeling was: *you* can't do that *here* – with equal emphasis on the 'you' and the 'here'. For us, that idea had been destroyed by punk, and by going to Europe.

Everything was up for grabs; nothing seemed impossible. We weren't angry punks. We didn't want to kick against the pricks. But we were energised. It was time to stop dreaming and make real the plan of forming a band.

Enter Johnny and the Self Abusers.

'Johnny' was John Milarky. John was the not inconsiderable force behind the group. Very sadly, his mum and dad had both passed away and left him and his brother some money, as well as the house. His co-conspirators were Alan Cairnduff and Allan McNeill. The former was a Dave Vanian type; Glasgow's first goth. There should be a blue, or perhaps black, plaque on a wall somewhere in the Southside. Allan McNeill was more of a Withnail figure. An Olympic-level drinker. Could put Shane MacGowan to shame.

Before we collided into the chaos of becoming a band, we would all go to a bar called the Doune Castle in Shawlands. It had a bierkeller downstairs where groups would play. We wouldn't hang out with John. His crew and our crew took up positions on opposite sides of the room, watching each other while also watching the bands on stage playing covers of Wishbone Ash and the Eagles. We would tut-tut away on our side. They would tut-tut away on theirs.

Once punk arrived, there was a rapprochement. We were all dressing quite outré by now, so we met in the middle and started to talk about music. John knew Charlie played, and we knew John played. John said he was putting together a group. In truth, the group existed only in his head – but he was raring to go. He had seen enough mediocrity in the basement of the Doune Castle to last a lifetime and had committed to a gig there before he even had a band. For his part, the bar manager had grown weary of John slagging off the live acts and so called his bluff: 'Can you do any better?' 'Yes, I bloody can!' He was quite verbally aggressive when he was drinking, John, in that spiky middle-class way. 'All right, you're playing here two weeks on Monday.' Hence why he had invited Charlie and me over to the house that Sunday morning. He needed to get the band out of his head and into the material world. He played 'Pablo Picasso' and shook our world.

We were in.

Our side of the equation was me, Charlie, Tony Donald and Brian McGee: the remnants of Biba Rom without Joe Donnelly, who was now in London. Although John, Allan and Alan had also gone to Holyrood, they were from the other side of the tracks. Borderline middle class. They had

90

gardens. They would speak to each other differently from our crew. Eye-watering insults, laughing, fighting, crazy bouts of drinking. They seemed to have more permission than us to be reckless. Charlie and I had never seen that kind of a devil-may-care flippancy before. They were mad. They were great.

Burchill/

The evening after we all finally met, Jim and I had a conversation where we agreed that we should get together with these three guys and see what might happen. After Biba Rom dissipated, we were still very much invested in the idea of having a band.

It was always two camps; two bands within one. They came from a very different background. An interesting bunch. Great fun to be around. Quite mad. They brought a lot to the party. And John was great. Witty and extremely bright, with a very dry, very funny sense of humour.

He had a house, which was unheard of: a guy with a *house.* We could rehearse in there because he didn't give a damn about the neighbours. We would wheel our amplifier a mile from Toryglen. By the time we got to his place the thing would be in bits, rattling all over the place.

We started learning a set for the upcoming gig: Kinks stuff, the Velvet Underground. Some of the first songs that we ever learned as a band were by the Stranglers, who I really liked. They bridged the gap between having punk energy and attitude while using keyboards and creating more interesting sounds. We never really felt that we wanted to thrash. Even the covers we were doing at the time had more musicality to them.

We also rehearsed some originals. The material Jim and I brought to Johnny and the Self Abusers was written before we hooked up with John, Allan and Alan. The two camps never collaborated. John was the writer on his side. 'Pablo Picasso' was based on the Jonathan Richman song, but he had a completely new take on it, which made it feel like an original.

Jim and I, meanwhile, came up with the songs in our camp. We had started writing together even before we had an outlet for the results. With only a guitar, Jim and I would get together in my bedroom. People often ask me, *How do you write a song?* The only useful answer I can give is: *You just decide you're going to do it.* The big thing is to start. We jumped right in from the get-go. Even then Jim had a good way with words, and I certainly felt that nobody owned the chords. We could do whatever we wanted.

I don't know whether Jim had any inkling that he was good at it or even had a desire to be a writer. I suspect he did. Creativity was always an ingrained part of the deal with him. As soon as he started coming up with words and putting them together, it was apparent that he had a great imagination.

By Easter 1977, we had written five or six songs that we could bring to Johnny and the Self Abusers. Two of them were 'Dead Vandals' and 'Saints and Sinners', which we later recorded as a single for Chiswick Records. It was getting real.

Kerr/

'Saints and Sinners' and 'Dead Vandals' were among the first songs we ever wrote, upstairs in Charlie's bedroom. 'Dead Vandals' is much the better of the two tunes. I listened to it recently. It's all there. Charlie was already playing with a great rock and roll feel. We had a bridge. Cool coda. Charlie added in some wild sax wails. It's like a schoolboy version of the Stooges. I can hear Iggy singing it. That was our first salvo.

We played 'Dead Vandals' at the Doune Castle, I think. It's a bit of a blur. But there is no doubt we went down a storm. The next five months were hilarious. They were also slightly terrifying. There was aggro at every gig. Either the band would fight with each other, or the audience would fight among themselves, or we would fight with the audience. Once we were outside Glasgow and Edinburgh, the gigs were often in pubs that would usually book heavy metal bands with an equally heavy following. We would turn up with our dyed hair and painted leather gear. Gulp. Quite often the local girls would be curious, which would only add to the tension. A few years ago at the British Airways lounge in Heathrow, I was spotted by a highfalutin businessman travelling around Europe. He made a beeline for me. 'I saw Johnny and the Self Abusers play the Isle of Skye hotel in Perth,' he said. 'It's the first time I've ever seen bottles flying *from* the stage!' I remembered that it was true. I might even have been the one sending them flying.

It was a mighty adventure, loading the gear into the trunk and setting sail. I loved getting in front of an audience and seeing that people liked it. We were finding out whether or not we were cut out for this way of life. Jumping in to see if we could swim. I discovered that I could. Duck to water. John would sing a few songs, and he would always get a good reaction – but I would get a good reaction, too.

We had the opportunity to support name bands like Generation X and the Jam. And we made an actual record. John Peel played it. It felt like we were going places.

Burchill/

In Glasgow, there was a record store on Queen Street called Graffiti. The Simple Minds album, *Graffiti Soul*, was named partly in its honour. A guy who worked there, Scott McArthur, became what might loosely be described as our manager. The store and the Rock Garden pub next door became a kind of communal gang hut where the punk and new wave tribes could convene and rehearse. We met people there who were instrumental in our development, none more so than David and Jaine Henderson. Jaine and Jim later became an item, and she and David were great friends and supporters of Simple Minds throughout our early days. They were fantastic people. Fun and eccentric, always up for a mad idea, and highly knowledgeable about film, theatre and books, as well as music. They taught us a lot. They were very bohemian and came at art – and life – from a completely different angle to us. It felt as though we had formed a little community of shared artistic interests.

At that time, a lot of the bands around the Rock Garden were getting singles deals. We somehow became one of them. Our first stab at vinyl posterity was a decent effort for the time, although we felt Chiswick got the songs the wrong way around. 'Dead Vandals' should have been the A-side. It was a more mature song than 'Saints and Sinners' and had more going on; I was a big fan of Chris Spedding at that time. Listening back now, it sounds as though I was trying to get his guitar sound. 'Saints and Sinners' was more of a punk thrash. That's probably what the label wanted.

Making a single felt like a tangible achievement. You banged about in a studio for a few hours and somehow the noise you made became a circular piece of 7-inch vinyl with your band name on it. Jim and I were listed as the composers. Regardless of the merits of the music, our single looked more or less like all the 45s we loved, made by our favourite artists. Suddenly, we felt like we were part of the game. We were in the mix. I thought, *Well, if we can do it once, we can do it again* – even though this band definitely wasn't getting another record deal. Johnny and the Self Abusers was the kind of crazy that wasn't built to last.

There were several tell-tale signs of an inherent volatility. The band's van was once involved in a notorious incident after McGee had had a massive argument with John. It ended with Brian throwing a wellington boot through the window of John's house. He got busted, because he was the only one of us who could drive and, upon closer inspection, the van was discovered to be full of wellingtons – and one pair was missing a boot.

Kerr/

The band was *The Young Ones* before *The Young Ones* existed.

After a while, John rented a flat in Wilton Street in the West End of Glasgow. That side of town was unknown to us. University land. Charlie and I still get nosebleeds when we travel across the Clyde. We are very much Southsiders.

The Abusers, one by one, moved into the flat, officially or unofficially. It was only for a period of a few months, but no one ever seemed to sleep. We listened constantly to *The Idiot* and *Lust for Life*, those two great Iggy Pop records, and *Marquee Moon* by Television. By day we would hustle for gigs. I started to lean more into a quasi-managerial role, dealing with bookings, phone numbers and cash flow.

We bought a van from a band called the Jolt, a Jam-type outfit from Wishaw. It was a converted ambulance with some old aircraft seats fitted in the back. Because he was the only one of us who could drive, McGee picked it up and drove it back to Wilton Street. We spilled out into the street and jumped in: 'This is my seat! This is my seat.' It was all very exciting.

We were due to play later that night, so McGee motored off to fill up the van. He seemed to be gone for an age. When he eventually returned, he was ashen faced. The room was deathly silent as he walked to the telephone, puffing morosely on a cigarette, picked up the handset and dialled. Six pairs of eyes followed him. When the person he was calling responded, McGee uttered the immortal words: 'Problems, Wullie, problems . . .' It transpired he had filled up the diesel tank of our brand-new van with petrol. *'Problems, Wullie, problems . . .'* Charlie and I still use that phrase today.

The Young Ones.

By this point, John didn't even bother wearing jeans. He just walked about Wilton Street nude, smoking and playing guitar. Very West End. Very bohemian. There wasn't a lot of that going on in Toryglen, but we got used to it. Apart from when we were eating.

There was an argument one day about the band playing a gig near Stirling. I wanted to do it. John really wanted to do it. Some of the other guys didn't. We were sitting in a circle on the couches, and he was standing in the middle – buck naked – with a ciggie, going around everyone as though conducting a court martial: 'Give me one fucking reason why you don't want to. Why, why?'

He was getting very upset.

The phone rang and it was for John. As he became engaged in the call he bent over a little. While that was happening – *hooray!* – the postman arrived with our dole cheques. We were all signing on at the time. McGee went around the room handing out the cheques to each one of us. When he reached John, without even looking, Brian took the cheque and deftly deposited it in the crack of his arse – where it remained. John was oblivious. We were rolling around laughing, but he was immersed in the conversation. As soon as he finished, he put the phone down. *Right!* And he was straight back into the court martial for the next five minutes. Oblivious. I can still see him getting more and more agitated as we became increasingly hysterical . . .

The vignette sums up life in the flat – and the band. Johnny and the Self Abusers. *The Young Ones*. It was a rite of passage, both personally and professionally. Our apprenticeship. It was the first time I had ever stayed away from home. I would go back to Toryglen once a week to take my dirty washing to my mum.

But it wasn't built to last, that's for sure. Within a few months, Charlie and I could see the writing on the wall. I don't recall any major fights or fallings out, but the project obviously had a finite time span.

One of the final Abusers gigs took place at a club called Terminal One, in St Enoch Square. This was the place most people only went after they had been knocked back from every other club in Glasgow. It was just across from the Gorbals and the first port of call for the guys from Easterhouse. It was heavy. Last orders for desperadoes. T1 didn't usually put on gigs but they had booked us for a Saturday night.

As we were waiting to go on, the promoter played a new song over the PA. He told us it was a 12-inch single. *A what?* It was the first time we had ever heard of such a thing. My head was already spinning from nerves and cheap cider when I heard a noise that I'd never heard before in my life. Then a sensuous wailing started. It sounded absolutely sensational. It sounded like the future. It was Donna Summer and Giorgio Moroder, 'I Feel Love'. I turned to Charlie. 'What *on earth* is making that incredible sound?' He said, 'It's a sequencer. A kind of synthesiser.' I had never heard anything like it. I swear right there and then I said to him, '*We have to get a synthesiser.*'

That may have been the penultimate Abusers gig. The last was at the Glasgow School of Art. We went on at two in the morning. I discovered a review of it a couple of years ago, and we didn't get a very good reaction at all. Perhaps that compounded things. We were also disappointed that Chiswick had taken four months to put out our single. We broke up in November 1977 on the same day that it was released. Super punk. Charlie and I had already resolved to take a very different path. We were going to form another band. We even had the name. We were going to get serious – and I was going to be the sole singer.

On the one hand, Johnny and the Self Abusers was a kind of comedy spoof on punk. Just look at the name. My dad called us Johnny and the *Elf* Abusers. At the same time, it was exciting as all hell, and we learned a lot. I can laugh at it, but I feel oddly precious about it, too.

It was as though we had taken a college foundation course on 'How to Be in a Band'. I maintain that without joining that group, there is a good chance that Charlie and I might have sat in the pub and spoken about our plans but never quite found the spark to get moving. There are always people who don't want to start something until it is perfect. Johnny and the Self Abusers definitely wasn't perfect, but it was a powerful catalyst. It gave birth to who we are now and what we still do.

Burchill/

We had started. We were young, with lots of energy and optimism. We had played shows and supported some big names. We knew how to write a song – whether it was any good or not. We had made a single. We had fun times and a lot of fights as well. Jim and I look back on it with great fondness.

The next stage was to take it up a level. There was a playfulness to the punk period, which was essential. It needed to be that way, because many of the people who got involved would never have started, or would have got thrown off track, if they had been saddled with grand expectations. All the same, Jim and I were deadly serious. When Johnny and the Self Abusers came to an end, we had a better idea about what exactly we were. We weren't a punk band, and we definitely wanted to add colour and power and more imagination.

13
Everything Is Possible

There is nothing impossible to him who will try.

– Alexander the Great

Mick MacNeil has only been playing keyboards in Simple Minds for three months when he tells us he will have to give up the band.

He loves our group but he says he is going back to playing semi-professionally in cover bands performing in social clubs, hotels and restaurants. He needs to make some money.

I can understand this. We are almost comically skint. The band is engaged in a constant fight for its fiscal survival. By the time we pay for a van, fuel, equipment hire, the booking agent, and express modest gratitude to one or two friends who have taken the trouble to help us set up, all that is left from our gig fee is the lint in our pockets. Any brass morsel that might remain is required to enable us to get to the next gig – where we will go through the same financial stress-test all over again.

Such is the glamorous life of an aspirational band dedicated to the long haul!

I give Mick the big sell. Three record companies are coming up to see us next month. The NME *is going to review our next gig. We're going places. You can hear it. You can feel it.*

Mick looks at me: 'Does stuff like that really happen?'

It's a great question. I love the way Mick speaks. No nonsense. Does stuff like that really happen? He means: To guys like us?

'Is it even possible?'

The rest of us are signing on, but Mick is still working in a factory. His boss is getting in his ear: 'Don't give up your apprenticeship. Think of your trade.' It is entirely reasonable for him to ask whether any of this is possible.

My reply is instant: 'For fuck's sake, Mick, everything is possible!'

Kerr/

And I believed it. Where on earth did I get the gall?

Over the years people have asked when I knew Simple Minds had the potential to make it. I believed we had something special as soon as I heard Charlie play the riff on a song called 'Act of Love'.

It was the first song we played at the first ever Simple Minds show, at Satellite City on 17 January 1978. It was also the opening track on the demo tape that helped secure us a manager and a record deal later that year. It was, for a while, our big song. To all intents and purposes, it was the first thing anyone had ever heard of Simple Minds. It became our rallying cry, our banner.

We hadn't blinked after Johnny and the Self Abusers ended. A friend of Tony Donald's dad called Jim Duffy owned a disused lamp and light factory in the Gorbals. The building entirely lived up, or down, to the description 'dilapidated'. Dark. Dank. Dirt. Debris. Bare brick walls. Twenty years later some City-type probably paid a fortune to live in it. The windows were smashed and the rain came in from every angle. Charlie put plastic bags over his shoes before he stepped across the threshold. But we had the run of it twenty-four hours a day. Plus, a lot of cute factory girls worked in the vicinity. They would come up to watch us rehearse. It was quite exciting.

Straight away we had a gang hut, a place to play whenever we liked while still picking up our dole cheques. At the time I would tell everyone that our first record would be called *Songs from the Light*, in honour of our new HQ. I still maintain it's a great title.

Mick MacNeil and his coveted synth hadn't yet arrived, but we wanted another guitar player to allow Charlie free rein. We put out an advert. Duncan Barnwell was a great man to have around for those first few months, not least because he came from outside our tight-knit circle. Dunc was a real non-bullshitter from Castlemilk. Still is. Salt of the earth. A bit older than us. A grown up. And a good player. He shook me up. He listened to our music and said, 'I've never heard a Glasgow band that sounds like this. This is outstanding.' Charlie didn't talk about how great it all was, he just plugged in and got on with it. Tony and McGee weren't handing out superlatives – but Duncan did. He was the first outsider to confirm that what I desperately wanted the band to be might lie within our grasp. His belief hit me like a jolt of electricity. We could be on to something after all.

We worked almost every day. We were barely a week into rehearsals when David Henderson said he had found us a gig. Great. I like a target. A deadline. We had a new band name even before the end of Johnny and the Self Abusers. Simple Minds, from the 'so simple minded' line in Bowie's 'The Jean Genie'.

It was in the storeroom of that freezing factory somewhere during the weeks when 1977 drifted into 1978 that Simple Minds found not only our name but our sound.

Although Charlie and I had written songs for Johnny and the Self Abusers, the pressure wasn't on. It was a free-for-all punk party. When he came up with a killer riff on 'Act of Love' it felt different. It fired my imagination. I started thinking about the excitement of what we were setting out to do. We rehearsed in the afternoon in the bombsite factory, and on the way I'd walk past Govanhill Library, mulling over the idea of the muse: a voice from within that appears to provide inspiration. The belief was accumulating. When Charlie played that riff, it made me think once again that we could do this.

Around the same time, we also wrote 'Pleasantly Disturbed', our first opus. I remember Charlie picking out the opening arpeggio. It was the first time I'd heard the sound of his Carlsbro amp, soaked in reverb, and it made the hairs on the back of my neck stand up. You can't fake that. They were standing up the way they would when I heard some of my favourite records.

Something about the timing of that riff prompted the image of blood dripping from a needle. It was metronomic. I could hear it. I could feel it. It presented the idea for the song. You write from what you're pulling in, meditating on, as you walk around inside your own head, tripping on the music. By this time, heroin was in Glasgow and the first zombie kids were starting to appear. There was something about those characters that fitted with the music.

> *Black lines call out from his face*
> *His heart beats staccato pace*
> *She says he's not killing time*
> *I just don't want him for no friend of mine*

Figures in black. A death trip. But true to the nature of Simple Minds, there is a glimpse of redemption: 'Streetlight!' I would have been thinking of the Velvet Underground's 'Heroin'. An expansive piece, possibly Lou Reed's most theatrical one. We were looking to write songs where we could incorporate some of the Citizens Theatre ethos; where we could conjure an atmosphere in which everything was almost motionless and yet filled with a taut, uneasy drama. As much as we loved some punk records, we still had prog roots – although it would have been terribly unhip to say so at the time. We loved the idea of expanse, of conceptualising.

If the question was: *What kind of band are we going to be?*, to my mind 'Act of Love' and 'Pleasantly Disturbed' provided persuasive answers; ones which said, 'We're not quite sure, *but it's going to be Simple Minds.*' That was a monumental realisation: we are going to be our own thing. We were already aspiring to something bigger than we could at this stage pull off, but it was clear that we already wanted to be more than a punk band.

We played both songs at Satellite City. We didn't arrive fully formed but we arrived with fully formed attitudes and a fully formed sense of presence, to the extent that people who were among the hundred-strong crowd that night still talk about it. We already knew that we believed in it, but would anyone else? To see that they did was the oxygen we needed to continue. From that belief comes the attitude, the body language, the whole culture of the band.

For my part, I was already in deep. Full on. One hundred per cent. Zen Buddhism states that we only need three things in life: something to love, something to hope for, and something to do. Right from the off, with Simple Minds I had my cause. I had found something I loved, I'd found something to do, and I thought I'd found a kind of purpose – and guess what, I might actually be pretty good at it. All of that was getting in my head. It made me the kind of character I am, or perhaps my character dictated the intensity with which I pursued this. I didn't just want it, I wanted it to be really good. I wanted it to be great. And if the first gig was great, I wanted the second one to be better.

I was always pushing; I still am. The root meaning of 'mediocre' is 'going halfway up the hill'. Just the sound of that word scares me. *Mediocre*. Imagine being damned to spend your life going halfway up the mountain and never reaching the top.

The idea of being considered mediocre gave me nightmares. It literally made me sick. Through Johnny and the Self Abusers into the early days of Simple Minds I suffered from terrible stage fright. I would physically throw up before every gig. I wouldn't eat on the day of a show. I would drink in a misguided attempt to 'calm my nerves'. I would still throw up. I'd take whatever else I needed to take to get up for it. I was pretty skinny in those days.

The stage fright was strictly pre-gig. As soon as the music started, I had an armoury. Not something to hide behind; something I could use to lead from the front. I believed in the music. I knew how good it made me feel and I felt empowered by it.

But beforehand – acute, debilitating stage fright. It came from wanting so much for it to be good. Every gig had to happen. I feared it not happening, because it would make me miserable and antisocial. Doubts would set in and take over: *Who do you think you are?* The fear was that it wouldn't be good or that it wouldn't work; or the crowd wouldn't like it; or I would look stupid. Afterwards, there was a great sense of relief. And then I would both dread and look forward to the next gig.

I was only starting out, but already I had come a long way from the stammering school kid who had been overlooked and advised it would be better not to read aloud in class. Although it was terrifying to put myself centre stage and risk humiliation, it was also an act of fearlessness. The sense of purpose it gave me, and its visceral nature, were hugely addictive. Also, people were starting to look at me differently, both friends and people I didn't even know. I took myself seriously, but you couldn't reasonably expect everyone else to take you seriously. Yet they did. They came, they watched and they wowed. Quite soon you weren't just Jim; you were that guy in that band. Which had a nice feeling about it.

But what if it stops being good? What if that feeling is taken away? The desire for it to really work made me ill.

I was in that fretful mode until the tour in 1980 where Simple Minds supported Peter Gabriel. We had just made *Empires and Dance,* and we were opening for Gabriel all over continental Europe. We got slaughtered by the crowd every night bar one. Recently, I started to think I might have been exaggerating how badly we went down, but I found a review of a gig we did in Torino where the writer said they felt sorry for the opening act. They were really good, he wrote, but they got killed. And yes, that's how I remembered it. People were throwing objects at us. We played five nights in Paris and we got destroyed on each and every one.

By this time, however, I knew we were right and they were wrong. This time there was a sense of enjoying the adversity. We were playing songs like 'I Travel', 'This Fear of Gods' and 'Thirty Frames a Second'. I knew we were great. I looked out at this sea of negativity and I thought, *You'll see! You'll be back!*

Burchill/

I remember Jim coming up with the name for Simple Minds. It's from 'The Jean Genie' but it also has a similar cadence to Talking Heads. You somehow just know when you have the right name; it's not even a question of good or bad, it just somehow seems to fit. Simple Minds sounded self-deprecating, but the idea was that the music was going to be quite sophisticated. Perhaps I'm post-rationalising. In any case, it seemed to work. Decades later, we tried to buy David Bowie's handwritten lyrics for 'The Jean Genie' when they were up for auction. We wanted to get our hands on it, but the price went from a steal to a fortune and in the end we left it.

It would have been very easy to drift in the gap after the end of Johnny and the Self Abusers. To have a lot of ideas, but not actually do anything. We were resolved to immediate action.

We always craved drama. 'Pleasantly Disturbed' was consciously intended to be widescreen. The guitar riff is to my mind quite generic, but it was enough to set an atmosphere running. It leads to a slightly pompous middle section. Jim and I were unafraid of showing our prog-rock side. We had older friends and brothers, so we knew a lot of progressive music. The Doors were a big band for us. We liked Genesis and Yes. We didn't have a Year Zero attitude where suddenly a band couldn't be influenced by any of that supposedly unfashionable stuff. It was always there. We used punk as a means of getting a foothold, but we had no intentions of being a punk band.

We were already thinking about how we could make our live performances look and feel different, even in tiny pubs. When we went to the Citizens, we were always impressed by how they put everything together. How clever it was, how they used music, and how they could convey so much atmosphere from a minimalist approach. It fed into our desire to add drama to our music and our shows. We had an intro tape. A little light show. We used props that David and Jaine Henderson would create. Anything we could cobble together to make it look like we had a show was up for grabs. Everybody was on the same page, and that generated more and more creativity.

Because initially we had Duncan Barnwell on rhythm guitar, I could play the lead – or get my hands on something else. I would try to get a useable sound out of any instrument. With Duncan in the band, if those sounds made their way into a song, then the guitar parts were still covered. I played violin on 'Pleasantly Disturbed', filtered through all sorts of effects, heavily under the influence of the Velvet Underground and Doctors of Madness. I was studying hard at violin at that point, really putting in the hours, but after playing it on the first album, I couldn't do it any more. Jim wanted me to play violin recently and I couldn't. It sounds OK on 'Pleasantly Disturbed'. It has the right atmosphere. Slightly out of tune. It was a sign that we didn't want to sound straight-ahead. No country, no blues, no rock and roll.

We started playing a residency at the Mars Bar in Glasgow every Sunday and it was very exciting. Quite soon, our shows there started to generate a buzz. People queued out through the door and around the block to see us. We felt that all the ideas that we had to make things slightly theatrical and more interesting were paying off. People were getting it.

I think of us as moving between two different bands at that time. We were evolving into the settled lineup that became Simple Minds. We were getting a following and we felt we needed to up our game. It meant identifying weak spots. One analogy is a football team thinking, *We're doing pretty well, but some areas need improving. To compete for the title we need to get the midfield sorted out.*

Kerr/

From the very beginning of Simple Minds, we have had to make difficult decisions. Before we were even signed we were putting the band before personal niceties.

A few months after Satellite City, we replaced Tony Donald on bass with Derek Forbes. We were trading up. Musically speaking, Derek was a £20 million signing. But it was tough. Skin was a close friend, but we were getting serious and he wasn't pulling his weight, which in our eyes was a crime. He would be drinking Black Russians and smoking cigars while we were humping the gear into the van. I'm exaggerating, but only slightly. Tony always seemed to have cash, while the rest of us were scrapping together on broo money – unemployment benefit.

Later that year, Duncan Barnwell left shortly after Mick MacNeil arrived on keyboards. Dunc's dismissal was complicated by the fact that his dad was the janitor of the school where we had started rehearsing. It lacked the urban edge of the Gorbals but it was a much nicer place to be; beautiful and warm, and close to Mick's house. Because of this, Dunc got to stay in the band a little longer than he might have otherwise. With Mick adding so much to our sound, the space in the music was becoming clogged up. Also, Mick was a pin-up. I remember one night watching two girls having the worst cat fight I have ever seen over Mick MacNeil – who was sitting on a wall, rolling a joint. Oblivious.

In contrast, Dunc didn't quite look the part. Even at that age, he had lost a lot of hair. Derek was merciless about it. As much as I understand Derek's later disappointment over leaving Simple Minds, he was ruthless about getting Dunc out of the band. It was Derek's constant jibing – which could be funny, but was too often laced with a darker edge, verging on cruel – that speeded up the process by which ultimately we decided to no longer have a second guitar player in Simple Minds.

Giving Duncan the bad news felt as brutal to us as it had months earlier with Tony. On both occasions, I recall Charlie and I taking the long walk to their houses, fully aware that we were about to deliver what for them would be a catastrophic disappointment. We decided that the best strategy was to dispense with any small talk and get straight to the point: 'We don't feel that you are right for Simple Minds and no longer want you in the band.' Hard as nails. I hated hearing those words coming out of my mouth. And while I am sure my eyes expressed a degree of empathy, it would have been accompanied by a steeliness that suggested there was little point in arguing. Then, the *coup de grâce*: 'It's nothing personal. Strictly business.'

Afterwards, Charlie and I walked home almost silently, both a little emotional but also suffused with a sense of relief. Our methods may have seemed a tad mafiosi, but our motives were nothing to do with machismo or exerting power for its own sake. We were pragmatists. That said, we came from a place where you had to fight for your dreams; a tough existence installed a certain grittiness. Barely eighteen years old, we were already recognising in those moments that the band was by now the most precious thing in our lives, and that the risk of appearing to be heartless bastards from time to time was already an unspoken necessity. It was just part and parcel of what we were convinced was required in order to do what was right for Simple Minds.

Nonetheless, I well remember the nervousness we felt on those occasions. I'm grateful that both Tony and Dunc made it easy for us. Skin was a bit nonplussed – 'Oh, OK' – but Tony was that way about everything. There was no falling out. I think he knew he could never be as dedicated or talented as we thought necessary. Tony remained part of the gang. He became a longstanding member of the Simple Minds road crew, but he didn't seriously pick up the bass again – which tells you something. Of all the people who worked with us in those formative times, he is perhaps the one we miss most today. He stepped aside without complaint and was loyal to the end. We lost Tony at the very end of 2019. I visited his grave the last time I was back in Glasgow.

Duncan also took the bad news in admirable fashion. He understood he was not being replaced. I particularly liked Dunc. His spell with us was short but it was one of the most critical periods. His belief in Simple Minds gave me great encouragement at a time I needed it most. He moved to Australia and many years later, during a period where again my faith in our future was being tested, out of the blue I received a message from Duncan willing us to not give up. It made a great impression on me. Here was a guy from our distant past still wishing Simple Minds the best. A solid guy and a good guitarist.

But still. For the sake of the music, for the sake of the cause, changes had to be made.

Burchill/

Getting rid of Tony was a symbolic sacrifice. It signalled how serious we were. We felt we had to move up a notch. We saw Derek Forbes play with another band and it was obvious he was a fantastic musician. We promptly poached him.

Shortly afterwards we recruited Mick, via my girlfriend at that time. Her best friend was Mick's girlfriend. We were on the lookout for a keyboard player – anybody! – and one night she said, 'Oh, my boyfriend plays. He's in a cabaret band and he has this weird thing called a syn-something.' 'He's got a synthesiser? *He's in!* No audition.'

Jim and I went to meet him in a car park at Murray's Pipe Works in Bellshill. He said, 'I'll play with you, but I'm not joining the band because I've got my trade to finish.'

'Oh, right.' A bit deflating. 'Who do you like?'

'Dr Hook & the Medicine Show.'

We thought, *This might be an education . . .*

Musically, both Mick and Derek came from completely different backgrounds to Jim and me. Mick's roots were in traditional music. His family is from Barra. He was, and is, an incredibly proficient musician: a great accordion player and a really good piano player. At the time he joined us he had limited gear. The task was to squeeze as much texture as we could from a Farfisa organ and a monophonic synth. Despite the differences in our musical upbringings, Mick just *got it*. He had a unique keyboard style because he was a such a great accordion player. Nowadays, when Simple Minds perform 'New Gold Dream (81, 82, 83, 84)', our keyboard players have a tough time because Mick played these fast accordion triplets on the keys. It's a Barra thing.

Derek, meanwhile, was our star signing. He had swagger; he was a total rock star. The fact that he was always a frustrated electric guitar player was key, because he would play anything rather than resort to what a conventional bass player would come up with. Likewise, I never wanted to play anything standard. I liked it when my guitar didn't sound like a guitar. Once Derek and Mick arrived, I could start to play far more colourfully.

That said, we had to school them both. The culture of Simple Minds grew out of mine and Jim's musical and artistic tastes. We used to laugh about it. Mick was listening to Dr Hook & the Medicine Show while we were listening to krautrock. He was playing ABBA in a Chinese restaurant while we were listening to Amon Düül. Brian, meanwhile, was a big ELO fan. Being young and dogmatic, we scoffed a bit at the time. Later on, we realised they were great in their own way.

There was therefore a period of getting everybody orientated and integrated. Jim and I were quite didactic about it. We put across the sound and the attitude of the music we liked and wanted everyone to pull in that direction. That continued for years. You lift ideas from other people and try and make them yours. When there's a group of you doing that, you slowly start to develop your own unique sound. It can never be planned. The aim is to create an open environment where interesting things can happen, where you have a chance of coming up with sounds that you had no intention of creating. In time, it becomes your style. Your technique.

We were very lucky. They were all so good. It was an exciting time. We had put together a great team and moved up a level. We were all very different personalities but we had so much fun. There was a lot of laughter and a real sense of a community. Mick came from playing in social clubs, and early on he talked to us about leaving. He loved the band but he had a full-time job and he needed to make money. We impressed on him that this band wasn't going to fold easily. He became invested in it.

Quite quickly, I started to feel that the musicianship was getting very good. Other Glasgow bands were having some success, but we felt that we were special. Pure arrogance. The joys of being young and daft. But being full of self-doubt doesn't get you anywhere. We knew we were doing something right. Jim and I knew the real deal when we saw and heard it. From going to lots of gigs, we knew the difference between bands that really were artists, that really drew you in, and others that just turned up and played. If you wanted to be the kind of band we wanted to be, you had to cultivate it, and you had to cultivate it very fast. We grew leaps and bounds at almost every gig.

14

Everything in Its Right Place

As a singer, you *are* the instrument.

– Jim Kerr

Very early on, somebody takes a photograph of Simple Minds playing at the Mars Bar.

I focus in on Charlie. Everything is in the right place. He has his collar up. A little star badge. The Flying V guitar. The face. The hair.

All angles.

Everything in its right place.

There is real precision there. Real artistry. He looks special. Because he is.

Of all the other local bands I have seen there is nobody like Charlie, with his Carlsbro amp, his pedals; his echoes and reverbs. He even plays the bloody violin.

I look at the photo and think: Man, he's something.

I look at the photo and think: Well, HE'S got a career.

Kerr/

I'm not a great singer.

I'm a great Simple Minds singer, but I'm not a great singer. Technically speaking, buskers in the street can sing better than me; that's why they're buskers in the street, because nobody could care less. Good singers are ten-a-penny. But a voice that draws you in can be precious.

Within the realm of pop music, the voice centres everything. I always say that I'm not a musician – meaning I don't play any instrument – but perhaps I'm selling myself short. The voice is an instrument. Actually, it's the first instrument. It's the sound of a human being, and that will always be the most beautiful instrument of all. Beyond that, some might say that life itself is an instrument: the more energy and imagination you invest, the more profoundly it resonates.

A lot of the voices that have pulled me in are non-singing voices: Lou Reed. Leonard Cohen. Johnny Cash. Tom Waits. If the voice doesn't *belong*, if it doesn't present the world of the music, there's a problem. It's just not going to pull you in.

I knew from 'Pleasantly Disturbed' onwards that my voice was right for what we were doing. I didn't know I could do it until the first gig, which was the first time I had to carry this thing. That was the first time where it was solely me as a frontman, and the first time I became aware of that special space out front. It's a special space in the same way that the voice is a special space within the music. I needed an audience to validate it. At our first gig, not only did the audience give a huge approval to the sound of this new entity called Simple Minds, but they gave a huge thumbs up to me and whatever I had conjured up for that.

I had found my voice.

Burchill/

The first time I heard Jim sing would have been with Biba Rom in his house in Toryglen. It was probably a Velvet Underground song. It was difficult to tell at the time what the voice was, but I immediately knew it had character. So many people have ordinary voices. They are good singers, but ordinary. Even now, when Jim and I don't like a band, it's usually because we don't like the singer's voice.

Years ago, we had a consultant who was fixated on doing a lot of market research and audience studies. I don't normally

pay attention to any of that, but for once it was quite interesting. He came back to us and said that quite a large percentage
of Simple Minds' audience, larger than you might expect, are
women. And they whittled it down to the fact that women like
Jim's voice.

But which one? He has had numerous voices.

In the early days I could hear the influences. I could
hear him trying to find his own style. Yet there was so much
intensity and conviction it always felt like his own thing.

During the eighties, I don't think we collectively realised
just how much character Jim's voice added to the band. He
has always had a very idiosyncratic way with melody, because
he doesn't think about music in theoretical terms. We did an
orchestral concert once with Alan Parsons. Alan said to me,
'Wow, Jim has a weird way around a tune; he finishes a tone
above the root note.' He does that entirely naturally. Alan was
saying it as a compliment, while pointing out that it was really
quite unusual.

Jim can be quite critical of himself, yet night after night
he blows me away, because he is able to convey all the many
moods of Simple Minds' music through the years. That
is much harder than it might sound. I'm thinking of him
performing a song like 'Belfast Child', where he is completely
exposed. Whereas songs from *New Gold Dream (81, 82, 83,
84)* require a very particular character. When Jim sings 'Big
Sleep', there is no bombast, none of the mannerisms that
you might usually find in a live setting. Those songs demand
poise and restraint, and he delivers.

When I compare him to a lot of other singers in other
bands, I see the originality shine through. Some people
approach music in a very technical way. They obsess about
getting things spot on. Jim and I have never really been
about that. From the start, it has been all about emotion and
expression. For me, he is the best there is at that.

Kerr/

So what about Charlie's musical voice?

It gives me everything.

Charlie's playing and writing are so evocative. Celestial. Bells and chimes. He paints an entire aesthetic in the most beautiful colours. So many of his lines, especially his great lead lines, are crushingly emotional.

Charlie doesn't really approach music from a rock and roll basis. His desire to build layers of sound is closer to the art of the chemistry class: he mixes this, he mixes that, and it's never the same twice. There is so much more going on than rock and roll – although he is a great rock and roll player with a great rock and roll feel.

Charlie will come up with a musical landscape and from that I will tell him everything I can see. The pictures are always there for me. Very rarely have they not been. I have been incredibly lucky. Not only does Charlie have an innate sense of melody, which gives me something to work with as the very basis of a song, he – as Mick MacNeil also did when he was with us – gives me incredibly strong atmospheres. The pictures are so vivid, I feel the setting for the song is already fully drawn. In a sense, given the way Charlie writes, the words are always there – without any discussion between us. It's my job to dig them out. Even now, when Charlie plays new music to me, the atmosphere is always rife.

Although he sits down with the guitar every day, since the early nineties Charlie has played piano a lot more. It is now his main writing instrument, because with a piano you have a much greater harmonic range. The pieces he brings to me nowadays are much more formal, but they always have three key elements: a strong melody, a strong atmosphere, and a strong emotion.

When someone doesn't fit into any particular category, they risk being overlooked in some of the more obvious ways. Charlie hasn't had a tenth of the recognition that he

115

deserves for the way in which he has sculpted a whole sound, his melodies, his subtlety, his beauty. He is such a fantastic artist. But the guitar players and the composers know. When Johnny Marr or the Edge or James Bradfield come to meet Charlie, they bow down. The connoisseurs know how special he is.

Burchill/

The guitar remains an endless source of fascination. I do a lot of jigsaw puzzles and crosswords, and the guitar has a similar attraction: *Can you solve this? How do you do that?* I sit down to figure out something and before I know it I have whittled away huge amounts of time. It's a game, at heart. One I never tire of. I take a guitar everywhere with me, and every day and night I am either listening, or changing tunings, or playing with tunes. It's a lifetime's occupation.

I have no idea where I fit into the 'guitarist' landscape. I'm not interested in awards. I don't hang out with other guitar players. I've jammed on stage with U2 and the Pretenders, but I've never worked on other people's records. I never wanted to be an overt player. What I do is more about texture and sound and, often, playing as little as is needed to get the job done. I've always believed that the idea is the most important thing, and at all costs it has to be melodic.

I dislike busy guitar players. I avoid power chords or anything that sounds like it is trying to be flash. Jim tries hard enough to get me to step into the spotlight and play solos, but it's not my style. I don't regard myself as being that kind of musician.

I watched a documentary quite recently about synaesthesia, the condition where the brain becomes confused and a colour can denote a certain word or a sound. It made perfect sense to me. It explained quite a lot of what I can't explain about what I do. It's not as though I visualise colour, it's really that you have to *see sound in colour*. Those colours come from all sorts of sources: film, theatre, books. It's not something I can easily write about, because it is so hard to explain. Provenance plays a part. American guitar players are incredible at what they do but I could never do that, because I didn't grow up in that world. Outside of America, there is perhaps more exploration because we are not straitjacketed by one culture.

Since the early nineties, I have played a lot more piano and keyboards in Simple Minds' music, and I often use those instruments to write. While making *Real Life*, in 1991, our producer Steve Lipson was the first to mention that I also had a distinctive style of playing keyboards. He spotted that I had an unusual way of voicing. I rarely play regular chords, and the same is often true on guitar. I hardly ever use the thirds in chords, it's usually only two notes. It's very Celtic.

Whatever the instrument, emotion is the number one criterion in my playing and writing. I would never give Jim anything to write to that I thought didn't have any intrinsic emotion. On reflection, I think that element is what has shaped Simple Minds as a band. Jim and I are not really songwriters. It sounds strange to say that, but for us the singer-songwriter method is too mundane. We are looking to capture the emotion. If that's not there, then nothing is there.

15
The Deal

The music business is a cruel and shallow money trench,
a long plastic hallway where thieves and pimps run free
and good men die like dogs. There's also a negative side.

– attributed to Hunter S. Thompson

Our manager Bruce is on the line.

'How about a worldwide record deal for Christmas? Sound good?'

Music to our ears, Bruce.

'If you can all come through to Edinburgh on Saturday morning, the lawyer from Arista Records will be here. The contract is ready to sign. They have agreed to all the terms you've asked for, Jim.'

A worldwide record deal? Fucking hell.

We haven't met anyone with one of those.

Worldwide? We haven't even played outside Scotland yet.

And as for giving us all the terms I have asked for: where did I get the gall? I am still only nineteen, signing on the dole, living in a tower block. That said, I have studied a bit about the music industry over the past year. I feel I know the conditions necessary for us to be able to do our best work.

Saturday can't come soon enough. Charlie and I trudge through the snow, from Crossbank Road up to Prospecthill Road, where Brian McGee is picking us up in his father's work van. We are already plotting and planning the months ahead: recording our debut album; taking Simple Minds' music out into the world; getting our hands on the advance to buy the equipment we so sorely need and right now can't possibly afford.

Fast forward to a couple of weeks later. Charlie, Mick, Derek and Brian are the proud owners of thousands of pounds' worth of shiny new instruments and amplification.

New toys for the boys at Christmas.

Me? I get a tambourine.

And a dream come true.

Burchill/

By the summer of 1978 we were thinking seriously about a record deal. Jim and Davie Henderson travelled through to Edinburgh to see Bruce Findlay, who had a chain of record shops, Bruce's, and a small independent singles label called Zoom. Bruce had gained some experience in the industry working with Café Jacques and Mike Heron of the Incredible String Band.

Courting Bruce was another sign that we were deadly serious. Unlike many bands, we didn't want to rope in one of our mates to be our manager. We needed an outside voice. Bruce was older. His tireless enthusiasm and advocacy came laced with experience and objectivity. In Edinburgh, Jim played Bruce our demo tape and he was impressed. He came to see us at the Mars Bar and he was even more impressed. He got it. We got him.

It was a coup to have Bruce on board. We all loved him, and his energy, humour and dedication played an enormous part in Simple Minds' success for over a decade. And Jim and Bruce complemented each other well. They bounced ideas off each other. Jim was always a co-manager in everything but name, he always had the overview and the vision, and I think Bruce recognised the positives in that from early on.

Bruce had no patience for the traditional idea of going down to London, cap (or cassette) in hand, to hawk our demo tape around the record companies. 'No, we won't do that,' he said. 'We'll stay in Glasgow. Those bastards can come up here. Just keep playing and word will get out.' It did. And they did

119

come. We knew that if you went down to London you became one of thousands of bands desperate for attention. We played hard to get. The idea was people would be more interested if we didn't flutter our eyelashes.

It worked. We signed to Zoom and by the end of 1978 Bruce had managed to convert that into a three-album deal with Arista. We were paid a £30,000 advance to make the first album. We could very easily have got lost at that point. It's a dangerous moment. You can fool yourself into thinking that you've already made it. Bruce was good. He told us that we needed to buy a van with the advance and invest in equipment. Nobody was going on any holidays. 'This is the easy bit,' he said. 'Now the hard work kicks in.'

Kerr/

I always struggle slightly when it comes to articulating why I was so disappointed with Simple Minds' debut album, *Life in a Day*. I relate a lot to Bruce Springsteen's complicated feelings about putting *Born to Run* out into the world. 'Part of it was, I was afraid of releasing the record,' said the Boss. 'For all the obvious reasons that people are afraid of exposure and putting themselves out there: *This is who I am, this is everything I know, this is my best, this is the best I can do right now.*'

I knew instantly that *Life in a Day* didn't represent who we were or the best that we could do. It's a competent record but it lacks character. It's too polite. Too slick.

We recorded at Abbey Road with John Leckie. Legends both. John had been a house engineer at Abbey Road where he had worked with the Beatles and Pink Floyd. He would later produce Radiohead and the Stone Roses. He's one of the very best. As an Abbey Road alumnus, I guess he must have scored some very cheap downtime there as a favour and had thought, *Throw them in at the deep end. It will be good for them.* Sometimes that works. But our only studio experience prior to this was making a demo in CaVa Studios in Glasgow,

On stage, I look around and he is right there, always; exactly where I expect him to be. Where I need him to be. I know him better than I know anyone, including my own family. – Jim.

We don't talk about what makes it work. We never have. It's never seemed necessary. Jim and I have always operated under the auspices of an unwritten manifesto. – Charlie.

My instinct is to look out for people. I felt a sense of responsibility from a very young age of having to take care of someone other than myself: 'You're the big brother. Hold on to him.' – Jim.

(Clockwise from top left) With my brother Paul; donkey-riding on the beach at Blackpool; with our mum, Irene, and Paul; with Paul, Mark and, far left, childhood friend, Frankie Reilly.

In my family, I am an archetypal youngest sibling. I suspect I must have been quite the afterthought, and as a result I had the luxury of being pampered. Mum and Dad doted on me. – Charlie.

(Top) On holiday at the Hotel Cardiff, Ostend (L-R): Dad, me, Jamie, John and Mum, with two staff members standing. (Right) 'The Bub'. (Above and right) Relaxing at home in Toryglen, and on holiday, with my brothers.

Jaine was an amazing person for all sorts of reasons. – Jim. With my first serious girlfriend, Jaine Henderson, 1977.

The hitchhiking trips were formative. Not just personally, but creatively. The experience filtered through into the music on the early Simple Minds records, which captured the feeling we had of an intense fascination for Europe. – Charlie. Jim during our hitchhiking adventures in Europe, 1976.

We bought a van from a band called the Jolt, a Jam-type outfit from Wishaw. It was a converted ambulance with some old aircraft seats fitted in the back. – Jim. Brian and David Henderson in the back of the van, 1977.

Biba-Rom only performed once in public, but its roots proved auspicious. Four of the original five members of Simple Minds were in that band. – Charlie. Biba-Rom in informal mode, c1975. (L-R): Joe Donnelly, Brian McGee, Tony Donald and Jim.

was only starting out, but already I had come a long way from the stammering school
d who had been overlooked. Although it was terrifying to put myself centre stage and
sk humiliation, it was also an act of fearlessness. The sense of purpose it gave me was
ugely addictive. And people were starting to look at me differently. – Jim. Fighting the
ink wars, 1977.

uite soon, our shows there started to generate a buzz. People queued out through the
or and around the block to see us. People were getting it. – Charlie. An early Simple
inds show at Third Eye Centre, Glasgow, 1978. Me on violin, Tony Donald on bass,
uncan Barnwell on the far right.

Charlie's playing and writing are so evocative. Celestial. Bells and chimes. He paints an entire aesthetic in the most beautiful colours. So many of his lines, especially his great lead lines, are crushingly emotional. The pictures are always there for me. Very rarely have they not been. – Jim.

We had an 'Us vs the World' mentality. We were living in a bubble, rattling around from place to place. Strangers in every town we played. In such circumstances, you lean in to each other. We were not going to be beaten. – Jim. Mick MacNeil, unidentified woman, me, Derek Forbes, Charlie, Brian. Out on the road, 1981.

We conceived *Real to Real Cacophony* by jamming together in a room in south Wales. Our producer John Leckie loved it. Under his encouragement, we ran amok. – Charlie. The Old Mill rehearsal facility, Rockfield, Wales, the room where we wrote much of *Real to Real Cacophony* in 1979.

The stakes felt very high. A lot of the music we were making then was so portentous, it seemed of another world. The emotions it evoked were so overwhelming. – Jim. Touring *New Gold Dream (81, 82, 83, 84)*, 1982.

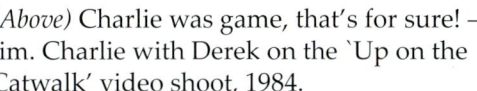

(Above) Charlie was game, that's for sure! – Jim. Charlie with Derek on the `Up on the Catwalk' video shoot, 1984.

(Above right) Bruce was a great champion of the cause, even more so than us. He still is. – Jim. Bruce Findlay, our talismanic manager from 1978 to 1990.

(Right) In a band, or in any collective endeavour, it is not an admission of weakness to accept when there is somebody smarter and more charismatic than everybody else in the room. I'd recognised it years before the band began. I recognised it on the bus to Toryglen when I was nine years old. – Charlie. Jim dreaming up new visions on the tour bus, 1984.

(Right) We were very lucky. We had put together a great team. We were all very different personalities, but we had so much fun. There was a lot of laughter and a real sense of a community. – Charlie. Band, crew and management mingle, 1984.

(Left) Even after Simple Minds became successful, Charlie and I would grasp any opportunity to go off on our own escapades. We had just read *Midnight's Children* by Salman Rushdie and craved a taste of that Indian experience. – Jim. Backpacking in New Delhi, 1984.

Marriage to Chrissie presented a whole other level of risk and reward. She was eight years older. She was a mother. She knew more than me, had read more than me, could sing better than me (better than most people). She could write. She was the real deal from the American heartlands. That was terribly exotic to me, coming from the high flats in Toryglen. – Jim.

It's so much easier when there are two of you doing anything. You egg each other on. Solo artists have it incredibly hard. I thank God I'm part of a creative duo within a band. – Charlie. With Jim by the beach, 1985.

playing in a basement for three hours. From there, we were pitched into the most celebrated studio on the planet. It was a bit of a stretch.

I felt the British class system pulsing through the very bones of the place. (I later learned that four Liverpudlian lads had had a similar feeling on the day they first pulled into the car park at Abbey Road Studios in their scruffy white van, a decade and a half earlier.) I hadn't experienced that anywhere else in my life at that point. It threw me. I've never been one for class warfare, but I started getting the sense that we were being (dis)regarded as complete novices; five northern oiks who were getting in the way while making our own album. *What are you doing here?* Some days, walking past the room where *Dark Side of the Moon* and *Sgt Pepper* were recorded, I thought, *Fair question: What are we doing here?*

Somehow, we had to find a way of justifying our existence. Not to John. John was brilliant with us and taught us so much. We were incredibly fortunate to have him in the first place. But Abbey Road and its British Establishment aura didn't work for us at that time. We could have done with being eased into this world, but we were thrown straight in. I felt like a football player who has never played in the first team and is suddenly told that on Saturday he's starting at Wembley. Tremendously exciting, and what a great break – but too much, too soon.

Burchill/

Abbey Road represented a world we had never known and I don't think Jim liked it much. I've rarely seen him intimidated but I think he was, a little. It was our first time dealing with session musicians. There were string players. Some guy came in to play sax. We were like little boys, with John Leckie holding our hands. He was a bridge between these Scottish scruffs and the somewhat stuffy Establishment world of Abbey Road, where everyone seemed terribly upper class;

all these people with names that we had never came across before. There were no Cecils or Horaces in Toryglen. *Where do these people get their names from?*

John was part of the fabric at Abbey Road. He was family there, but at the same time he was firmly on our side. And so playful to work with. I loved making the album. I have no bad memories of it.

At the time, I thought that we had made quite a proficient record. There were tracks on there that had potential. Everybody at Arista kept saying how much they loved 'Chelsea Girl'. We were told it was a hit. I honestly couldn't hear it. It was obviously indebted to the sound of *The Velvet Underground and Nico*. Two chords. The guitar parts are so generic. It's what you do when you're just learning to play. Similarly, 'Life in a Day', which was released as the first Simple Minds single, was very naive. At the time of writing them, me and Jim definitely didn't think either of those songs were destined to be hits. And indeed, they weren't.

When I listen back to *Life in a Day*, I hear an early shot at a band trying to forge an identity. Unsurprisingly, it doesn't really sound like us. We went into Abbey Road with songs that Jim and I had written together mainly on guitar. The album reflected what we had done as a songwriting partnership in the years leading up to getting the band together. It didn't have much of our collective band identity in it, and I think that irked Jim. Jim being Jim, by the time we finished it, he was already way ahead, plotting the next move. Some bands release an amazing debut album and it can be the kiss of death. The pressure is on instantly. Whereas we had a bit of headroom. We had somewhere to go.

Kerr/

Just before *Life in a Day* was released Simple Minds made our first ever live television appearance on *The Old Grey Whistle*

Test. Almost fifty years later, through the power of YouTube, our terror is still palpable.

First of all, we couldn't believe that we were there. This was a show we had all grown up with, that all the greats had been on. Bob Marley. Patti Smith. Bowie. Talk about imposter syndrome. Bruce had pulled off a masterstroke getting us on.

We had never been inside a television studio before. We had never played live without an audience before or sung to a camera. So yes, we were terrified. I especially resembled a deer caught in the headlights. After the recording, my recollection is that we felt that we had completely blown it. We hadn't been ourselves. There was an air of stunned silence driving back up to Glasgow over the Pennines. But we were too close to it. Whenever I watch it now, I can still see the fear – but man, it's cool. Mick, Charlie, Derek. What style. And although I'm definitely jittery, I think you can tell that this was a band that was going to go somewhere.

16
Real-ism

Ever tried. Ever failed. No matter. Try again.
Fail again. Fail better.

– Samuel Beckett, 'Worstward Ho'

In the van on the way back to Glasgow after making Life in a Day
*we hear an advance copy of a debut album by a band that is getting
a lot of attention.*

Unknown Pleasures *by Joy Division.*

Instantly, I think, We've blown it. *I am determined we have to
be better.*

Charlie and I love bands. We want Simple Minds to be a real band.

*We change the way we work. We become a proper collective; a
writing, recording, performing machine.*

Within six months we release our second album, Real to Real
Cacophony. *Bombs.*

A year after that we release Empires and Dance. *Bombs.*

*These albums are strange, atmospheric and highly experimental.
They alienate our record company and sell next to nothing – yet we
feel we're getting somewhere. They far better reflect the kind of band
we want to be.*

*Simple Minds are garnering good reviews but there is no glim-
mer of a commercial breakthrough. At heart, and at twenty-one, I
worry that this precious thing could be taken away from me.*

*All we can do is put our faith in the only thing we know how
to do.*

To go on stage and win the battle every night.

Burchill/

Jim and I were never precious about trying to retain the Simple Minds songwriting credits for ourselves. Our attitude was the more the merrier, because then you have a bigger ideas pool. In theory it should be a lot easier – and in practice, it was.

We hadn't got around to writing as a collective before we made *Life in a Day*. We didn't have time. Life was moving fast and we already had a store of songs that Jim and I had written. Almost by default, therefore, the album drew from that stockpile of material. We were just trying as a band to make the songs sound more imaginative.

The next album was a statement – to ourselves as much as anyone – that we weren't satisfied with repeating that formula. The band had bedded in and we wrote accordingly.

I would suggest that it's quite easy to hear that we conceived *Real to Real Cacophony* by jamming together in a room in south Wales. A lot of it was just being weird for weird's sake: there are tracks that are 100 seconds long; tracks in a 9/8-time signature with a middle section in 7/8; quite a few instrumental fragments; a couple of Kraftwerk rip-offs. It is a wild potpourri of sound distilled from lots of bits and pieces that we had lying around. John Leckie was back and he loved it. Under his encouragement, we ran amok.

If I think back to making those early records, we were very lucky that somebody indulged us: me standing in a cupboard with a saxophone I couldn't play; the bass line playing the letters X and Y; a French girl reading a short story and the rhythm track being an 8-mm camera. Someone was paying us to do that! We were lucky to get away with it. I honestly think that. It was so earnest. When you're young, you think wilful experimentation will instantly turn you into the Beatles or Pink Floyd.

The sound of Simple Minds during that period grew out of thousands of hours of unguided playing, with no thought ever of writing 'a song'. We used to stay up all night. I would try to make a guitar sound like a keyboard; slowly we developed a language between the guitar and Mick's keys. Add to that bass lines that sounded like someone playing a guitar. That was the way those early records started. It was very much about how all the elements were interwoven together. It's how we wrote for years afterwards.

Jim would give it all a context and a shape to the extent that it became possible to hear what a piece of music might want to be, but these were never quite actual *songs*. In fact, we had a bit of an attitude about the notion of 'songwriting'. I hear people pontificate often that unless you can sit down and play the chords and sing a top line, it's not a 'proper' song. Nonsense. Try playing anything from our first four albums on an acoustic guitar. You would have a hard time, yet it's still good music.

That said, we emerged from that period with a few solid pieces. I wrote 'Changeling' on the guitar: a picking riff at the front, and a sequence heavily influenced by the Rolling Stones in the verses. That was almost a proper song, and it became quite popular in the incipient New Romantic clubs in London. Rusty Egan and other influential DJs would play it regularly, though it was never going to be a hit.

We had 'Premonition', which had a really powerful groove and was another strong track. On *Empires and Dance* we came up with 'I Travel', a part homage to 'I Feel Love', which remains a regular fixture in our setlists today.

But at the time we weren't overly concerned about being songwriters. At a certain point that changed. We thought we had better at least try to write some material that had a fighting chance of getting played on the radio. That view started coming into focus around 1982. Before that, we were freewheeling.

Kerr/

I knew we were making great music.

After a shaky debut album, we had started doing the business on record, even if it felt like an uphill struggle to keep going.

Although *Empires and Dance* in particular was well-received by a few UK critics and featured prominently in some end-of-year polls in the music press, reviews were mixed. Sales were worse. With little promotion and virtually no radio play, the album sold very few copies on release or throughout the period that followed.

Objectively, it was our third commercial failure in a row. A cynic, and we knew plenty of those, could easily have said that after three misfiring album releases, the only thing Simple Minds had definitely succeeded in was submerging ourselves in the mountain of debt we owed to our record company at the time.

We never pinched pennies when it came to recording; it's one reason why those records still sound great decades later. We always invested in the best, using top-notch studios and name producers. Neither of which came cheap. The results justified the expense, but we were under increasing pressure from Arista. I was still only twenty-one, and I worried that our record company would tire of our loss-making efforts and pull the plug. I tended to internalise a lot of these worries; Charlie, as usual, kept his head down and played on.

From one perspective our band looked like a failure – and there's no shame in that. Everyone fails. It is a fact of life, a necessity, even. Those who succeed are those who do not give up when they fail. But I would watch and listen as every night the crowd went bananas when we played 'I Travel', 'Changeling', 'Today I Died Again' and the other powerful tracks that we were creating, and I thought: *No way. Not possible. Our story is just beginning.*

We knew long-lasting music careers needed time to develop. We were continually making gains from the experiences we were learning out on the road, building a loyal following one gig at a time, much like my father would build a foundation wall: cementing one brick and then another.

The early history of Simple Minds felt very much like that. We had to build it up stone by stone. Being local heroes was one thing, but we already knew that the world did not stop at the Scottish border. We had to start afresh in every new territory, playing to rooms all around the United Kingdom, then in Europe, in Canada, the United States and Australia.

I lost count of the number of times we turned up at a venue to play to an empty room, or to the proverbial three men and a dog. But almost every time we did, the promoter would come back afterwards and tell us he had never seen three men and a dog go quite so crazy. 'You guys are happening. Come back again!' That was the oxygen we needed, or at least I did. And for me, it was always there. Even the rehearsals sounded great.

It meant that as Simple Minds toured almost constantly during those years, the next gig was still the most important gig in the world, whether it was a pub in Maastricht, a dive bar in Boston or a sold-out hometown club. The stage was our nightly proving ground. It engendered an *Us vs the World* mentality. We were living in a bubble, rattling around from place to place. Strangers in every town we played. In such circumstances, you lean in to each other. We were not going to be beaten.

There was a soundman we worked with at the time called Frank Gallagher. Frank hailed from Banknock, near Falkirk. During the period when Talking Heads were the hippest band in the world, Frank mixed their live sound. He was, and remains, possibly the rudest guy on the planet. And a dear friend.

When he wasn't with Talking Heads, Frank worked on a couple of the early American tours with Simple Minds. These treks were incredibly hard. Once we were outside of New York and Los Angeles, the shows could be very dispiriting. Pulling in, we already knew there would be hardly anybody there. We would play a university hall with a thousand capacity, and less than a hundred people would show up. Tumbleweed. 'Oh God, here we go again.'

Even I would have my doubts. Sometimes I expressed them quite forcibly. 'I don't know what we're doing here! It's a shithole. The gear is no good, the monitors are crap. I can't hear myself.' Frank was having none of it. 'I wish *I* couldn't hear you, pal – you're fucking miles out of tune.' He was a self-pity annihilation machine. The merest whiff of defeatism was shredded mercilessly. 'What are you gonna do about it, fucking greet? Go crying home to your mammy? Cunt! The promoter told me Echo & the Bunnymen played here last week and went down a storm, so you'd better get on with it!'

I am not paraphrasing. Frank was brutal but brilliant. The band already had its own never-say-die attitude, but at times of disappointment or exhaustion it could slip – and when it did, boy, would Frank remind us of why we were there in the first place. 'You'd better do the business, boys, or we're wasting our time here.'

There was struggle, but the struggle was often enjoyable as the improvements in our records and live shows became undeniable. Whatever doubts or fears I had, they never deterred me because I could hear it and feel it. I was much more arrogant then, but I think you need a kind of arrogance when you're young in order to believe you can achieve your goals.

It was a nightly crusade to put the band across in the best light, and it is still a crusade. But the feeling these days is less combative. Nowadays, I say quite often to our band, especially the younger ones who might sometimes be nervous before a show: 'What are you worried about? People are here because they already love you. They have sacrificed not only their money but their time and have been looking forward to this night for weeks. They're already into it. The game is almost won. All you have to do now is be brilliant – *every night.* In Simple Minds, you have to be really brilliant every time. Worry about that. But don't worry about the audience.'

That's something I learned over time. Back then, we needed to feel that every show was a battle. We fed off that intensity. Once we came through that period, we could be a little less attritional. We didn't have to fight the audience. They were going to come with us anyway.

17
A Vision Thing

There are two basic kinds of professional . . .
There's the professionalism that does something
well enough to earn a living from it. And there's
the professionalism that creates a commitment so
intense that the earning of a living happens by the
way. Its dynamic isn't wages but the determination to
do something as well as it can be done.

– William McIlvanney, *Laidlaw*

Simple Minds are rehearsing and I take a moment to breath it all in.

Everyone in this band brings something special. I love being in the middle of it. Love hearing the noise we make.

I am obsessive. For me, this isn't work.

Every waking second of every day, the only thing I think about is Simple Minds.

Kerr/

Because I didn't have to fake my enthusiasm, I soon found that my role in the early days was not so much group leader as horse whisperer.

I was already shaping things. Every great band knows how to spin its own stories, create its own myths. As a non-musician, yet someone who works with melody and words, I regard the ability to communicate through storytelling as a core competence. In my case, that means not only writing songs but crafting a narrative around the band and convincing people – including, crucially, my fellow band members – to then engage in that narrative and to believe in the story that I have created around us all.

I'm not so modest to overlook how important that was in the early days of Simple Minds.

Although never designated as such, I grew into the role of leader. From day one, though certainly not responsible for the music, I was responsible for just about everything else. Before we had a manager, it was up to me to decide on the strategies. Why me? No one else seemed to have any.

That continued even when we had Bruce. I felt I could see the whole movie in my head. I just had to figure out a way of explaining it.

My evolving style of leadership was based on using influence, suggestion and gentle coercion rather than any expression of authority. I tried to get the rest of the band to think differently, or get them interested in things they wouldn't otherwise have been interested in. Hardly the alpha-male type, I was as much a novice as anyone else to this game.

I had no desire to dominate the efforts of my band mates. We worked together in harmony with the shared aim of achieving results that went far beyond anything we could hope to do as individuals. But if the ability of a creative collective to achieve remarkable things hinges on how well they can pull together – then someone has to decide which way to pull.

Burchill/

Jim very quickly became the leader in Simple Minds.

There are usually several reasons why the singer becomes the singer; vocal prowess might be one of the least important. In a band, or in any collective endeavour, it is not an admission of weakness to accept when there is somebody smarter and more charismatic than everybody else in the room.

I recognised it. I'd recognised it years before the band began. I recognised it on the bus to Toryglen when I was nine years old. I don't think the others in the band recognised it – or if they did, they were unwilling to accept it. Their conception of the internal dynamic stemmed more from identifying the various musical roles that people played within the group than looking at the bigger picture and what that required.

Jim was never a ball-breaker. I know. I was there.

Kerr/

Every organisation needs someone ultimately to make decisions, and in our organisation, I always had plentiful ideas that in turn led to a clarity of vision. My band mates increasingly looked at me to take the initiative. There was rarely any challenge to any suggestions I would make. No one else seemed hungry to take on the responsibility or the workload.

With hindsight, and such realisations take a long time, I can see that there were decisions I took which I thought were so blindingly obvious there was no point talking them through with the band. Much later I might have thought, *I should have discussed that; I should have checked it was all right.* And perhaps at times I simply took our roles for granted. My attitude was that we each had our positions, and what was important was that everybody excelled in their designated position, because then the combined force was going to have so much more impact. So, of course, the singer is going to get almost all the credit. He's the goal scorer. In terms of public perception, it doesn't matter about the assists. *Who put the ball in the net?*

That said, at certain times in Simple Minds the dynamic has been subject to a certain amount of fluidity. As much as me and Charlie were always best friends, there was a whole period during *Sparkle in the Rain* and *Once Upon a Time* where Mick and Charlie were joined at the hip.

Musicians have a code, a shared language. In terms of socialising, they were drinkers, first at the bar. On tour they would go off and ride into the night. At the end of a tour, they would go on holiday together, while I would be despatched to Canada for another three weeks to do promotion. At the time, I thought it might have been a nice gesture if I were paid for the additional work. We had a disagreement about it. There was a vote. I lost. Charlie and Mick vetoed it.

They were tight. They had opportunities to converse when I wasn't there and come back with a shared take. It makes me laugh sometimes when Mick will now say, 'I knew Jim and Charlie would always agree about everything.' Not at all. My recollection is that, for a period, I had to get certain decisions past Charlie and Mick.

18
Colours Fly and Catherine Wheel

Sure do miss the drugs . . .

– Johnny Cash

Charlie and I spend the night before we start recording the fourth Simple Minds album, Sons and Fascination, *in Ladbroke Grove Police Station.*

There has been an unfortunate incident at the Russian Embassy.

Earlier, we visited the HQ of our new record company, Virgin, in Vernon Yard, Notting Hill Gate. We have extricated ourselves from Arista and things are looking up. We leave the office with armfuls of new records.

Virgin's wonderful Australian A&R Ross Stapleton played a big part in getting us signed to the label. He lives in a flat next door to Vernon Yard, which he shares with some other people. Ross invites us over. Scotland are playing a World Cup qualifying match that afternoon, so he hands around a few beers and we watch the football. Ross says, 'You guys like acid, don't you?' Well, now and again we have been partial. Why not?

We figure that we'll come up in a few hours' time.

Wrong.

As we are watching the game the giggles overwhelm us and everything starts getting silly. Ross's flatmates are coming back from work. They walk in to find two Scottish guys tripping, freaking out at Alan Rough, the Scotland goalkeeper, with his massive perm and his huge plastic hands. We can't deal with it. 'Look at the size of his fucking hands, man!' We tell Ross we have to get out of there.

135

We emerge into what suddenly seems a hostile and confusing world. We are so out of it, we can't quite fix our coordinates to return to Shepherd's Bush, where we are staying. Every time we try to stop a cab, the driver hears us gibbering and giggling and drives off. The weather is fine so we amble down Bayswater Road, heading towards Holland Park. We're thinking, This stuff will wear off soon.

Wrong again.

After a time, we hear music and see lights coming from the other side of a high wall. A garden party. Nice. We should pop in. They are playing 'Gimme Shelter' by the Rolling Stones. Clearly, we are being cosmically beckoned to join the fun.

So begins the not undemanding task of getting up and over the wall. In what seems like an instant, blue lights are flashing around us. 'Ello 'Ello. What's all this, then?

The police begin to ask problematic questions. Such as:

'What are you two up to?'

What follows is a case of my brain telling me not to say something, and my mouth not taking any notice. I try to explain to him that we are in a band. We're called Simple Minds. There is a snort.

'How come I haven't heard of you, then?'

He is wearing the Dixon of Dock Green *helmet and all the trimmings. My mind screams:* It's the fuzz!

I mean to say, 'Well, we play the universities and colleges. We're a student band. Arty. Perhaps not your thing, officer.'

What I actually say is: 'We don't make music for police. You wouldn't have heard of us, all right?'

He then informs us that we are attempting to break into the Russian Embassy and we are, to quote, in deep fucking trouble. I explain we have to start making our new record tomorrow. Or is it today? 'Not likely. You're going nowhere.'

We are so out of it, I realise later that they are taking us in for our own safety. At Ladbroke Grove Police Station, they split up me and Charlie and put a bit of pressure on. 'Where did you get the drugs from?' We stick to the same story: we were in a pub, we had a pint, and after that we don't know what happened.

We don't have any acid on us, so eventually they tell us to sling our hook. We are still flying. As a beautiful blue dawn breaks, we sit on the steps of the police station, dazed. I tell Charlie I'm going to liberate some milk from the crates sitting outside the store across the road, which hasn't yet opened.

It is six o'clock on a summer's morning in central London. By three o'clock in the afternoon, I will be singing the vocal on 'In Trance as Mission', the opening track on Sons and Fascination.

Years later, when people ask, as they often do, why Simple Minds can't make 'those' kinds of records any more, I will tell this story as a means of explaining that art is a product of a specific set of circumstances: time, age, reality, experience; of the sun shining on our acid-fried faces at six o'clock on a summer's morning in central London. Where, for just one moment in time, I hear the holy backbeat . . .

Kerr/

In terms of drugs, Toryglen gradually earned its reputation. Hard drugs didn't really come into the area until the latter part of the seventies. When we were going to gigs as young teens it was all about scoring a bit of hash. Again, Tony Donald led the way. Always old beyond his years and with a ready stash of cash, Skin was the first person we knew who could roll joints. For me, hash never really appealed, outside of the idea that it was somehow cosmically connected to music.

What became a bigger deal for me and Charlie was acid. Just before the dawning of punk and Johnny and the Self Abusers we had a delinquent phase – which we revisited a few years later. The appeal of LSD was that it was mind expanding, which is ideal when you have nowhere to take it and nowhere to go once you have.

In Toryglen, we would drop acid, go to a disco and then roam the streets for the rest of the night – absolutely out of our minds. Charlie and I have very fond memories of doing that, the fits of giggles and all the ridiculous behaviour that went with it. We would egg each other on. Charlie is very brave. When we took acid he would just pop it. No questions asked. He was game, that's for sure.

One of the first nights that me, Charlie and a few others went on a trip, we thought we had come down sufficiently to venture home. However, we were still getting the visuals. I had gone into the bedroom where my brothers were sleeping to be presented with two monkeys. It was the funniest thing I had ever seen in my life, but Paul was particularly unamused, screaming at me to stop laughing and turn the light off. From the next room Mum and Dad heard the uproar and came to find out what was going on. My dad took one look at me and clocked what was going on, but he said nothing.

While all that was happening, down the street Charlie went to bed but couldn't sleep. He decided to have a bath. In doing so, he became convinced that hundreds of little spiders were crawling out of the wall. He woke up his mum to give her a hard time about not cleaning the bath. She said, 'I don't know what you're talking about, Charles. I can't see any spiders.'

There was a delinquent naughtiness, a cartoon mischief, to taking acid. We loved how it made the city look and sound. We noticed we could hear things differently. We loved cruising through the streets at night and spending hours at hot-dog stands. It was a rite of passage, which seemed connected to the music. In our naive, uninformed way, this was what the Beatles did. This was what Pink Floyd did. It seemed that we were getting a toe in the water of that kind of culture.

Periodically, we jumped back in.

Burchill/

Acid by its very nature creates unreliable narrators. My memory of the 'Russian Embassy' incident is a little different to Jim's. We were in Newburgh in Fife, working on *New Gold Dream (81, 82, 83, 84)*, when 'Promised You a Miracle' charted. We were told we had been offered our first ever spot on *Top of the Pops*, which was a huge deal. It felt like we had finally made it, or at least jumped up several levels. We came down to London and it was all very exciting. Being on *Top of the Pops* was surreal. It was made even more bizarre by the fact that Jim and I got put in jail straight afterwards. On acid.

We had gone to Ross Stapleton's house after recording *Top of the Pops* and watched Scotland play football on television. It was the night Jock Stein died. Admittedly, we performed 'Promised You a Miracle' on *Top of the Pops* in April 1982 and Jock Stein died in September 1985, but to me it was definitely the same night. That's acid for you.

Ross gave us a pile of records, and Jim and I wandered up to Notting Hill Gate, off our heads. We were standing in front of a record store, tripping on all the album covers, and the next minute we were huckled by the police. They knew there was something up. They said they'd had a report that two people had broken into the record store and taken some records. That was merely a pretext. The truth was they just didn't like the look of us.

At this point, Jim delivered one of the all-time great quotes.

The policeman said: 'Right, what do you two do?'

'We're rock stars.'

'What band are you in?'

'Simple Minds.'

'Never heard of you.'

'That's cos we don't make music for cops . . .'

It was worth a night in the cells, that line.

On reflection, I think the only reason we took acid was connected to the music. People used to say you could always tell when a band had never taken a trip. It wasn't a compliment.

Kerr/

There are a few good acid tales. I particularly like the one about us tripping in the desert and thinking that TV evangelists were coming to shoot us.

On the bus in America when we were touring *Sons and Fascination*, we had a long overnight drive through Arizona. Or perhaps it was Texas. Beforehand, somebody had told us that this was the best drive for taking a trip; out in the middle of the desert while the sun was coming up. We got our hands on some peyote. We were quite excited.

Once again, we bit off more than we could chew. We took the peyote and stopped the bus in the desert. Everybody else was annoyed but Charlie and I were flying. I'm sure we were a pain in the arse, but our mindset was: *Come on, it's the desert. You have to trip! Jim Morrison would have.* It had all the weight and significance of a sacred ritual. We both carried a flag for that. We kept everyone up all night having quasi-religious experiences, and when the sun came up, we got off the bus and wandered into the wilderness. Charlie was wearing mirrored sunglasses. He said, 'I can see the world through your eyes.' We were *flying*.

We thought by the time we reached our next stop we would have come down. But we hadn't. We were still very much airborne. It was a Sunday morning in what could have been El Paso. It might as well have been Narnia. We checked into the motel and Charlie was still really *very* high. He called me up in my room and said, 'You have to come and see this.' His voice had taken on a quite sinister tone. I went to see him, and he was acting like Dennis Hopper. He had switched on the evangelist channel. An evil-looking guy, as they all were, was asking for money. Charlie was muttering: 'I hate these cunts, I hate these cunts . . .' And he was well within his rights to do so.

A telephone number was flashing across the screen. Charlie had a brainwave. 'Right, I'm calling them.' 'No, no, that's not a good idea.' These were local stations, and these guys were heavy. 'I'm calling them . . .' Halfway between completely terrified and ending myself laughing, I grabbed a bedsheet and stuffed it in my mouth. Charlie was shushing me, deadly serious, as he dialled into the programme.

It was a tinpot local station, but they were on television, so it looked like a big deal. He dialled. Immediately, on the screen the telephone lit up. 'Hello. This is Sunrise. What is your message for today?' Behind his mirrored glasses, Charlie started into it. 'Excuse me, I have something to say to you.' 'Go ahead, sir.' 'Youse people are fucking evil. Youse are the *devil*.' I was terrified. I thought they were going to hunt us down and kill us. They said, 'Please leave us alone, sir. Please leave us alone. We will call the police.' But Charlie was hanging in there: 'No, you listen to me for a minute . . .'

That was some peyote.

In the early days of Simple Minds, we were speedy. My stage fright stopped me eating and amphetamines took away the hunger pangs. In addition, it enabled us to stay up all night and not get tired. Great! When we were in the rehearsal room, we just wanted to keep going and play for as long as we could. At that time, Simple Minds were in the full glow of collective creativity. We didn't need drugs to make great music. Did speed or acid or cocaine make Mick MacNeil write that beautiful melody, or Charlie write that fantastic riff, or Derek write that amazing bass line? No. But working for twenty hours non-stop certainly helped the output.

Later, it was a less effective spur. I'm thinking of a particular occasion in New York. That afternoon, we had come into the city by road from Pennsylvania. Charlie, as ever, had got talking to our driver. It quickly spiralled into a scene from a Scorsese movie, where one thing leads to another in a process of rapid escalation. Charlie said to the driver, not entirely seriously: 'Can you get us any *real* cocaine? None of the cheap crap. This is New York. Could you get some real Colombian coke?' The guy looked like we'd mortally offended him and his entire family. 'Can I get you great *cocaine*? I can get you AK-47s, helicopters, hand grenades. I can get you fucking *anything*!' We were pissing ourselves laughing. He made a promise to

Charlie: 'I'll drop you off and I'll be back in fifteen minutes with the best stuff ever.' And he was.

Charlie and I made a pact not to touch any of it until after the gig. In the car going to the soundcheck, he said, 'Shall we just have a wee taste, just to make sure?' Possibly our worst decision ever. I could barely speak, never mind sing. We had forgotten that in America all the big knobs from the record company come back to say 'hi' before the gig. That way, they don't even have to stay to watch the show. By then, paranoia had taken me over. I couldn't see anyone. It was a disastrous gig. I ran into one of the risers during the first song and cut my head but didn't realise it. Blood everywhere. A nightmare.

Anyway, that was all Charlie's fault. And it was probably one of the last times.

Burchill/

Having dabbled with drugs recreationally for a relatively short period of time, as many young people did from our generation, particularly those involved in the music industry, there came a point when it became first apparent and then very obvious that they were hindering rather than stimulating the creative output.

Without any great debate on the subject, those kinds of substances were simply no longer around.

Kerr/

Once my daughter Yasmin was born, I called it quits in terms of getting high. I didn't like the idea of it. I was going to be away from her a lot and, yes, I could say that I was away working, but is it really work when you're spending your time in toilet cubicles? The vibe was always a bit seedy in terms of how you scored drugs, but in our younger days I felt that it was good, honest juvenile delinquency. As it did for many others, the allure and false glamour associated with the clichéd notion of sex, drugs and rock and roll tricked us into believing we were invincible; that the thrill of the moment was all that mattered. Naive? Certainly. But what else were we to think when our heroes included the Beatles, David Bowie, Iggy Pop, Lou Reed and Jim Morrison, all of whom made incredible music during their years of dedicated chemical exploration.

Later, it became part of the rock and roll eighties. When the drugs were free, it felt different. Once we had enough money to pay for them, it just didn't feel right. You realised that you were spending as much on a party night as your dad would earn in a week.

Looking back, I appreciate my personal good fortune in escaping without any serious addiction. Coffee soon became my sole drug of choice. These days, a double espresso takes care of all my needs whenever I feel like setting the heart racing and kicking my brain into action.

19

Scrawling on the Wall of Sound

The task of a writer consists of being able to make
something out of an idea.

– Thomas Mann

*Let's talk about Glasgow right now. Nineteen eighty-three. I am
walking at night along the Clyde and communing with the remnants
of a proud past that is regarded as proud no longer. We are being
told that our city is finished, seen off by decades of industrial decline
and incessant doom-laden forecasts.*

*Yet a number of Glasgow's younger citizens, artists, writers,
poets and painters are daring to incorporate a new kind of civic
belief into their work. I am merely one, visualising with full faith
that rather than becoming 'a futuristic wasteland', as predicted for
so long by politicians and faux-intellectual media commentators,
Glasgow will instead evolve into a powerhouse of new hopes and
dreams. It will rise again and again to the challenge of renewing
and reinventing itself, much as rivers always will in Hermann
Hesse's* Siddhartha *(and, coincidentally, in much the same way
that Simple Minds will always strive to do).*

*I have no intention of attempting to convey this kind of lyrical
complexity in a song. I know my strengths – and weaknesses. I
simplify. I focus on the rain. Different kinds of rain that represent
things both clear and obscure to me. Healing, revitalising rain, a
timeless rain, falling to scour away the dark days of recent history
and clear a path for the future.*

I am thinking of the 'real rain' to which De Niro's Travis Bickle refers in Martin Scorsese's Taxi Driver. *The same silent rain hidden within the lyrics of Peter Gabriel's 'Here Comes the Flood'. The rains that made it possible for Al Green to be washed clean and reborn in 'Take Me to the River'. The same rain found in 'What the Thunder Said', the final section of T. S. Eliot's* The Wasteland, *in which ancient mythologies combine to suggest the prospect of redemption and spiritual renewal. The poem ends with a vision of 'cleansing rain', the possibility of continuous rebirth.*

I draw in all that moisture and squeeze it tight:

'Come in, come out of the rain!'

Kerr/

You can get in a real mess with the words.

What is a lyric? For me it is when an emotion has found its thought and that thought finds expression in words. Likewise, music isn't simply *the notes*; it is emotion set to a beat. I don't see myself as a wordsmith so much as someone who sprays slogans on top of a musical picture. Scrawling on the wall of sound with a jargon that I think is fitting.

Which is not to say that what I do is in any way offhand or casual. 'Waterfront' is a good case study. When all the influences on 'Waterfront' are laid out line by line, it is possible that listeners might be able to see and hear them in the song. But I don't really want them to be seen. I'm not looking for intellectual brownie points. I want listeners to be swept along by the essence of it, distilled into a simple chant set against a throbbing blues powered along by Derek's mighty bass riff and even mightier reverb.

That's what I think I do well. Capture the essence of a feeling.

The one thing I did, always, was listen obsessively to the music. I listened to it a million times more than the band. I listened while they were working on it, I listened to it in taxis in London, I listened to it on top of mountains. Play. Pause.

Rewind. Repeat. I listened to it until it was talking to me. I learned instinctively to have the right word, on the right beat, on the right rhythm. The right tone. I tripped on the music until I heard things I would swear were there.

Once I felt I was seeing the pictures clearly it was time to go into the studio and sing them into reality. The penalty taker's walk. Terrifying. Often, and this was particularly the case on *New Gold Dream (81, 82, 83, 84)*, I didn't come up with the words until the very end of the recording process. I wasn't lazy. I would be worrying away at the lyrics all the time, but I wanted to deliver my part with assurance. The guys had worked on the music for weeks in the rehearsal room, then for weeks in the studio. The stakes felt very high. A lot of the music we were making then was so portentous, it seemed of another world. The emotions it evoked were so overwhelming – not only did I have to nail a melody, but I had to nail the right atmosphere and somehow try to make it all feel *right*.

Only then was I ready to take the long walk to the penalty spot. Sudden death shootout. It's only the belief that you are setting the right pictures to the music that gives you the conviction to take the kick. How many times have you seen a player miss a penalty before he has even hit the ball? He strolls up too casually because he isn't sure. Or he just blasts it over the bar. Too soft, too hard, too high, too tricksy. All down to lack of belief.

So, I would wait until I was ready. I wouldn't hit the top corner every time, but it wouldn't be for want of care or effort. Afterwards, someone might turn around and say, 'Jesus, Jim, you really nailed it.' Often not. There was usually a positive reaction from the band, but Charlie would really get it because we had read the same books. He knew what the references were. '*That's* a chapter from Borges! *That's* the movie we went to see in the West End on that rainy Tuesday night!' He would know where all the snapshots were from. And we had taken the same drugs.

Burchill/

With many of the songs on the first few Simple Minds records, I would know the books that inspired the lyrics. Not literal words; just a notion. A feel. We passed around a lot of arty novels and plays and movies that were fodder for Jim to get writing. If you were to ask Derek or Mick about the lyrics, I don't think they could tell you very much about them. I don't mean that disparagingly. Simple Minds was definitely a gang, creatively and personally, through the making of all our early music, but when it came to the words there was a much stronger connection between Jim and me.

I have a memory of Jim singing one of our early songs, 'In Trance as Mission'. The words literally poured out of him – and they were *fantastic*. I was transported by them. It felt like being taken on a mysterious adventure. You might not know what the song is saying, but you know you are travelling somewhere interesting. I have always loved '20th Century Promised Land'. What a title! Works so well with the music. With a lot of the quite eccentric sounds Simple Minds made early on, Jim did an incredible job of not simply capturing the essence of it but actually enhancing its strangeness.

On *New Gold Dream (81, 82, 83, 84)*, he didn't come in with the lyrics until the final couple of days in the studio. But he delivered. I never doubted that he would. Quite recently, Bono chose the title track as one of his top sixty songs, and he quoted some of the lines. Even though I sing them (to myself) on stage every night, there comes a point when I'm not necessarily consciously thinking about the content or their meaning. When I read the particular section of 'New Gold Dream (81, 82, 83, 84)' that Bono quoted – 'Setting sun in front of me, worldwide on the widest screen' – it struck me afresh how inspired it is. It captures perfectly where we were as a band at the time, and where Jim was as a person, as well as a greater, more universal optimism. All that shining promise: the gold and the silver and the glittering things. During that period Jim's positivity fronted us. It drew people in.

Kerr/

With our breakthrough album, *New Gold Dream (81, 82, 83, 84)*, I loved the notion of there being an entire concept behind the words. It extended to the title. It wasn't enough simply to call it *New Gold Dream*. No, let's have all these numerals running behind it. Subconsciously, I was saying:

This is serious!
You have to listen to this!!
This is more than pop music!!!
We're talking about epochal stuff here, pal!!!!

It wasn't arrogance, or delusion. I believed in it completely. I thought, *If I'm crazy, so be it, but the music we are making demands this kind of language.*

That was my job: to convey that. It still is.

We were a band whose songs were created through intense collective jamming among the musicians but, in hindsight, a lot of *New Gold Dream (81, 82, 83, 84)* is classic songwriting. At the time we didn't really know what we had in our hands. We belittled ourselves for many years, but when Charlie and I made the Simple Minds *Acoustic* album in 2016, we broke down songs that I never thought would work acoustically and discovered that they were beautifully constructed.

'Glittering Prize', though I say so myself – man, that's a great song. This is not someone spraying on a wall. It's an amazingly well-crafted piece of work. Recently I was in the car and 'Someone Somewhere in Summertime' came on. I don't know how I wrote that lyric and melody, and yet I don't think it could have been better. The expression is perfect for the music. The longing in that song, the hopefulness, could not be more precise. It's not just a big jam with the right words painted on it. It's an actual *song*. You feel sad when you're meant to feel sad, you'll feel heartbroken when the bridge comes in, then suddenly a light appears around the corner and there is a wholly satisfying payoff. It's proper songwriting and proper lyric writing. We just never realised it at the time.

Still, I'm no wordsmith, in the sense of the Leonard Cohens and the Bob Dylans of our trade. Of course not. I'm not even in that ballpark. But nor do I have the desire to be so.

One final verse. Part of my job is knowing when *not* to write words; when not to sing. Simple Minds have written some fantastic instrumentals. On 'Theme for Great Cities', probably our greatest, I could have come up with something, but the music was talking so eloquently already. I thought, *Let's leave it. It will be fantastic.* The title was my contribution. It said everything. The music didn't require anything else from me. By calling it 'Theme for Great Cities', the music opens up in front of you. It couldn't have been called anything else.

Much of the time, if I had a title that I felt was a good match, I was halfway there.

Burchill/

It is still unusual for Jim to come up with a fully formed lyric before there is any music. However, there might be titles. If I'm working on a piece of music, giving it a title, even a working title, opens a door for me. It suggests a direction. While that's developing, usually quite quickly Jim will have some lyrics. I can tell when he's on to a good lyric because he will put it on the song right away. When I get that, I usually feel there is a fighting chance that we are on to something good.

Still, quite a lot of times when we've been working on a song for a while, the point where Jim goes in to sing it will be the first time I hear the lyrics.

Over time, Jim became not just a songwriter, but a writer. Like any writer, themes recur. Travel and rain often show up. Rich colours. Celestial language. People might find it strange given I'm in a band where I have enjoyed a very long and successful songwriting partnership with my best friend, but I usually don't know what his lyrics are about. In reality, it's not so strange. Lyrics are a deeply personal proposition. Sometimes even the singer doesn't have access to a complete understanding and, in any case, Jim isn't the kind of writer who trades in singer-songwriter-type lyrics. His language is so subjective and imaginative, it would be difficult to piece it all together without additional clues. But I have no desire to ask, 'What does that mean?' I love the mystery. Asking would take the fun out of it.

Sometimes, when we have reached a point where we know we're on to something good but we are still going around the houses, he will feed me a clue. When I get that information, it opens up a whole new area about where the song can go. *Right! That's the mood. That's the context. We should go in this direction.* At other times, we'll be working on a song and it's almost as though he decides impulsively to tell me what it is about. And it always surprises me. Only after talking to him about 'War Babies', for example, did I realise that it's about a broken marriage.

I have never asked Jim to change a word that he has written. The lyrics are his department. They are what makes Jim Jim, and what makes us us. Sometimes, when I first hear a lyric, I might think that a line or phrase doesn't scan terribly well – in that moment, I'm using my technical head. That's a mistake. I always know that as Jim revises the words, they will start to take focus. You have to really trust in his process. Many of our song titles and album titles are unusual. There's a lot of quite abstract imagery. It's another reason why I can't intervene or meddle with it. It's coming from a particular place and, within the context of Simple Minds, the only person I know who can do it is Jim.

Kerr/

Chorus to fade.

Charlie never writes words and perhaps that's surprising. Engaging in conversation with him is fascinating. He's incredibly well-read and well-informed. I suspect there might still be an underlying sense that he prefers to communicate through music. Or perhaps it's the old-school thinking that in all the best bands the singer writes the words – a theory to which I tend to adhere.

There are groups where the singer doesn't write the lyrics, and I always think, *How can you sell it if you didn't write it?* Our job is all about expression. It's coming from deep inside. Then again, the first time I did reluctantly sing someone else's words, apart from on cover versions, the results weren't too bad. Even then, my biggest aversion to recording 'Don't You (Forget About Me)' stemmed from the fact that the lyrics were not the kinds of words I would write, and thus sing, and that therefore I wouldn't be able to feel them. But part of being a showman is the ability to act it out. And if you act it well, you make it believable.

20
Walking Between Worlds

Only connect.

– E. M. Forster, *Howards End*

Two thousand and twenty-four. Milano. The final show on the European leg of our global tour. An hour before we go on, I can't walk from the bed to the bathroom in the hotel room. I opt for denial. I don't tell anyone. Getting up the stairs from the bus to the dressing room is agony. I think, Bloody hell, this is going to be interesting.

I manage to get myself on stage. It's amazing what adrenaline can do.

Once there, it helps that there are a few old showbiz tricks I have learned over the years.

After four songs, I sit down on the riser and I apologise. I tell the crowd: 'It's really tough tonight. I'm in physical pain.'

I am speaking to them in Italian. They love that.

'The only other move was to cancel the show,' I continue. 'That is never going to be an option for Simple Minds. But tonight, I need you to help me . . .'

They love that even more. Lesson one: the crowd is rooting for you. Before I have even finished my speech a huge roar erupts around the arena.

And we live to fight another day.

Kerr/

I realised from our very first gig that singing is only a part of my role on stage. The bigger element is to become a human

152

transmitter who can create a shared experience between audience and band, one that is able to unite and uplift any room or venue we find ourselves performing in. How to do that most effectively changes as the context changes.

After *New Gold Dream (81, 82, 83, 84)* took Simple Minds for the first time into large venues and major outdoor festivals, I began to give serious consideration to how these places worked.

We would see other artists on the same bill as Simple Minds, musical giants like Elvis Costello and Van Morrison, and realise that their music didn't cut through in that kind of space. Some of our earlier material, too, felt ill-suited to such venues. So what *would* cut through? We would have conversations about it – and then 'Waterfront' came along. To this day, that song is perfectly constructed to grab an arena or a stadium by the scruff of the neck.

There are two ways to go in a stadium. You can go big, or you can do the opposite and make it very intimate. To pull the music right down, with just the voice and a piano or a guitar, can be highly effective. To seduce thousands of people into rapt silence is a powerful skill. *Tingle.* Or you bring out the big guns. *Bam!* Anything that falls in between those extremes often doesn't work so well.

As a singer and as a frontman, I'm hyper aware of the stage. It's the altar. A holy place. In Taormina, there is a magnificent ancient Greek amphitheatre, and when I wander around it, I can feel all the weight and beauty of its past still present within its tiers. When Simple Minds have toured America in recent years, beforehand I will google the history of some of the theatres we are visiting. Never mind that the Beatles played there – Charlie Chaplin played there, the Marx Brothers played there, Judy Garland. Mario Lanza. Frank Sinatra. These are sacred places.

Everybody takes a different approach to being a front person. There is no single right way to do it. What you transmit, how you create an atmosphere where some transcendental connection can occur, is a very personal thing.

A rock concert is by definition transformative. When you pull into a town or city for a few hours with your trucks and your sound and your lights, the aim is to turn the place upside down.

Depending on where the bus is parked, I will often see the audience coming in. I like that. It reminds me why we are here and what the next few hours are all about. The big concrete arenas can feel soulless backstage when you are sitting in them night after night. Perhaps once a week I might even venture into the audience incognito, wearing a bunnet and glasses, and try to connect again to what it feels like to be part of this experience from the other side.

Watching the audience beforehand frames the transformation. As they pour into the venue, people are already excited – but the body language by the end of the night, when this *thing* has happened within those walls, is something else again. What exactly has occurred is difficult to pinpoint. It's not tangible in the same way as sport, where a winner and a loser and a definitive result are recorded. At a great gig, some profound collective experience has taken place – but what, exactly? And how? The singer shook his leg, the guitar player jumped up and down, and they played their big songs. Well, yes, but something else, too. People forgot the worries of their day; the music transported them – all of us – to some higher place.

The front person is in a unique spot to channel that transformation, standing in front of the band, placed symbolically between the audience and the musicians. It's a shamanistic role: *Listen to this! Come with me! Look what this is doing to me; I'm feeling it as well!* The front person is a conduit, somehow part of both sides and, hopefully, connecting them. Anything that interferes with that connection is a cause of frustration. I hate gigs where I stand in the middle of the stage and the aisle is so wide, I feel as though I'm singing to no one; or where the barrier is so far away that it feels I can never quite reach out far enough. Overly zealous security personnel used to annoy us. That doesn't really happen any more.

As the man up front, you reach out and grab the crowd – and you grab the band, too, if needs be. A show is a two-way exchange of energy. As much as the audience is invited to suspend reality and become lost in the moment, the same applies to the band. We have played shows when family members or close friends have died that day. We have still gone on. We *needed* to go on.

The process requires you to be both in and out of your own head. You don't want too much time to think on stage. Just do it. The song I worry most about singing is 'Belfast Child'. There's too much space. Too much time to think. And boy, do I think! My mind goes wandering in the spaces between the lines. Not to anywhere profound. Just wandering. *Those tiles for the bathroom wall . . . are they too expensive? What am I going to eat tomorrow?* It shouldn't happen, but if there's a glimpse of space the mind can scamper through the cracks and allow reality to break in. Then comes a bum note or a wrong word or a slight panic descends, and you have to scramble back into the moment.

The physical transformation that occurs on stage can be staggering. I was visiting my nephew's wife recently here in Taormina. She practises Pilates. She had seen some Simple Minds shows on our 2024 tour and she said, 'I'm impressed, you can still do that move where you go down onto your knees and then bend over backwards.' I said, 'Yes, but I couldn't do it now.' 'What do you mean you can't do it now? Let's try it.' And indeed, I couldn't do it. I joked that I can only do it when I'm getting paid. The true explanation is that adrenaline is a far more powerful force than money.

At the same time, there is an act around whatever I do on stage. My partner Yumie will say my face changes before

I go on. My entire physiology alters. I'm preparing to play a role.

Yet as much as there is a construct involved, the essence of what I do isn't a construct. It's coming from a wholly natural place, it's simply that the essence is magnified; shaped and played about with. The values in the music are my values. The dreams in the music are my dreams. But simply to get to the point where you can even dare to say, 'Hey, look at me!' to thousands of people, there has to be a construct.

Otherwise, I'd be the biggest pain in the arse in the world.

21
Let There Be Love, Pt 1

Love leaped out in front of us, like a murderer in an alley
leaping out of nowhere, and struck us both at once.

– Mikhail Bulgakov, *The Master and Margarita*

Sydney, February 1984. Another sliding-doors moment.

Simple Minds are in Australia as part of a bill that includes Talking Heads, the Pretenders and the Eurythmics. An unbelievable lineup. We interchange as headliners every night.

It is the day before the gig. I emerge from the elevator at the Southern Cross Hotel and walk into the reception where a group of fans is waiting. I am going to the local radio station and we are late. Someone says, 'Just ignore them, we need to go.' I'm not going to do that, but I know I need to be quick.

My head goes down and I avoid making eye contact as I sign autographs. I am particularly aware of one voice. It is saying, 'Jimmy, I love you. I love you, Jimmy, I love you!' My head stays down while this voice keeps up its rather incessant chorus of admiration. Within a few minutes the fans disperse and only one character remains. I glance up. They are wearing a hoodie and sunglasses and a big, big smile: 'Jimmy! Jimmy, I love you, I love you.' I look again.

It is Chrissie Hynde.

She says she loves not only me but Simple Minds, Scotland, Glasgow. I will later learn that her father is, in true American fashion, very proud of his Scottish roots. She says she wants to see us play. That can be arranged.

We have a warm-up gig the next night in a sweaty Sydney club. Everyone who is anyone in town shows up. Robert Plant is here. It is all quite intimidating. Chrissie is in the front row. She has come on her own. No band mates, no girlfriends, no record company chaperone. She has had a bit to drink. Correction: she has had a LOT to drink. Afterwards she comes backstage, and we chat. I say, 'I think I should get you home.' We go out into the car park to find a taxi . . .

And that is that.

In a car park in Sydney, a tipsy rock goddess takes advantage of me.

By September we are married. It's rock and roll time. Accelerated movement. Sliding doors.

Kerr/

Until I met and married Chrissie Hynde in 1984, I'd always been something of a stoic character. The eternal bachelor.

When I first started hanging out with Charlie seriously, from the age of fourteen, for a long while there were no girls around. We were brought up in a boys' world. Neither Charlie nor I had sisters. At secondary school, there were no girls in our classes until we were fifteen. They were intimidating creatures. Alien. Otherworldly. How did you talk to them? Where did you start? I was still a weird teenager. Stuttering away. The idea of approaching a girl was terrifying. My dad didn't tell me anything. My mum would tell me to be nice. I might go to discotheques and school dances and get off with someone; that might even happen a couple of times. But there was nothing serious.

Both then and now, Charlie has always been incredibly private about that side of his life. When we were young, it was typical among my other friends and I to joust about our exploits, talking about what happened and, more often, what didn't happen. Charlie never did that. Not once. To this day – though we're a bit long in the tooth for all that now

– it is a no-go area. He was always very discreet and quite mysterious, romantically speaking.

Shortly after we had left school, I was seeing a girl called Carol McDonald. Very sadly, she later passed away in a tragic accident. At the time, Carol wanted to be with me more than I wanted to be with her. Finally, I had to own up and let her down. It took a long time because I didn't know how to do it. I asked my mum, who said, 'Be honest, but be a gentleman.' I nodded dutifully. 'And don't ask your dad for advice, because he doesn't know anything . . .' Righto.

I let Carol down, but she wasn't for turning. She didn't accept it was over. Awkward. About a week later, I went to a party and Charlie walked in holding Carol's hand. She looked at me as though to say, *Well, how do you like THAT?!* Carol and Charlie subsequently dated for two years, but he never said anything to me about it. There was never any acknowledgement that I had been seeing Carol beforehand. Not that it was ever a problem, but I found it quite interesting. I put my hand up once again and admit that there are levels to Charlie Burchill that I don't know at all.

When we started the band and discovered that girls would come and talk to us, what a blessed relief that was. We didn't have to engage in all the nervy preliminaries, because they would invariably make the first move. It didn't matter how average looking you were. Something about musicians and bands, for a certain type of girl, was like a moth to a flame.

My first serious girlfriend was Jaine Henderson. That was 1977. Jaine was an amazing person for all sorts of reasons, but one of the greatest things about meeting her was that she worked in a record shop. We instantly had something in common to talk about, and she had already travelled widely and experienced so many things. Jaine died in 2024. We remained great friends right to the end.

Aged twenty-four when I met Chrissie, I had still never lived with a woman.

Burchill/

When Jim and Chrissie happened, it happened very quickly. We were sharing a bill in Australia and one day Chrissie came on to the Simple Minds bus to travel to a show. I thought, *Oh! Interesting.* Because we didn't know Chrissie very well at that point – or at least, I didn't.

I asked Jim, 'Why is Chrissie travelling with us?'

'Um, I've been seeing her.'

'Oh, really!'

Suddenly they were together. It was fast. I don't remember thinking, *Well, this isn't going to last.* I felt it was a good match. Chrissie is a bit older, and I believed that it might work. I thought she was great. I still do.

Kerr/

How to sum up Chrissie Hynde. Mercurial is one word. In Sicily, we say a person is *lunatico*. It literally means that they change with the moon. Well, I've never known anyone change moods as quickly as Chrissie. Remarkably so. In the heat of the battle you think, *Oh my God, where is this coming from?!* But she doesn't bear a grudge, she is very kind, and she is generous to a fault.

I vividly remember the first time I went over to her house. In the corner of the room there was the Fender amp, the leather jacket, the Stratocaster . . . and a big teddy bear. One side was saying, *I'm rock and roll, don't mess with me.* The other was saying, *Come and play.*

I had known Chrissie's name from before the Pretenders, back when she used to write in the *NME*. She then proved she could walk the talk with her band. And how. Before I met her in Sydney, I was already a huge fan. Her voice is so incredible it can sometimes overshadow the quality of the writing, which is also formidable. 'Private Life' is still my favourite of her songs: 'Your sex life complications are not my fascination / Your private life drama, baby, leave me out.' Wow.

Chrissie was the real deal from the American heartlands. That was terribly exotic to me, coming from the high flats in Toryglen. She liked Simple Minds, which was a relief, although she couldn't stand Talking Heads. Thought they were 'phoney'. We were already having arguments about that.

Very shortly after we got together in Australia, she went on tour to America with the Pretenders for months. We spoke just about every day on the phone. I didn't know what was going to happen. She had been in a relationship with Ray Davies which was unwinding; me meeting up with Chrissie possibly helped nudge that along. They had a young daughter, Natalie. She was trying to work out how to deal with it all.

By September of that year, we were married. We were desperate to be together, but we were like ships in the night. So, we jumped the broom. It was Chrissie who suggested it and it was all tremendously exciting. We were married in Central Park in New York. Chrissie is very private and was, quite rightly, very protective of Natalie. As a result, the wedding was done undercover of the night – in broad daylight.

I consider myself to be a pragmatist, but when I look at my life, most of the really significant decisions I've made, I have made in a heartbeat. I'll go around the houses for months on the minutiae, but the life-changing stuff, whether in business or in my personal life, I'll decide on in an hour.

From the outside our marriage may have looked a little stereotypically 'rock and roll', or somehow flippant. Far from it. The timescale might suggest that, but the emotions were the same emotions anybody else would have had. My father and my uncles married young. That's what you did, particularly in our neck of the woods: you met someone, you fell in love, you got married. With Chrissie and I, all the other practicalities – how the schedules were going to work, where we were going to live – were set aside.

There was, however, a logical aspect to it all. I was marrying someone who did the same job as me, who understood what was involved, rather than somebody who would have to tag along, perennially in the shadows. Naively, on paper I thought it would work. Now, it seems absurdly young and quick. If my son were to do that, I would have something to say about it. But you don't get to fall in love with Chrissie Hynde every day of your life.

When I met her, Chrissie was in a tough place. She was trying to put together the new Pretenders lineup while still mourning the death of her two friends and band mates, James Honeyman-Scott and Pete Farndon, and the fracturing of the original group. On top of that, Chrissie and Ray Davies seemed not to have been a good relationship. She never said anything to me, but I saw the net result. Let's just say Chrissie was sorely lacking in confidence. She had lost her zest. I thought, *I can help! My band can help!* I think she had temporarily forgotten the joy involved in making music with your friends. When she met Simple Minds in Australia, she joined our gang for the remaining time, and she got a real kick out of being around us.

I was clearly looking for something, too. It may sound glib, but the challenge involved in being in Simple Minds felt less urgent by the mid-eighties. We were up and running, heading to the big league. Being in the band was always a challenge, and remains so, but marriage to Chrissie presented a whole other level of risk and reward. She was eight years older. She was a mother. She knew more than me, had read more than me, could sing better than me (better than most people). She could write. She was the real deal. *And* I fancied the pants off her; *and* she just happened to feel the same way about me.

How exciting is that? And what a challenge!

When we got together, Chrissie said – half-joking, I think – something along the lines of, *I can't be with anyone who isn't vegetarian* (although, funnily enough, I don't think Ray Davies was). I responded, smiling: 'I'm a vegetarian . . . and my name is Pinocchio.' I had been a butcher boy for four years. By the mid-eighties vegetarianism was in the air in certain circles, but it wasn't in the air in our part of Glasgow. We were still getting used to pineapples. Vegetarian essentially meant quiche. Nut loaf? Forget about it.

However, the next day I thought, *Jim, you are a man of your word.* So, I made the switch. More than forty years later, I have never again eaten meat, although strictly speaking I am not vegetarian because I eat fish. It was quite a turn up for the books. Chrissie wasn't quite as militant in those days as she has since become. Not long ago, Simple Minds and the Pretenders were planning on playing some dates together. We really wanted her on the bill. Chrissie said she would do it, but only if each venue sold exclusively vegetarian food. We went back and forth exploring all the options, but there was no compromise to be had. Eventually I said, 'Let's leave it. I'm not telling a truck driver what to eat. You can, if you like. I'm not. Each to their own.'

There are a couple of myths to dispel from the time when I first met Chrissie. There is a story that it was Chrissie who talked me into finally agreeing to Simple Minds recording 'Don't You (Forget About Me)'. That's nonsense. After we had recorded it, I was nervous about how it might be perceived, and she said: 'Get over it. People love it. It sounds great.' That's the story.

I have also heard claims that during this time I would make negative comments about Ray Davies on stage as some kind of provocation towards him. That is 100 per cent false. Complete fantasy. I would never waste my time doing something like that.

Chrissie and I didn't directly influence one another. We never wrote together or swapped lyrics. Our jobs were so different. Chrissie is a songwriter. It's between her and her guitar. I belonged to both a partnership and a collective. However,

I did influence her production choices for what became the biggest-selling Pretenders album, *Get Close*, released in 1986. I knew that she would benefit a lot from working with Jimmy Iovine and Bob Clearmountain. Likewise, Jimmy was getting up in my ear about persuading Chrissie to take a meeting with him and Bob, in the hope that she would see the sense in working with two guys who were red hot from the success of working with Simple Minds on *Once Upon a Time*. I think it worked out well for all parties.

Once Upon a Time was written very much when I was still in the heart of that relationship. There was a kind of creative transference that occurred during that period. Rather than feed each other musical ideas, Chrissie and I would feed off our lives together. At that time in London, we went out a lot. We would visit all the great independent cinemas and talk about movies. Chrissie had a lot of interesting people turning up at her door. Brian Eno would come around. John McEnroe would stop by. It wasn't a glitzy thing. They would come over in the morning for tea and toast. There would be great conversations, and some of those thoughts and some of those emotions would infiltrate the songs.

Charlie was cock-a-hoop about it all. Charlie loved her. 'Wow! *Chrissie Hynde, man!*'

Burchill/

I have always loved Chrissie. She was of a slightly older generation from us, and to my mind those few years' difference gave her a certain amount of wisdom and an alternative perspective to us on many things.

I have fond memories of a time when Jim and I had an argument while we were writing. I can't now remember what the argument was about – but Chrissie was on my side. Yes! I also remember being at her place in London when I wanted to buy some clothes for John Giblin's young kids as a present. I was going to jump on the train, but Chrissie insisted on taking us into town and showing us around all the best places.

She is that kind of person. Beneath a certain spikiness, she is incredibly thoughtful and generous.

Kerr/

When I look back, I can see that there was obviously a hunger to have something more in my life. Chrissie came with Natalie, and it felt right to have another child soon. When I first met her in 1984, we were both touring extensively for much of that year. By September, we had found out that Chrissie was pregnant, and we got married. Yasmin was born in March 1985.

The timing was great and not great.

When we first met, there was a vague notion that 1985 wouldn't be such a busy year for Simple Minds. That proved to be a wildly inaccurate prediction. 'Don't You (Forget About Me)' was released in April and, unexpectedly, exploded. Simple Minds barely stopped spinning for the next two years. I think sometimes Chrissie forgets that. She would say, 'I took a year off. Why couldn't you?' But whereas Chrissie could call all the shots with her band, I couldn't. I was part of a collective and we had worked all our lives for this moment – or something resembling it. We had to grab it. I couldn't say I was downing tools for twelve months just as everything was coming to fruition.

Yet I have always felt guilty, to a degree, about the timing.

Fatherhood was new to me – doubly so, because I had never known girls. For most of the first period of being a dad, I really wasn't around much. Saturday Dad. That was often how I felt early on, which is why I later wrote 'Saturday Girl', the B-side to 'This Is Your Land'. It was hard as hell. I don't think I'm the only father to have felt that.

Chrissie did a fantastic job. She was, and is, a great mother. You never saw her with the kids at any public events. The children went to a normal school. It was privileged, yes, but there was a real effort made to try and keep their lives as low key as possible.

By the time I *was* more present as a father, things with Chrissie were coming apart. From that point, the girls spent a lot of time with me. No nannies, no minders. Just me. Natalie was always there. She knew I wasn't her dad, but she and Yasmin were a gang and we had great times together in Portugal, in France. Even until they were teenagers, they would come up to Scotland and run up hills, ride ponies. That family time was very precious to me.

Burchill/

When Yasmin was born, Jim was twenty-five. To me, that was young. I had no intention of having kids at that time, but I think Jim was ready for it. He was always that bit more mature than me. I wasn't surprised. I was excited for him, particularly because both our families are very male dominated – and then along comes a daughter. When Jim told me her name, I planted a jasmine tree in the garden at my parents' house. I watched it grow as she was growing.

It was a great thing, but it was a frenetic period for Jim; 1985 was a crazy year for Simple Minds. However, I never had any sense that marriage and parenthood were going to change the course of the band. Both Jim and Chrissie knew the score. I don't think either of them thought that there was going to have to be any great sacrifice. They just carried on as a creative couple working in rock and roll.

Kerr/

There wasn't any one factor or event that finished my first marriage. It was a gradual realisation, I think, on both our parts. We ended up really not spending much time together. When I met Chrissie, Simple Minds were entering our stratospheric period. Afterwards, when we had finished touring *Once Upon a Time*, I was in Scotland. I had bought my first flat, in South Queensferry, and Simple Minds had just bought a house on Loch Earn where we were building a studio. I hadn't quite thought about how all of that was going to look. Being away on tour for six months, then leaving my family behind to come up to Scotland to work, Monday to Friday. Never at home. Inevitably, there were frustrations. Chrissie and I were in the same game, but that only gets you so far. The head understands; the heart is a different matter. First, it was, *I'm missing you*. Then it was, *I'm lonely*. Finally, *I'm not feeling you any more*.

Knowing the person that I have become, I have a slight sense of embarrassment at thinking that the relationship could ever have worked out. But I stand by the notion that you don't get to choose who you fall in love with. There is a kind of gallantry towards the end of a relationship when you realise that you can never make the other person happy. I realised that and so I quickly moved aside when Chrissie indicated it was over. That's the meaning I give to any relationship: *What can you do? What are you going to bring to this?* When I thought I no longer had the right answers to those questions, or I couldn't or wouldn't be able to provide them for this person, I stepped aside. We had the means to get in and get out quickly and move on. Again, that might make the marriage seem flippant. It wasn't. When there are children involved, that is the last thing it ever could be.

Burchill/

It is quite something to see Chrissie and Jim now. Two intelligent people who, when all the dust died down, probably realised that the marriage was never going to work but who have retained a great friendship out if it.

Kerr/

I'm very happy to say that I still have Chrissie in my life, but it's a different Chrissie. There are times when we're not in touch so much and then periods where we have a lot of contact. I care about her. I didn't have a big brother or a big sister to learn from, but I have learned a lot from her.

I am still a fan. She is still *Chrissie Hynde*! I hear her in the supermarket every Christmas. It's nice. She is one of the true American greats. When she tours the US, they all turn up to see her: Dylan, Springsteen, Paul Simon. That tells you that she is the real deal.

But I also see her as a mother and a grandmother. We talked recently when she was playing some shows in Scotland. Within that conversation, we said how we would both love our grandsons to go to university in Edinburgh. The kind of conversations all grandparents have. We have shared history and connections. My partner Yumie and Chrissie are good friends. Yumie stayed with Chrissie for months, helping her with the kids when she was younger. She is managed by Simple Minds' manager, Ian Grenfell. Far be it from me to say I influenced any of that. But I influenced *all* of that!

Chrissie shows up when it matters. She was fantastic when both my mum and dad were ill. On stage she still dedicates 'Hymn to Her' to my mother. She came to see Dad very near the end of his life. She just turned up unannounced at the front door. He was so energised he found the strength to go into Pollok Country Park for a walk with her. Chrissie took a great photograph that day that she ended up turning into a painting. It was a beautiful thing to do. She loved him and he loved her.

At his funeral she was so supportive and yet oddly vulnerable. Sarah Brown has been working with Simple Minds for over fifteen years. She is an incredible vocalist. At my dad's request, Sarah sang 'Danny Boy' at his funeral. Afterwards, I said to Chrissie, 'Come over and meet Sarah.' She said, 'I can't! Really, I can't. I'm just stunned at how good she is . . .'

Those two sides are still there: the leather jacket and the teddy bear.

22

Hey, Hey, Hey, Hey!

Be careful what you wish for.
You may receive it.

– W. W. Jacobs, 'The Monkey's Paw'

It is late spring 1985. The someone-else's song we have grudgingly recorded as an afterthought for a film we don't particularly rate is blowing up big. 'Don't You (Forget About Me)' is steaming towards the top of the charts in the States – but I have bigger problems.

We have established that Jimmy Iovine is going to produce the next Simple Minds album. When we meet in New York he tells me, 'You'd better have something up your sleeve. This thing is going to be a number one.' I tell him we don't even like the song – which isn't quite true, but we don't love it. The lyrics are a bit . . . He shrugs. 'You'd better have something up your sleeve.'

Jimmy is an absolute ball-breaker. He thinks lyricists are born bullshitters. He might be right. 'You always say you're going to do something, none of you ever fucking do it. You're always scraping around at the last minute, procrastinating, driving everybody nuts.'

I assure him it won't be that way with me. He is smart enough not to take me at my word for a second. Back home, he starts calling me every few hours. He wants me to fax him lyrics daily. There is no hiding place.

Bloody hell.

My daughter Yasmin has just been born. The house is in chaos. I'm spinning myself the whole pram in the hallway Cyril Connolly line. I need to go away and get the work done, if only to get this madman off my back.

I decide to go to Nice to write. I go alone. I stay in a very ordinary little place. As the weeks pass, 'Don't You (Forget About Me)' rises to number five, then four, then three. I come back early to the hotel one evening. I've been out sitting on the rocks with my Sony Walkman, writing words and melodies for our new music. There is a message for me: 'Congratulations from Gil Friesen, President of A&M: you are number one in the Billboard charts.'

Bloody hell.

This might never happen again (spoiler: it doesn't). I should probably celebrate. But what to do? I don't drink, but I go down to the bar where I usually have a coffee. I ask the barman for the best champagne he has. Cristal? So be it. Open her up.

I tell him that I just want a sip – and to give everyone who comes into the bar a taste. He asks me what I'm celebrating. When I tell him he looks at me with amused Gallic scepticism. Every time someone new comes in the bar, he gestures over to me: 'Monsieur, he is rock and roll! He is number one!' They look at me sitting on my own with a bottle of Cristal and their eyes seem to say, What on earth is going on here?

In the end I have more than a few sips of bubbly. As a non-drinker, I get blotto. Later, I realise that this strange evening will rather neatly sum up the collective confusion and ambiguity Simple Minds feel about the success of 'Don't You (Forget About Me)'.

Do we like it? Do we love it? Do we even care?

Open that bottle of champagne!

Kerr/

We have a strange relationship with a few of our biggest successes, 'Don't You (Forget About Me)' being the most obvious example. A song achieves everything you ever wished for, yet you feel conflicted because it didn't happen in exactly the way that you had hoped or imagined. It's an irony that I appreciate a little more the older I get.

We didn't want to record 'Don't You (Forget About Me)' for *The Breakfast Club*. It wasn't our song, and I didn't feel the lyrics were words that I would write or sing. Bruce was trying valiantly to talk us into doing it; we were dragging our heels. By the end, he was on the phone every night. Having tired of the stick, the final carrot he dangled, which was surprising because Bruce knew how we worked, was to inform us that the songwriters, Keith Forsey and Steve Schiff, were talking about offering us a share of the publishing. That didn't shift the dial. I told Bruce there was no chance we were going to take even 1 per cent of their publishing. It wasn't our song. We were also getting serious pressure from the US record company, A&M; Gil Friesen just so happened to be an executive producer on *The Breakfast Club*.

When we eventually agreed to do the track, we recorded it in a single afternoon in north London. We relented because we thought it would get the record company onside and help us get a bigger push in America. Then we more or less forgot about it. No one even remotely imagined it would have the kind of success that it did. Nobody thought *The Breakfast Club* would become the movie that it was going to be. And never in a million years did anyone think this song was a US number one.

It was therefore all very confusing when it happened. There were mixed feelings. We were thrilled by the success and the opportunities it presented, but there was an instant nervousness and unease attached to it. We knew what we had put into it. We made it what it was; what it is. It is Simple Minds in sound and spirit. But it still wasn't our song.

Burchill/

For a while, Jim and I had been having discussions about breaking America. We thought that we needed to spend some sustained time in the States and do all the work that bands had to do to get a foothold, which can be summarised as: playing the game. The fact that we were committed to working on breaking the band over there was the reason we eventually agreed to record 'Don't You (Forget About Me)'. Even though we held out for quite a while because we were intrinsically against doing someone else's song for a Brat Pack movie, recording it was a statement of intent to our label that we were ultimately willing to cooperate in order to improve our profile in America. We were even thinking about getting some form of US management; the legendary Bill Graham wanted one of his team to look after us at one point.

As such, when 'Don't You (Forget About Me)' went to number one in the US it felt like a huge moment of arrival. I was still staying with my mum and dad, although by then we had left Toryglen. Bruce called up: 'Are you ready for this? You're number one in America!' There would have been no great celebration at my end. It had been heading that way for several weeks. When Jim and I talked afterwards, I remember him saying to me, 'Right, we need to get on with this.'

Through the years, we have been overly hard on 'Don't You (Forget About Me)', as well as Keith Forsey, who co-wrote the song and produced the track. We have talked it down too much, which I now feel was a little cheap on our part. We should have taken ownership of it. We didn't write the song but, believe me, it wouldn't have been a hit had we not done it. All the input came from us. Deep down I think we always knew that it was a brilliant pop song, but we weren't big enough to come out and say it. It's strange: you create this incredibly successful thing, yet it doesn't quite feel yours. And we were worried about the image that it put across. Pop stars. Sell-outs.

It's yet another example of the core Simple Minds pathology: *This is great, but what happens next?* There was particular panic about following up on the success. On the one hand: *Wow, number one in America!* On the other: *What are we going to do if the song that we wrote is released next and gets nowhere?*

With that kind of pressure, we knew we had to work with somebody who could take us to another level. Acutely conscious of the number one hanging over us, we needed to make a coherent record with really strong songs. At that time, Jimmy Iovine was renowned for being 'The Song Guy'.

We were fortunate. We had 'Alive and Kicking' waiting in the wings. It was reassuring to have that in our back pocket while trying to follow up a colossal hit. It was our own song and a far better one than 'Don't You (Forget About Me)', and it ended up reaching number three in America, which put a few insecurities to bed. A change in Jim's writing is evident from the opening line: 'You turn me on.' Jim would never usually write a lyric like that, but it wasn't an intentional attempt to be more commercial. It was just a placeholder lyric. When Jim told Iovine he would change it later, Jimmy said, 'Over my dead body!'

In some ways that little detail is indicative of the bigger shift that was taking place.

Kerr/

While 'Don't You (Forget About Me)' was ascending the charts we were in the rehearsal room with Simple Minds' new bass player, John Giblin, working up the songs for *Once Upon a Time*: 'Oh Jungleland', 'Alive and Kicking', 'Sanctify Yourself', 'All the Things She Said'. Jimmy Iovine was a commercialist, but the kind of commercial music that Jimmy liked was the real deal. Tom Petty. Bruce Springsteen. These people sought success on their own terms. Next to them, I sometimes felt we were some obscure oddity, blown into Jimmy's orbit by a freak gust of wind. But the songs we were writing gave us confidence that we were on the right track. By now, the jamming days were done. Everyone had places to live and home studio set-ups. There was much more focus and cohesion to the writing.

Once Upon a Time did extremely well for us. I still think it's a great album, but not everyone agreed. We worried about the perception that Simple Minds had sold out, no matter how nebulous that concept is. In the face of such huge and unexpected success, did we appear overly desperate? Should we jump on this wild horse galloping towards us? Now, I wish someone had told us straight: *Look, this is the game you've chosen. In for a penny, in for a pound. Stop faffing about!* That would have made sense to me. But no one said that, and at the time I didn't have the wherewithal to think it clearly.

I understood the criticisms we faced about selling out. I didn't like it, but I understood it. I had always loved the music press. I had grown up with it. Even now, I hold some of the best journalists in the same esteem as my favourite artists. I knew the deal. I had seen all the greats be ridiculed for cutting through commercially. You go from having a rarefied appeal to being on every radio station and having your song played at weddings. It's a turn off to the connoisseurs. I got it.

We had never been immune to a critical mauling. I remember one of our first London reviews in *NME*. We had been told afterwards that the writer in attendance had really liked the show. We couldn't wait to pick up the issue and read about how amazing we were. On the day it came out, I flicked through to the live reviews pages to be confronted with a picture of me and the headline: 'Trapped in the Cellar with the Ghost of the Seventies'. A complete pounding. Had you kicked me in the stomach, it wouldn't have hurt anywhere near as much. I didn't understand. We had gone down a storm in the room, but some higher being had cast a lofty eye over it all and decided we were terrible. At those times, a small internal voice is saying: *How can you do this to me? I'm trying my best here!* Another voice is muttering: *You're dead, pal.*

Every band has to go through that. Trial by fire. I still have their addresses. I know what schools their kids go to.

By the period around *Once Upon a Time*, I had built up some defences to the negative reviews that came in. I would rationalise it: *I was there, I saw the audience going crazy. The records are selling by the truckload. Give me peace.* But there is always a dissenting voice inside your head, one that is actually louder than the critic's voice. It speaks to you even during the gig. It says many things, but the gist can be reduced to two words: *You're crap.* If you allow that voice even a glint of light, it can live there permanently. That uncertainty never goes away, unless perhaps you are Paul McCartney. Or Sting. He seems fairly immune to self-doubt.

Success at the level we had reached can't be strategised, but the notion of a new commercialism was in the air; it was beckoning us. Bowie was in the stadiums. He had made *Let's Dance* and I'd loved it. Springsteen had finally gone mainstream with *Born in the USA*. Roxy Music had broken through in America. I adored all those crisp, punchy Bob Clearmountain records. I wanted to work with Bob. I wanted to work with Iovine. I wanted to work with Americans in New York. And let's see if we could do what precious few of our peers had ever done. Because just think how many British bands had tried to break America and failed.

For as long as I could remember, America was the cultural telescope to the stars. Through its lens, we spied the far shores of what might be possible. America, through its dominance in music, sport, entertainment and publishing, was the Pied Piper. America played the tune and the world danced. My parents' generation swooned to the golden age of Hollywood, Elvis and Frank Sinatra. Despite the silliness of the Clash stamping their feet and singing 'I'm So Bored with the USA', for working-class teens in the seventies and eighties, whether in the Gorbals, Camden or Salford, America was still the biggest and brightest window to the world beyond where we lived, beamed in through the screen of the Granada TV rental in the corner of the room.

America transmitted cultural messages to the planet. To cut through in the US presented the greatest challenge and the greatest reward of all. Selling out? As though it were that easy! We might as well have said, *Let's go to the moon and see if we can not only survive but thrive up there.*

It helped immensely that fate played another ace. MTV launched in the summer of 1981. In the incipient video age, MTV possessed the power to put groups such as us in the corner of living rooms all over the world. That was a holy grail. They were showing hair-metal bands and pop stars, but they were also playing Depeche Mode, Echo & the Bunnymen and the Cure. By 1985 Simple Minds had a fair chance of getting played on MTV under our own steam. But what a stroke of luck that at the very moment when some level of success in America seemed even remotely possible, we became associated with a hit song and a hit movie and a more accessible musical approach that by then felt natural to us.

Sliding doors. We could never have planned it that way.

You win; you lose. We broke through with 'Don't You (Forget About Me)' and *Once Upon a Time* and we took a critical hit. Everything we did became widescreen. When I reflect on that period now, I realise that virtually the only time anyone ever saw Simple Minds was in front of a huge crowd. Not only do you need a certain kind of sound for that, but you need a different kind of projection. You can't be cool in those places. I knew that I had to be much more exaggerated, and sometimes I was trying too hard. But how can you be trying too hard when there are forty thousand people at the back of a stadium and no video screens? In striving to reach everyone, it's easy to appear overblown and *just too much.* I didn't know that then. These things only become apparent in hindsight.

I could see why we might get it in the neck. And we did. Even people at Virgin, our UK record company, who I would have expected to be very happy for us, said: *Oh, we're going to lose you; you've gone all American.* But by the eighties, the choices were quite stark. You were either a band like Magazine and effectively redundant, without a record label; or you were having to develop the sharpest elbows and make sure you were going to be on the cover of *Smash Hits* and on MTV. There was no in-between.

Burchill/

We were overly protective of our honour at the time. Wary of being seen as sell-outs or pushovers, we asserted our independence in ways which could be self-defeating. Even as we were enjoying huge success in the States, there was a kickback. There was a definite determination to ensure we weren't bullied into doing what the US record company was telling us were the correct things to do. They wanted us to play their game. We kicked back.

I stand by a lot of our choices, but it was not a smart move to leave a colossal song like 'Don't You (Forget About Me)' off *Once Upon a Time*. There was certainly room for it. *Once Upon a Time* is concise, there are only eight tracks, and yet we refused to include our biggest hit on it. That's where Jim slipped up for once in his life. It was a moment of madness. We thought we had eight better songs, and we really dug in our heels. Bruce was aghast. The record company couldn't believe it. It was plain arrogance. *This album is going to be so great nobody will even bother talking about 'Don't You (Forget About Me)'.* Sure!

Our stubborn self-belief has taken us a long way, but on occasion it has backfired.

Kerr/

We didn't put our number-one song on the album. How about that? Pure gall. 'Screw it, it's got nothing to do with us.' We wanted to make the point that we thought *Once Upon a Time* was a great record, and we didn't need some song from a movie to prove it. 'America, you'll never take us alive!'

Trying too hard again. I don't recall anyone challenging it, but the record company would have been horrified, and Bruce would have protected us from their horror. When we released a new digital version of *Once Upon a Time* in February 2025, 'Don't You (Forget About Me)' was finally included. It took four decades for common sense to prevail.

I can sum up our relationship with that song, and that period, with a phrase I would often hear from my mum and my granny: *Never look a gift horse in the mouth.* What a gift it was, from out of nowhere. To this day, it's still our bread and butter. And as much as a part of me might not enjoy saying that, I'm grown up enough to know that is what it is. Something else that often gets overlooked and should always be celebrated is the amount of enjoyment that song has given people all over the world for forty years. That's a gift, too, and one I increasingly appreciate.

We should be falling on our knees with gratitude in front of 'Don't You (Forget About Me)'. I just don't know that we are.

23
Ch-Ch-Ch-Ch-Changes

I think about my father. He never reached heights like me.
But in a lot of ways, he had it better. He had his people.
They had their standards. They had pride. Today, what
do we got?

– Tony Soprano, *The Sopranos* pilot episode (David Chase)

Blood makes you related. Loyalty makes you family.

– Mafia boss Totò Riina to the Palermo judge
who sentenced him

Australasia, 2017. Our final shows with Mel Gaynor.

For a while now, Mel has seemed less committed. He doesn't seem engaged. Or happy. Sometimes I get a little antisocial about it. I don't hold back.

Eventually, I realise that it is time for a change.

There is no showdown. But the next time we are looking for a drummer, Mel won't get the call. Instead, Charlie and I will resolve to bring in somebody who is excited to be part of Simple Minds.

We need that. We need to strap on a couple of new engines. It keeps us energised. And it's the least Simple Minds deserves.

Kerr/

Then and now, Charlie and I can be merciless when it comes to Simple Minds. A bit mafiosi. As soon as there is even a hint that you're no longer invested 100 per cent, or your presence is not conducive to what is best for the band – then it's over. And out.

For many Simple Minds fans, Mel Gaynor is a big part of our story. A powerhouse drummer. One of the best. Mel first played with us in 1982 and last got the call at the beginning of 2017.

We fired Derek Forbes in 1985 because we felt he wasn't committed to the cause just as we were hitting the big league.

By then our original drummer, Brian McGee, so essential to the metronomic bedrock of *Empires and Dance* in particular, had already left the band. He bailed in 1981 straight after the recording of *Sons and Fascination*.

Mick MacNeil left in 1990 following the *Street Fighting Years* tour.

Bruce Findlay, our talismanic manager, also exited during that period.

From the very start of Simple Minds, we have needed more than music. We needed our own distinctive vision, something that would evolve and become unique to ourselves. Along with that vision came an attitude and work ethic that have become our modus operandi.

The downside? For a vision to be fulfilled requires both directives and boundaries to be imposed, otherwise chaos quickly ensues. Not everyone we have worked with is able to understand the importance of this to both Charlie and me. As a result, they eventually discover that they are no longer invited to continue contributing their talents to Simple Minds. Or that they no longer want to.

This is where Charlie and I perhaps slip into the mentality of the generation that came before us: *You don't know how lucky you are.* It could be viewed as a deficiency in us both. But we simply cannot get our heads around why anyone would leave the band. Leave for *what*?

Burchill/

Having to tell Derek he was no longer in Simple Minds was the toughest professional decision I've ever had to make. I cried the whole night beforehand – but it had to be done. He saw it coming. He'd had a lot of warnings. In our band, you only get so many.

It was a shame. He just wasn't around at the time we most needed him to be. Jim, more than anybody, told him he had to get it together because we needed to keep focusing. And it was anything but focused from Derek. The stakes were high. It was precisely the wrong time for him to take his eye off the ball. We told Derek that, but he was quite stubborn.

Derek leaving was sad. I was a little hurt when Mick left in 1990, but he was getting cranky. He and Jim had had a big fight. Jim happened to be in the right which, believe it or not, isn't always the case. When Mick called me up to tell me he was leaving, his parting words were, 'We've done this for ten years and it's time to move on.' When it became apparent that there was no reconciliation to be had, Jim and I resolved to get on with it. A few years ago, Mick said to me, 'I've never regretted my decision to leave.' I was very happy to hear that. It would have been terrible if he had.

As for Mel, we miss the big man. He could be very funny. But there had been issues for some time that were quite exasperating. I'm not sure he was very happy. It felt like a natural drift apart, and by then we were looking for different subtleties in the sound. Meeting the current Simple Minds drummer, Cherisse Osei, was a stroke of amazing good fortune. She's theatrical. She takes on a lot of responsibility. She is on top of everything and never makes a mistake. She's got incredible focus.

Cherisse ticks every single box. Jim is convinced that if Prince were still alive, he would have nicked her.

Kerr/

For me, ultimately it all comes down to specific character types. After a couple of years of touring, Brian McGee was homesick. He wanted to be back in Glasgow with his fiancée, living a relatively normal life – house, family, security. Patently a long-lasting career with Simple Minds was not for him. Fair enough. Not everyone is built for the marathon. Some are born for the sprint.

Derek was our rock star, and in the end we felt he enjoyed playing that role more than he enjoyed turning up to rehearsals to play the bass.

Mick tells the story of being in a room in Dublin watching the TV to see if 'Belfast Child' had got to number one. It had – and he says that he didn't feel anything. He was numb. He just wanted to go home. To me, that is a sign of someone who is no longer cut out for being in the band. You don't have to go into all the other reasons why. It's clear he wasn't feeling it any more.

Ten years is a long time. Chances are Mick's character predetermined that a decade was as long as he could do it before he no longer enjoyed being in Simple Minds – or any band, seemingly. Despite his incredible talent, to my knowledge Mick has never attempted to form or join any other collective unit since leaving.

It's not as though anybody let us down. The fact is, not everyone is cut out for the dynamics of being in a band long term. Former members might harbour grievances that Charlie, or more likely me, did or said something they objected to. I would counter with some realism. In a band with five or six guys there is always going to be grief, power struggles, jousting for position. Within any collaborative creative entity, such matters are par for the course. They might even be healthy. To a degree, it is *Lord of the Flies*. Deal with it.

These aren't criticisms. They are all great guys. We laughed a lot and created a lot of wonderful music together. I'm proud of the work we did. There are fraternal, familial links between us that will always endure. But I'm not a fan of airing dirty linen in public. There are men that came back from wars and never spoke about it. Keep it in house.

Burchill/

When the original lineup of Simple Minds gradually dissipated, some ex-members vented their frustration and grievances on Jim — from a distance. They certainly didn't do it at the time. Unfortunately, because he was the leader figure, Jim got the brunt of it. I got off scot-free, when the fact is we agreed on everything. I still feel bad about that. And they were cowards, because they couldn't say it to his face.

More recently, there has been a lot of bullshit revisionism coming from some quarters. The truth of the matter is, aside from Mick, there are former band members who are lucky that they got any writing credits at all, never mind on every track across multiple Simple Minds albums. I'll leave it at that.

Brian was in the band for three years. Derek was in the band for six years. Mick hasn't been in the band for thirty-five years. Jim and I have kept Simple Minds going for almost fifty years. We are still doing it, and very successfully. We pride ourselves on being the band that never split up.

Kerr/

The number of changes to the Simple Minds lineup through the years is mentioned quite often in dispatches – but not so much when it comes to the Cure, not so much with Echo & the Bunnymen or other bands of a similar generation. U2 are the outliers. The great exception that proves the rule. Nearly fifty years in with no exits or entrances. But even they have come close to falling to bits at times. *Achtung Baby* was a hard delivery. We were around for some of it. It could have gone either way.

Change is inevitable. If an organism, a business, is going to last, not everyone is going to grow at the same pace. Anyone looking through the history of the band and the different lineups might think, *Can Jim and Charlie not just keep this thing together?* The fact is most people who work with Simple Minds stay with us for long periods and they're usually keen to come back. Sandra Dods started in 1981. Our manager Ian Grenfell, our brilliant bass player Ged Grimes and Sarah Brown are now past fifteen years with us. We've been working with Gordy Goudie since the early 2000s. Cherisse has been with us for almost a decade. Nowadays, that's rare. It tells me that people like to work with us, and we know how to show our gratitude, which is as it should be. We certainly haven't sacked many people.

At the same time, Charlie and I know our worth. I'm not afraid of appearing vain when I ask the question: *Would a Simple Minds-type band have happened were Charlie and I left to our own devices?* Yes, I think it would have. Do I think the other original members would have come up with a Simple Minds-type band without us? Well, there's a clue in what has happened since. I mourn the lack of creativity that has come from Mick, in particular, since he left the band. There must be so much more to give with those talents. But it hasn't materialised. From any of them. Last I heard, Mel had relaunched himself as a singer.

There is something sacred about Simple Minds to Charlie and me. If you don't know how lucky you are to be part of this adventure, or if you are going to be in any way casual about it, or turn your back on it, you are turning your back on the sacred. That may sound absurd, but I can't put it any other way. In which case, you will be part of Simple Minds' storied history, but not its future. Meanwhile, we will already be looking to the next riff, the next song, the next album, the next tour.

That's just the way we are.

24

Mountaineering

This is your Everest!

– Bruce Findlay, backstage at Live Aid, JFK Stadium,
Philadelphia, 13 July 1985

Backstage at Live Aid. The preamble before the moon landing.
Prior to lift-off, our manager Bruce Findlay is trying to summon
up the words to capture the momentous sense of occasion.
Characteristically, we poo-poo it.

Undeterred, Bruce is directing most of his inspirational verbosity
towards me. What begins as a bit of a Bill Shankly pep talk becomes
practically Churchillian: 'To each there comes in their lifetime a
special moment when they are figuratively tapped on the shoulder
and offered the chance to do a very special thing, unique to them
and fitted to their talents. What a tragedy if that moment finds
them unprepared or unqualified for that which could have been
their finest hour.' All that.

I am far too distracted by the clock ticking down on the Portakabin-
cum-dressing room wall to give Bruce the attention that he merits.
He's unphased. 'This is it, then. This is your Everest, boys.' He
doesn't mean we have climbed Everest; he means that we have
finally reached base camp. 'You can see it. This is your moment. It's
only fifteen minutes; a sprint. You have to hit your marks.' By now,
he is working himself into a lather and slightly slurring his words.
Method Churchill, perhaps. Nevertheless, we get the gist. In the
last agonising minutes leading up to the biggest performance of our

lives, his words add to the collective nervous energy, already at a feverish peak, as he further underlines the opportunities that might come our way if Simple Minds deliver during our three-song set.

It isn't that we are unaware. Having just had a number one after feeling we had never really had a fair crack at America, within months everything we dreamed about has been put on a plate in front of us. We are feeling pressure to live up to the hype. But it is much too overwhelming to truly consider anything other than the task at hand at this moment. Instead, we horse around, pretending to be oblivious, continuing the usual banter and mutual piss-taking that is all part of the waiting-to-go-on ritual.

Meanwhile, America and a worldwide television audience of a size never witnessed in the history of worldwide television audiences awaits. Something like ninety thousand in the stadium and over one billion people on telly. (How do they measure these things?)

'Actually, boys, I got that wrong.' Drawing on a joint being passed around, Bruce is still talking. 'It's even bigger than Everest. Jesus Christ . . . Live Aid! More people around the world will see you play these songs than watched Neil Armstrong take the first steps on the moon. Imagine that?'

I really don't want to imagine this. 'Cheers, Bruce!' I say, hugging him first, then shaking his hand. I restrain myself from wringing his neck. 'No pressure, then . . .'

Burchill/

In his book *Surrender*, Bono writes that his memories of performing at Live Aid are sullied by the rather impressive mullet he was sporting that day. I feel his pain. I haven't watched footage of Simple Minds at Live Aid for a very long time, partly because I can't bear to look at what we're all wearing. Jim opted for espadrilles and baggy white harem pants. I chose some kind of cerise blouson. Of all the things to wear on a day like that. *Really, boys?*

No question, the unexpected success of 'Don't You (Forget About Me)' gave Simple Minds our spot in Philadelphia.

The film and the song became a hit in the early summer of 1985. Without that, we certainly wouldn't have been asked to play in the States. In the end, it was more a matter of geographical convenience. We were recording in America and were suddenly hot there. Otherwise, I imagine Bob Geldof would have corralled us into appearing in London at Wembley Stadium. From our perspective, we would have performed anywhere on earth for such a worthwhile cause. As much as we didn't expect to play in Philadelphia, we didn't feel we had been fast-tracked into this spot. We'd had big success in Europe. We had done a lot of groundwork. For years we had been planting the seeds and they were coming into bloom.

The day itself was a carnival. Everywhere you looked there were famous people. At one point we were in a little shed with Jack Nicholson, who was making one of the telephone appeals for donations. It was surreal. Security was lax; we could walk around quite freely. Famous people were wandering all over the backstage site just to catch a glimpse of other famous people. The sun was shining and there was a feeling of goodwill. Everybody was in a good mood. Strangely enough, I wasn't particularly nervous. The whole day was so unlikely, it felt like there was no pressure. The event was so much bigger than any band, and I had the feeling that nobody was being judged.

As was often the case, Jim's dad Jimmy was with us as we were getting ready. We were on our side of the revolving stage, and on the other side there were lots of people with their gear set up. I was with Jimmy, checking my equipment, when Bo Diddley appeared. He was performing that day with George Thorogood, who was playing in the slot before us. I plugged into my amp, very quietly, just to make sure it was on. Meanwhile, Bo plugged in his big square guitar and started playing at full volume. He looked at me and said, 'Plug in and play, young man!' Jim's dad was watching all this, smoking his pipe: 'Who's that old git there?' 'That's Bo Diddley, Jimmy. He's a legend.'

We opened our set with a song that we had never played before, one nobody had ever heard: 'Ghost Dancing'. We'd barely written it. Typically, Jim would decide such things, in terms of running orders and setlists. It was a bold move, but not unusual for us in those days. Because we knew that we were going to finish with '(Don't You) Forget About Me', the two remaining song choices were quite open. We didn't have any other massive hits, so we reasoned that anything we played was going to be relatively obscure to such an enormous audience. In which case, let's go for something energetic that we can get our teeth into and make an impact.

Bruce had a huge fight with Bill Graham, who was running the show. Our set ran over, and Bill was going crazy at the side of the stage to get us off. There was a short period when Bill was considering managing us in the States. Perhaps that's why he never did.

There was a moment at Live Aid during my solo on 'Promised You a Miracle' when Jim came over to me and placed his hands on my shoulders. He would do that a lot in those days. I'm not sure he was marking anything particular that day, but there is no doubt that during those fifteen minutes the momentum that had been building for Simple Minds over many years reached a kind of symbolic peak. Not Everest, perhaps, but we had arrived at a place we had always dreamed about. We just never guessed that it would be Philadelphia.

Kerr/

Aside from Bruce's Churchillian soliloquy – which Charlie doesn't recall at all – I remember lots of little details and moments about Live Aid. Most of them are relatively inconsequential in themselves, but they build into a bigger picture. One of my clearest memories is trying to track down my dad before we got into the car to go to the stadium. He had gone missing. It turned out he had been helping Bob Dylan to bed. They'd been up all night in the hotel, Dad and Bruce and Kirsty MacColl and God knows who else. Bob was steaming. Which may not come as a complete surprise to anyone familiar with his performance later that day.

With a resigned yet palpably anxious air, backstage someone mentioned the unmentionable not long before we went on: 'Do you think this is right, to begin with a new song?' My feeling was, *Yes, it's absolutely right.* Why? 'Because it's a great song and most people haven't heard of us anyway, so who cares.' The sheer nonchalance, given all that was at stake! We had done something similar at Phoenix Park in Dublin in the summer of 1983, supporting U2. We opened with 'Waterfront', which we had literally written the day before. Classically Scottish. Very Glasgow. 'Ach, fuck it. It'll be great.' Youthful arrogance, perhaps, but also a kind of humble faith in the power of the music to deliver. When I reflect now about opening at Live Aid with a song no one knew and which we had never played before, I can see that there was a fair chance we were committing career suicide. My only logical explanation is that we weren't really thinking about the international TV audience, because that was too overwhelming. We were thinking about the crowd in front of us and how to get them jumping up and down. We didn't know the consequences. Or perhaps, more accurately, we were *pretending* we didn't know the consequences.

I regret now that we didn't pay more attention to Bruce's speech; that we didn't join him when he raised a plastic cup full of fizzy wine to his mouth and energetically punched the air. *What idiots we were!* Here we were at the higher climes we had always aspired to, and Bruce was daring to remind us of the fact. We should have looked up and around, soaked it all in. Having said that, Bruce was daring to remind us of the fact while holding on to a chair, barely upright, with a joint in his hand, saying, 'Come on, lads, let's *focus.*'

We did focus. And we did deliver, I think. It was over in a flash, there and gone. Those were fast times, and we were already moving on.

Burchill/

As usual, there would have been no great celebration after Live Aid. We were immediately looking forward. We went straight to Bearsville in upstate New York to make *Once Upon a Time*. We knew we had something special up our sleeves.

It's fair to say that Jim and I are the worst at celebrating any of our supposed achievements. You really wouldn't want to go to a Simple Minds Christmas party. Bruce used to try his best: 'It's been a great year; we need to get together and cele-brate. I've got you gifts!' One Christmas he had leather bags specially made for each of us and gathered us all together to present them to us. Very thoughtful. Straight away, Derek started ripping his apart. I asked what he was doing. 'I'm looking for the bung. Where's the money?!' I said, 'No, Derek, the bag *is* the gift.'

That was about the closest we ever got to a party. Much later, we organised a Christmas meal at a restaurant in Edinburgh. There were four of us: me, Jim, Dougie, our technician, who was hilarious but the most po-faced man on the planet, and Sandra Dods. Sandra has handled our accounts for ever. She is a brilliant woman, 'band mother' with a dash of Miss Jean Brodie. She also drives us nuts. There we were, this strange quartet, having Christmas dinner in Edinburgh. Jim not drinking. Dougie dry and monotone. Sandra checking our table manners. I thought, *Jeez, this is the most depressing Christmas party ever . . .*

In general, we tend to let key moments pass by unmarked. In the old days, whenever we received a gold disc we might have had a drink with the record company, but we would never have rubbed our hands together and said, *Right, let's go and celebrate.*

As soon as we finish something, Jim is on to the next project immediately. What drives that, subconsciously, I don't quite know. At the time of Live Aid and 'Don't You (Forget About Me)' in particular, I think there was a lot of working-class anxiety. Almost a nervousness. We thought, *We had better crack on before this all falls apart.* The worst fate on the planet seemed to us to be given a taste of it, and then have it taken away. It's not often that you hear anyone admit it, but if you come from our background, often the underlying force that drives you is the absolute determination not to have to get up and go to work at seven in the morning in the dark and freezing cold. I've never quite got over that. I still have nightmares about it. Ironically, there are times now when we end up doing that on tour. We get back to the hotel at two in the morning from some festival, and then it's up and off again at half-past six. I think, *Hang on, I thought I'd escaped this years ago . . .*

Kerr/

On a micro level, at the end of a great gig, taken in isolation, you have ten or fifteen minutes to savour the afterglow before you are already moving on to the next one. Not only are you moving on to the next one, but it is amazing how within a couple of days, that killer gig could have happened two years ago. It's that far gone. You really don't have the time to look back.

Bruce was always great at recognising the moment as it was coming, and afterwards he would want to celebrate and remind us of what happened and what we'd done. Bruce was a great champion of the cause, even more so than us. He still is.

But neither Charlie nor I are particularly good at celebrating any of our achievements. Charlie has always been a quiet worrier. He worries if things aren't going well, or if he thinks things might not go well. Even after something great has happened, he won't say, 'We did well, that was amazing.'

193

It just doesn't happen. Likewise, we don't openly fawn over each other, give each other hugs or declare how much the other means. It's just not the way men from our background behave. We are Glasgow guys. Emotionally speaking, our generation doesn't lay it all out.

Not everything needs to be said.

25

Don't Look Back, Never Look Back

But you, children of space, you restless in rest,
you shall not be trapped nor tamed.
Your house shall be not an anchor
but a mast.

– Kahlil Gibran, 'On Houses'

I have come back home to Toryglen after a tour.

I go for a walk, and I bump into someone I know.

We talk a little and then he says, 'Those guys that have moved in near you. They're a bad lot.'

'What guys?'

'Junkies. Watch your ma in the lift.'

Burchill/

Jimmy Iovine has always loved 'Oh Jungleland'. Even today, he plays it to other musicians and barks at them: 'Now *there's* a band that can play!' Musically and melodically, I always thought it felt slightly generic. The chorus sounded like I had heard it somewhere before.

Lyrically, however, the verses are brilliant. There's a line that has always stuck in my head: 'In the city, get out the city pretty quick / I've got a prayer I'm going to sing it you.'

It's got such narrative swagger.

I can still see it all happening.

Kerr/

'Oh Jungleland' transmits all the joy we experienced when we lived in Toryglen. But there is sadness there, too. Because it's also a goodbye. By the time I wrote the song both mine and Charlie's families had physically left, but I harboured a profound memory of looking out from the eleventh floor and taking in the fact that this was the last time we were ever going to be there. And thinking about why we were leaving.

The buildings had been cheaply built, and they were beginning to fall apart quite fast. The original residents had started to move out. New faces were coming in. In the late seventies, there had been talk about heroin, but the fears were often sensationalised in the media. I remember one boy dying of an overdose and it being terribly shocking. He was a friend of Charlie's brother. It was in the local paper. It was a big deal.

Fast forward only a few years and heroin seemed to be everywhere. Once I discovered that it was impacting the flats around us, I was very alarmed. It led to discussions about moving, although my parents never asked for anything. In fact, my mum was still working in Greggs, and she would come home and say, 'The poor wee junkies came in today and we gave them all the broken pies.'

I spoke to Bruce. I told him I had to get Mum, Dad and Mark out of there. Bruce advised a chat with the bank manager. I was out of my depth. I didn't really know what a mortgage was, and I hadn't spoken to my parents, but I started looking in the newspapers at houses for sale. I found a place in Pollokshields, not far away on the Southside of Glasgow. I knew my dad liked the area and that it was near Pollok Country Park. This house looked like a Swiss chalet. Coming from this modernist high rise flat I thought, *Great, we'll get a Swiss chalet!* The price was sixty-eight grand. You always remember, don't you?

I got myself in shape to see the bank manager. Suit. Shirt. I bought a little briefcase, and inside it I took along album reviews and press cuttings. When we sat down in his office I was impressed; he knew who I was. He said, 'My daughters have been to see Simple Minds. You're doing great, Jim.' I thought, *This is a doddle.* He knew the house – 'Looks like a Swiss chalet!' – and agreed it was a good price. 'So,' he said, 'how are we going to do this? What can you give me as a guarantee of regular income?' 'No problem,' I said, and I opened my briefcase and showed him my cache of rave Simple Minds reviews: *Band of the Future! One to Watch!*

He said, '*That's it?* That's what you're giving me? That isn't how this works. You need to give me a deposit. How much money do you have?' I told him I didn't have any. By this point we had made *New Gold Dream (81, 82, 83, 84)* and we'd had some minor hits, but we still didn't have any money. 'But you've been on *Top of the Pops*, you've been in the charts.' I said, 'It's on the way, it's coming soon.' He got the gist, but he needed evidence of *actual money.*

He wondered whether I had any pop-star pals who could lend me the cash. A light went on in my head. I spoke to Bruce. A couple of days later I received a phone call from the bank manager, who was practically wetting his pants: 'Hello Mr Kerr. Richard Branson phoned me!' In his position as our boss at Virgin Records, Richard had agreed to take on the deposit for the mortgage, which was an amazing thing for him to do. My brother Paul contributed as well. So wee Mark Kerr upgraded from Prospecthill Circus to a Swiss-style chalet in the leafy suburbs. I still jibe him about that. We left Toryglen, and a little later I wrote 'Oh Jungleland'. The tower blocks were finally demolished in 2004. The shiny promise of the New World lasted less than forty years.

Soon afterwards, as a band we were quite well off. We were becoming, at least in theory, the kind of people Margaret Thatcher would have liked: the aspirational working class, starting our own businesses, employing people, getting mortgages. That only dawned on me later. She would have been very proud of people like us. Quite the irony.

Burchill/

While we were away on tour, a lot of people we knew started becoming addicts. Guys who grew up below me when we were kids were dying of heroin overdoses; not one, but three or four. There were lots of rough parts in the Circus, suddenly, but for some reason the block that my family lived in became the worst of them all. It was such a sad decline.

By then, Jim and I were out. We were rarely home anyway, and we had managed to bypass the introduction of the hard-drug culture coming into our area. Returning from touring we could see it and I realised that we were lucky. It's too easy to get dragged into that scene. It's like a tide. Before you know it, the waves have taken you too far out. You don't always have a choice.

Toryglen was turning. I wanted to get Mum and Dad out. There was nothing holding them there; my brothers were leaving and going their own way. However, it took a while for the money to accrue. We had 'made it' and we were skint. We were always responsible with the advances we received. We did everything right. So many bands got deals and blew it all on the Enjoyment Club. We put it back in to either touring or buying equipment.

We never talked about money. We never wanted anything. There were never any flashy trappings, no big lifestyle shifts. Even when the rewards started accumulating, nothing really changed. Bruce advised us to gets cars and set the cost against tax. But Jim and I were never interested in cars.

The one big change was that everybody started buying houses for their parents. In 1984, I bought a bungalow in Carmunnock. It was a nice area, albeit en route to a suburb just a little further out on the fringes of Glasgow that was regarded as properly upmarket. We were faux-posh. Nearly there, but not quite. It cost forty-two grand. You always remember, don't you? I only sold the house about ten years ago.

I bought it for my parents, but I stayed there when I was home until I finally bought my own place in the late eighties. By then Simple Minds were looking for a property in which to set up our own residential studio. In the process, I came across a house on the west coast, in Wemyss Bay, near Largs. It was an old baronial castle that had been divided into apartments. I moved in by myself and had most of the ground floor. Jim went to the east coast, to South Queensferry. I went west. Both of us by the water.

I never considered relocating to London, as Jim did when he met Chrissie, and again when he married Patsy Kensit. Back then he was living on Lansdowne Road, just off Holland Park, which I thought was very exciting. Jim came to know London well, but I'm not sure it was a city that ever quite suited him, temperamentally. Most people move to London with a clear motive, drawn there because there's a lot of activity, an excess of energy and options. That isn't Jim speed. He's much quieter than that. As much as he loved London, it never suited his character.

Kerr/

The first home I bought for myself was a flat in South Queensferry, a village just outside Edinburgh. The apartment overlooked the magnificent Forth Rail Bridge. I was with Chrissie by then and I thought we would spend time there, perhaps hoping that by stealth Scotland would become the place for us to put down roots as a family. Chrissie loved Scotland but, in the end, it didn't quite work out that way.

Chrissie owned a house in London, and we spent most of our shared time there. Later, in the nineties, I lived in London again, with Patsy Kensit. I liked the city, and I still do, but

I don't remember ever being creative there or settling into a rhythm and having a group of friends. I have been lucky enough to travel far and wide and initiate friendships all over the world, but for some reason not in London. It has never felt like home.

Stephen Hendry, the world champion snooker player, later moved into the same apartment complex in South Queensferry. He knocked on my door one evening. It was at the time Sky TV was launching Sky Sports, which broadcast all the big live football matches. In those days you needed to buy a subscription and have a satellite dish installed to receive the channels. Stephen had come around to see whether I fancied getting a dish for the building. Perhaps, he suggested, we could ask all the other residents if they would like to chip in? I tried to picture this. Imagine: Jim Kerr and Stephen Hendry turning up on your doorstep asking for ten quid a month to watch the football.

'Let's not go chapping on all the neighbours' doors, Stephen,' I said. I think we sorted it out between us in the end.

26

Your Name in Lights

The wise man thinks of fame just enough to avoid
being despised.

– Epicurus

*I realised long ago that being famous inevitably involves
disappointing people, falling short of their expectations.*

*I catch a faint whiff of it still. Today, I am out and about in
Taormina, minding my own business. Bunnet. Glasses. No one's
idea of a rock star.*

Even so, I am spotted:

'Jim Kerr! What are you driving these days?'

'A Vespa.'

The face falls. I have failed them.

Where's the Porsche?

Kerr/

I felt a bit embarrassed at being a pop star. I wanted it when
I was up there on stage, but I didn't want it when I was
going for a pint of milk. I felt daft. After *Once Upon a Time*,
Simple Minds built a studio on Loch Earn in the Highlands
of Scotland. It was a great bolthole. In the woods. Up in the
hills. A place to hide. I did a lot of hiding. I stopped going to
clubs, because there was a pressure to live up to an impossible
image and I didn't like it and couldn't do it. That sense of
discomfort is multiplied tenfold when you marry another
rock star or, later, in tabloidese, an 'actress/sex kitten'.

201

The suit of fame never really fitted. It fitted on stage, but nowhere else.

Burchill/

Thankfully, we didn't wake up one day suddenly famous. Our ascent was so gradual that we never really saw it. We would just be playing bigger venues the next time around and selling more records.

Fame creeps up on you, but parts of it will always seem discordant. I still find it odd that a stranger might know who I am.

It begins with playing live in your hometown and the occasional person recognising that you are in band. They might view you a little differently armed with that knowledge. At the beginning, you go from being 'Charlie', to 'Charlie in Simple Minds'. It's a change.

I remember the feeling of first hearing Simple Minds on the radio. Very surreal. Slightly disembodying, but a fantastic thrill. Then there are reviews. Judgement time. Every artist claims they're not interested in reviews – but they are, and at first you take the bad ones personally. If you could take a course on how to be in a band for the length of time that me and Jim have, one section would be called: 'How to Manage Criticism'. It's impossible for everybody to like your music, and sometimes it can be brutal. You need to figure out a way of dealing with it.

Then our first *Top of the Pops*. A true landmark. We've made it! Now everybody will recognise me because I've been on the telly for three minutes – and of course they didn't. Thankfully. *Top of the Pops* was great for our parents. Not because we were now famous – we weren't – but because it was tangible proof of our progress, as well as an achievement they could tell their friends about that they could all understand.

With me, Jim and Bruce, at each new point on the ascent I remember having conversations where we would say, 'Right, we need to go to the next level. We need to really take this thing seriously.' But it was never born from a desire to be famous.

Bruce would always say, 'Great! The hard work starts now.' Jim was always thinking about our next move. Mick was so introverted that he never had any intention of being a rock star, although he looked the best out of all of us. So we just left Derek to the spoils! Nobody's head was ever turned because we knew, potentially, that around the next corner it could all disappear. We had good people surrounding us who came from the same backgrounds, and they kept our feet on the ground. It was a useful reminder of who we are and not to get ahead of ourselves. They would not have tolerated us getting carried away. In my case, Jamie was a great leveller. He was always championing Simple Minds, as was my oldest brother John, but the thought never entered their heads that they had better treat 'wee Charlie' as some kind of a star. I was still living with my mum and dad. Whenever I came home it was straight back to reality.

And yet I can argue with myself against such noble talk. There is always a part of you that thinks, *Wow, I could be famous!* We might say that we do what we do for the love of the music, but it's not only that. I remember seeing John Lennon being interviewed and being asked why he wanted to be in a band in the first place. He looked at the interviewer as though it were the stupidest question in the world. 'To get rich, famous and laid!' Everyone has that in them. Because if you don't have that, why are you doing it?

But I don't think any of us at any point ever regarded ourselves as 'rock stars'. We felt that being motivated by fame and fortune was a bit crass. Jim obviously received by far the most attention, even if it wasn't always directly related to the music. It might be, *Oh, he's married to Chrissie Hynde.* Or later, *He's married to Patsy Kensit.* Very superficial. It never created any problems within the band, I always just felt very sorry for him. Celebrity is not Jim's thing. It's difficult when you see someone you know so well attracting what, for them, is all the wrong kinds of attention. It was quite painful to watch Jim go through that. Fighting with the paparazzi. There was an episode at Edinburgh airport and it stayed with him for days. His son was there and it was horrible.

On the other hand, it comes with the job.

Kerr/

At one point it wasn't even fame. It was celebrity. Photographers outside the door. Paparazzi in the trees. It's not often I would say that I was naive, but it really didn't dawn on me that it would be like that. I hated it. I got to know one of the main paparazzo guys later. He said, 'I can still feel that punch you gave me.' I said, 'You asked for it. My kids were there. I told you.'

The ultimate bargain would be to play an arena or stadium gig and then immediately become anonymous. That would be fantastic. You've been paid a fortune, had all the adulation, gone to the best restaurant afterwards – and the next day nobody could care less. Bliss. And yet, anytime you put out a record or put a gig on sale, you want the spotlight. You can't have it all ways. When I think of the heady days of high fame, I think of being in a place where I wanted all the exposure I could get for the music but naively felt, *Hey, I should be allowed to go about my business completely unbothered.*

But who would feel sorry for us?

I've got a good radar these days. My profile compared to the eighties and nineties is much reduced, but even now aspects of fame can be a pain. I'm grateful I have a real life and a real personality to come back to. I remember looking at Prince in the eighties and being struck by the idea that this 360-degree wraparound artistic identity was invented by a lonely wee guy in his bedroom. He appeared before us more or less fully formed. Fascinating, to be so deliberately the architect of your own public persona and to be able to sell it to the world so completely that we can't see a real person behind it. But you have to live with the consequences. You can't be ex-Prince. He ends up living in his own studio and dying in the elevator there.

For the longest time, I feel I've known my strengths and my weaknesses. When that is the case, at least you know what's an act, and what isn't.

27
Mandela Day

Music is a great blessing. It has the power to elevate
and liberate us. It sets people free to dream. It can unite
us to sing with one voice.

– Nelson Mandela

I have gone on holiday with my dad at the end of the Once
Upon a Time *world tour. Things are not good at home. I need
to get away.*

*I have never been to Africa. We certainly aren't going to South
Africa; apartheid is still in force and under the terms of the cultural
boycott I won't set foot in the country.*

*We come to the Gambia. It is a beach holiday but today we have
taken a trip over the border into Senegal. We visit a historical fort on
the coast where, for hundreds of years until the nineteenth century,
African slaves were shipped to the Americas.*

The iron chains are still fastened to the walls.

*We walk through the portal through which thousands of enslaved
people passed to board the boats – from there, we can't follow. How
could we? The reality is stark, horrific. Unimaginable.*

*There aren't many occasions when I can remember seeing my
father getting obviously emotional. This is one.*

Kerr/

When Jerry Dammers came to see me and Bruce Findlay a
year later, the images from that trip to the Gambia were still
fresh in my mind, as was the awareness of the contemporary

legacy of the Senegalese slave forts. The apartheid regime in South Africa symbolised the last dregs of slavery and colonisation.

In Britain, Jerry had made Nelson Mandela a mainstream figure. When he had written 'Free Nelson Mandela' and recorded it with the Special AKA in 1984, he introduced Mandela's name to large swathes of an entire generation for the first time. Prior to the song, Mandela was very much a ghostly presence, locked away for decades. In a sense, Jerry had restored the jailed African National Congress leader to flesh and blood.

At that time, the idea of music being the lingua franca of the world still held some credence. Inspired by Live Aid, Jerry had resolved that a mega pop concert was the most effective means of continuing to exert pressure in the fight to end apartheid. Rattling tins and holding cosy church fetes wasn't going to cut it. He wanted a packed Wembley Stadium and a roster of artists that could draw an international audience.

There were many inspirational figures behind the scenes, but the Mandela concert would never have happened without Jerry. It followed on from all his other activism within the realm of music. But let's not forget that outside of that cossetted world, on the frontlines, innumerable campaigners and militant crusaders had given their very lives fighting in the pursuit of championing human rights and ending apartheid.

I was under no illusions about any of that – and how insignificant our role was in relation. But how great that Simple Minds were now in a position where we could play a very small part. Jerry came up to Edinburgh to see us. His pitch was blunt: *If Simple Minds agree to this, it will happen.* I think he had Mark Knopfler waiting in the wings. If Simple Minds signed up, he said, Dire Straits would also come in – and then we were away. Perhaps it was flattery. If so, it wasn't required. I was happy to take Jerry's bait. Bruce was,

207

too. The game was on. I didn't have to sell it to Charlie and Mick. They were up for it.

We would have done the concert anyway, but as Jerry was leaving, I said: 'Here's the deal. Everyone who takes part has to write a new song. Everyone has to state their case. It can't just be about turning up and getting the kudos when you happen to have a new record coming out that week.' Well, I don't know what happened to that idea. It would have been a real statement had every major artist written their 'Biko', their 'Free Nelson Mandela', their 'Sun City'. In the end, Simple Minds were the only ones who wrote a new song: 'Mandela Day'.

Burchill/

We wrote 'Mandela Day' before we had moved into our own new studio to work on the next Simple Minds album. We had rented a beautiful house in Dunoon, where we started writing and doing preparation for *Street Fighting Years* with Trevor Horn and Steve Lipson.

We were in Dunoon when Jim said to me, 'We should write a song for the Mandela concert, rather than just play our old songs.' I had three chords. They were, in fact, derivative of one of our earlier songs from *Sons and Fascination*: 'Seeing Out the Angel'. For some reason, I don't know why, I played it on the guitar and Jim was inspired. That was the basis of the song. We added an extra chord as a tag chorus and that was it. 'Mandela Day' was done. It was written very quickly.

Everyone was so committed to the idea of the concert. There was a good buzz. The political aspect felt right. It wasn't a divisive thing.

Kerr/

Within weeks of meeting Jerry, the Nelson Mandela 70th Birthday Tribute concert was announced, to be held at Wembley Stadium on 11 June 1988. Jerry had told me that the BBC were interested in showing the whole concert live, dependent on the lineup. I guess someone wasn't entirely paying attention at Broadcasting House. Live Aid was unambiguously a charity concert. Deep down in the semantics, you perhaps could get into an argument about the political factors that had caused the humanitarian catastrophe in Ethiopia, but you couldn't really make a political case against raising money for famine relief. Geldof did a great job, and with the BBC coming on board, for the first time a stadium concert became a global news event.

The BBC had loved Live Aid, and they no doubt saw another chance to get behind a global concert championing human rights. But the BBC's charter is to be nonpolitical and non-partisan, and of course the Nelson Mandela tribute was *absolutely* a political concert. When I heard about the BBC coming on board, I suspected there were going to be fireworks at some point. And indeed, motions were raised in the House of Commons by the Tories about the BBC supporting 'terrorists'.

The BBC stuck to their guns but, even so, as it got closer to the event the vibes began to fray a little. We were friends with U2, and I just assumed that Bono and the boys would be there. I took it as a given. Simple Minds had worked a little with Amnesty International, but U2 and other artists such as Sting and Peter Gabriel had very deep ties with them. It transpired that Amnesty International and elements of the anti-apartheid movement were at loggerheads, because the entire premise of Amnesty International is to support only nonviolent protest, whereas the ANC had taken up arms in its struggle. Some artists were caught in the middle of that. I must say, hearing the arguments on both sides, I was disillusioned. I thought, *Jesus, even here the internal politics take over.*

Peter Gabriel *had* to be there, in my view. It was due to the influence of artists like Peter that we had been raised within a musical culture that displayed an element of empathy and reflected an awareness of what was going on in the world. But Peter was also closely connected to Amnesty International, and his involvement became ensnared in that. First, he was doing it. Then he wasn't. In. Out. In the end, we invited him to join Simple Minds on stage to sing 'Biko'. He couldn't really say no to that. We quite consciously made him an offer he couldn't refuse.

Everyone behind the scenes was very enthusiastic for Peter to be involved. It was a different story with Stevie Van Zandt, Bruce Springsteen's right-hand man who had recently left the E Street Band. Whenever we mentioned his name, it was met with some variation on the phrase: 'Do we really need him?' Yes, we do! Stevie had arguably done more than almost any artist when it came to raising the profile of the anti-apartheid movement in the US. He had put together Artists United Against Apartheid. He had led the way. But Stevie doesn't hold back, and the powers-that-be were afraid that in the middle of a song he would launch into some prolonged political rap – a fear that was not entirely without merit.

Even so, I was amazed that they were so reticent to book the man who had put together 'Sun City'. Periodically I would ask: 'When are you going to call Stevie and invite him?' 'Oh, we will, we will . . .' Nothing. Finally, it was, 'Oh, there's no room.' It was appalling. Against that backdrop, we got Stevie over to London and we snuck him on to the bill. I don't know whether he knows that. He would be horrified; he probably thinks he was the first name on the list. In reality, we had to sneak him in under the radar. He came on at the end of our set to sing 'Sun City' with us.

This wasn't just another concert. It was political, and it was controversial. We got stick. My dad and dozens of our friends and family travelled down from Glasgow to London to be there on the day. For many of them, and certainly for Dad, the cause held real significance. Disgust at South Africa's apartheid regime was particularly strong in Glasgow. In 1986, the City Council had even renamed one of the city's squares Nelson Mandela Place. Students at the university drank in the Biko Bar. When I returned to Glasgow on the Monday after the concert, I was one of 15,000 people who marched to a rally in Glasgow Green, where we gathered to demand the end to apartheid.

But there were other views in our home city. The same morning, I saw the first edition of the *Daily Record*. On the front page was a picture of Annie Lennox and an article in which my name was prominently displayed. The headline? Just Scum. The newspaper had interviewed the so-called maverick Scottish Tory politician Nicholas Fairbairn for his views about the Mandela concert, knowing precisely the kind of nonsense he would spout. Fairbairn was a cartoon caricature of a man; a clown – but a dangerous one. The *Record* duly put his poisonous views all over the front page. I never quite forgave them for that, even though I could see what they were doing. They wanted to play both sides, but I thought it was outrageous to have our motives and those of so many others vilified in such a cheap way.

Other people asked why on earth we were doing this: politics and music don't mix. That's a point of view, I suppose, but artists by their very nature are usually idealistic. The ones I love are, in any case. Not to say that every band should do what we did, but many people gave their lives to fight for the end of apartheid. I felt that if we couldn't contribute some small effort to that cause after a decade of making music, what was the point in having a platform in the first place?

It turned out to be a great day. In the middle of this thunderous show, with all its grand gestures and raucous rabble rousing, Tracy Chapman came on with an acoustic guitar to sing 'Fast Car' and blew everyone away. Magical. The producers, of which Jerry was one, worked hard to ensure all aspects of the cause were represented, down to the artwork on either side of the stage. It couldn't just be a bunch of well-meaning white blokes. There was a strong representation of Black artists, from Whitney Houston to Salt-N-Pepa to Harry Belafonte. There was reggae and rap, and an incredible roster of legendary African musicians. Hugh Masekela. Miriam Makeba. Youssou N'Dour. Salif Keita.

As a musician, these kinds of events are always tricky. You are at the mercy of factors outside your control. So many things can go wrong. It's nerve racking. The set itself was a sprint. Half an hour. It was imperative to get off to a good start (once again, thank God for 'Waterfront'). And yet within the sprint there were a lot of targets to hit. I wanted to make sure that I brought into focus the whole point of us all being there, because it wasn't an ordinary festival spot. At the same time, there were scores of other bands playing, and I wanted our band to be the best. That never goes away, certainly not in Simple Minds.

We knew that we didn't want to be too po-faced about it all. Agit-prop only works if you are entertaining people. If Peter Gabriel's 'Biko' didn't have such a beautiful, stirring melody and such starkly poetic words, I would only have listened to it once. It still needs to be great music and great entertainment. Thankfully, we had written a beautiful new song, 'Mandela Day', which we debuted that day.

As a bonus, Johnny Marr joined us to play a cover of Eddie Cochran's 'Summertime Blues'. If Johnny had been around us growing up in Glasgow, Charlie and I would have been in a band with him. No doubt about it. He's our kind of person.

Burchill/

Funnily enough, I bumped into Johnny Marr when me, Jim and Mick were given an Ivor Novello Award in 2016. He told me that he and his band played 'Life in a Day' every night in the dressing room before they went on stage. I was laughing. He said, 'Honestly, we do!' I thought, *That's a weird one.*

Nothing from *Life in a Day* would have worked at Wembley Stadium, that's for sure. It was Jim who came up with the idea of Johnny joining us on stage. After leaving the Smiths he had semi-officially become part of the Pretenders, and earlier in 1988 Simple Minds had played two festivals with them in Brazil. I jammed with Johnny at a football stadium in Rio. We got on well with each other – and Jim really liked Johnny, too.

For the Mandela concert, Jim suggested that we should do the cover version of 'Summertime Blues' by Eddie Cochran. A brilliant idea. It's a great track, and nothing like anything we had done before. He also suggested we bring on someone we liked as a guest artist. How about Johnny? Before the show we were staying at the Halcyon Hotel in London and Johnny and his wife came up to the room. We socialised and tried out a few things. It was pretty loose and good fun.

Any nervousness tends to peak in the run-up to these events. The general feeling around the concert was very positive. There was a fantastic pre-gig get together involving the artists and many of the people involved in anti-apartheid organisations. I got talking to Hugh Masekela and Miriam Makeba. Terence Stamp shot the breeze. A nicely eclectic bunch of people. There was a lot of goodwill and mutual curiosity. Not many people acting like stars. It's hard for people to act like a star when there are so many famous people in one room.

On the day of the concert, there was too much going on to get nervous. We brought in a percussionist called Leroy the day before and gave him carte blanche: *Play anything! Play what you want!* He loved it. He was great. It was a little wobbly doing 'Biko' with Peter Gabriel because we hadn't rehearsed with him. On one song, Mel gave me a hard time because he thought I was supposed to be starting it. He happened to be wrong. I said, 'You were supposed to start it, ye dafty!'

All of that was going on. The usual. Once you're on stage, it's just a gig.

Kerr/

When you support worthy causes, you always ask, *How much does it really matter?* You raise a few quid. Everyone leaves feeling great. But does it really change anything? Even while we were doing the concert, a voice in my head was saying, *You're getting above yourself. Who do you think you are?* At the same time, another voice was saying, *The world gave you a microphone. Say your piece.* There was a constant internal conflict.

There was a second Mandela concert at Wembley in April 1990. The Freedom Concert. Simple Minds played a short set. This time the great man himself was out of captivity and able to attend. I won't ever forget that moment, seeing Nelson Mandela restored to flesh and blood. A colossus. Living history. Living *vindication.* In the room with the artists, he said a few words that will always stay with me. He thanked all the musicians, and then he said something amazing. I'm paraphrasing, but the essence was: 'When no voice was allowed, somehow we always heard the voice of the artists, the writers, the authors, the movie makers, the painters, the musicians, and that gave us sustenance. Because you can't lock up a song. It's in the air.'

I thought, *Wow, it DID matter.*

The first concert very much got its point across, but no one should get carried away in thinking that it turned the course of history. Apartheid was clearly unsustainable. Mandela was going to be set free. All the gravity was travelling in that direction. But the British government at the time was dragging its feet. It was stalling. I understand now, being much more grown up, that so much of this was about money: vast investments, multinational dividends. I regard the 1988 Mandela concert as the final rapier thrust by a younger generation intent on embarrassing global governments into getting their act together to finally rid the world of the stain of apartheid.

It was one of the most poignant events that Charlie and I have ever taken part in. Riding on the coattails of Jerry, we met some incredible people, among them many battle-scarred ANC diehards, as well as Archbishop Desmond Tutu, who was a dynamo. These people had devoted their lives to this cause. We most certainly had not. But we showed up and pinned our colours to the mast. Pride has never been part of Charlie's and my make-up. Very rarely do we sit back and reflect. When that time comes, however, I think we can look back at that day with some pride.

Burchill/

After all that excitement, Simple Minds went back into our new studio to finish the next album. In retrospect, I have sometimes wondered whether, for Jim, the Mandela concert gave context to the title and even the themes of *Street Fighting Years*. We already had 'Mandela Day', and I am certain the idea of putting our own version of 'Biko' on the album arose because we had played it with Peter at the concert. We recorded it fast, and it was after the show.

In some ways, the concert set the tone for what came next.

28
Soul Crying Out

I don't need time. I need a deadline.

– Duke Ellington

We are about to start work on the new Simple Minds album. I already know deep down that my marriage to Chrissie Hynde is over. The writing is on the wall. I can feel it.

Obviously, this is profound and overwhelming, but I am adamant that I am not going to write a forlorn set of lyrics.

The classic creative mantra is: write about what you know.

Well, I think, how about: DON'T write what you know?

Kerr/

When it came to writing songs for the next Simple Minds album, I arrived at the notion of addressing the big themes rather than looking too deeply inside myself. I was brought up not to be self-indulgent, emotionally speaking. I was also brought up to try and make sense of the world around me. That is my father's influence. It doesn't stem from an intellectual impetus. The first stage is empathy. *Do you feel this? Does it hurt inside to hear about this injustice?*

I had read a book called *Street Fighting Years* by Tariq Ali, a compilation of his writing on the pressing themes of his generation: Vietnam, Ireland, Cuba. From my perspective, the equivalent themes for my generation as the eighties progressed included Thatcher, apartheid, ecology, Ireland – still – and the Poll Tax. It wasn't a strategic plan but looking

216

I haven't watched footage of Simple Minds at Live Aid for a very long time, partly because I can't bear to look at what we're all wearing. – Charlie. Performing at Live Aid, Philadelphia, 13 July 1985.

Drawing on a joint being passed around, Bruce is still talking. 'More people around the world will see you play these songs than watched Neil Armstrong take the first steps on the moon. Imagine that?' I really don't want to imagine this. – Jim.

One of my clearest memories of Live Aid is trying to track down my dad before we got into the car to go to the stadium. He had gone missing. It turned out he had been helping Bob Dylan to bed. – Jim. Dad relaxing backstage at Live Aid.

I don't think any of us at any point ever regarded ourselves as `rock stars'. We felt that being motivated by fame and fortune was a bit crass. – Charlie. On stage during the *Once Upon a Time* tour, with our great backing singer Robin Clark.

I felt a bit embarrassed being a pop star. The suit of fame never really fitted. It fitted on stage, but nowhere else. – Jim. On the set of the video for 'All the Things She Said', 1985.

Success at the level we had reached can't be strategised, but the notion of a new commercialism was in the air; it was beckoning us. Let's see if we could do what precious few of our peers had ever done. Because just think how many British bands had tried to break America and failed. – Jim. With guitarist Carlos Alomar, husband of Robin Clark, backstage on the *Once Upon a Time* tour.

Even while we were doing the concert, a voice in my head was saying, You're getting above yourself. Who do you think you are? At the same time, another voice was saying, The world gave you a microphone. Say your piece. – Jim. Performing at the Mandela 70th Birthday Concert, Wembley Stadium, 11 June 1988.

Once you're on stage, it's just a gig. – Charlie.

It was due to the influence of artists like Peter that we had been raised within a musical culture that displayed an element of empathy and reflected an awareness of what was going on in the world. – Jim. With Peter Gabriel and Steven Van Zandt at the second Mandela concert, 16 April 1990.

(Left) In retrospect, I can see why people may have regarded it as an incongruous match, but I wasn't aware of that then and I wouldn't have given a damn in any case. I had met somebody who very obviously had a lot going for her. Patsy was witty. Exciting. She was young and energised. She was very beautiful. – Jim. With Patsy Kensit at the movies.

(Below) It's a rock and roll cliché. You have your own studio. You start taking years to make records. – Charlie. Our studio at Dalkenneth House, Loch Earn, Perthshire.

Every review and everything I read about Simple Minds hammered us – and me, in particular. That's all part of the deal, but it had eaten away at my confidence. I felt lost. In the quieter moments I could contemplate walking away from it all. – Jim. Simple Minds in the dog days of the new millennium.

The pressing questions were: How do we get the engine of this rusty car started again? And if we do get it going, how far and in what direction can we take it? – Jim. Performing at Ahoy, Rotterdam, 3 November 2003.

Ian tells the story that at the time most of his friends said he was crazy to take us on. We only found that out recently. I thought it was hilarious. – Charlie. Jim with Simple Minds manager Ian Grenfell at the Roundhouse, London, 2 March 2012, during '5 x 5 Live'.

We have to deliver every night. A quality in performers that isn't highlighted often enough is consistency. U2 always want to be there. Elvis Costello always wants to be there. Springsteen always wants to be there. Simple Minds, I can assure you, always want to be there. – Jim. With Bruce backstage during his Broadway residency, October 2018.

(Left) My father was quiet, quite diffident. There was a real sweetness about him. He was a dynamite guy. A gentleman. Open-minded about everything and everyone. – Charlie. Spending time with Dad in Umbria.

(Right) John Burchill (far left) and Jimmy Kerr (far right) at a function, with Celtic's Lisbon Lion legend Tommy Gemmell in kilt.

Jimmy became a huge part of the Simple Minds story. We travelled all over the world with him, and not only on tour. He became a second father to me. – Charlie.

Charlie's dad was, genuinely, the politest man I have ever met. Always whistling. A happy and very clean-cut guy. Quiet, decent, friendly. A proper gentleman. Just like his youngest son. – Jim.

My father is where my intellectual curiosity comes from. He was always worth listening to. Always interesting. There would always be a point to him telling you something: 'Listen to this, Jim. It's important.' I'm glad I did. – Jim. With Dad, Forest National Arena, Brussels, 2013.

We still want to evoke a group feeling around everything we do; to present the latest version of Simple Minds while still being true to its original essence. – Jim. Simple Minds, 2025. (L-R): Ged Grimes, Cherisse Odei, Jim, Gordy Goudie, Charlie, Erik Ljunggren, Sarah Brown.

Charlie talks to everybody. He knows every waiter and every chef. He'd only been here three months and already the town was ringing to the cries of, 'Charlie, Charlie!' – Jim. Charlie with our great friend, Antonio Chemi, in Taormina.

When we met our partners, both Charlie and I were coming out of a kind of carnage, albeit at different times. Both Yumie and Win Hong helped sort out all of that while still allowing us space. – Jim. Yumie (left) and Win Hong (right), at the OVO Hydro, Glasgow, March 2024.

Taormina excels at all the things you loved as a child. Great pizza. Fantastic ice cream. The beach. Zipping around on Vespas. The food is great. The light is incredible. This is a healthy place, but you need to be healthy to live here. It's all hills. Taormina keeps us feeling young. – Charlie.

Chrissie Hynde used to say to me, 'Jim, you're going to end up as an old guy sitting in Italy growing tomatoes' – which has turned out to be not quite true. I grow olives, not tomatoes. – Jim. Helping out at the olive harvest, Taormina, October 2024.

The process the two of us began when we were so young is something I don't see ever ending. – Charlie.

Beyond everything he has brought to my life and to Simple Minds, Charlie has always been great fun. He still is. – Jim.

back I can clearly see why I was writing songs like 'Belfast Child', 'This Is Your Land' and 'Soul Crying Out'.

I wasn't convinced that it was going to make for a commercial record, but it was a gauntlet thrown down. As a writer, at some point I felt I had to grapple with the issues of the day. By now people were asking about my position on certain topics. After a while you have to say something other than, 'Buy my new record.' I didn't speak about any of this with Charlie or Mick. It was hard enough to shut out the voice in my own head saying, *Come on now, Jim, who the hell are you? Taking the entire history of Ireland, putting it into a pop song, and trying to make it rhyme? Pretty glib. Don't touch it.*

I give great credit to the artists who had influenced us, such as Peter Gabriel, Stevie Van Zandt and Bruce Springsteen. They provided impetus and inspiration. I loved what Prince had done with 'Sign o' the Times'. In the first two verses he covered everything from HIV/AIDS to the crack epidemic; nuclear Armageddon to the global political situation – but it was still incredibly sexy and funky. You could dance while being educated. Or just dance. There was something in all of that which appealed to me.

In the end, on *Street Fighting Years*, we mislaid our dancing shoes. We flunked the funk.

Burchill/

Halfway through making *Street Fighting Years*, or perhaps even later than that, Jim came up with the title for the album. We ended up with tracks like 'Belfast Child', 'This Is Your Land', 'Mandela Day' and 'Soul Crying Out'; a cover of 'Biko'. Statement songs. I have always thought that Jim's writing comes from a very optimistic point of view. Everything is shiny and bright; glittering and golden. This time, he was taking on big issues. On 'This Is Your Land' he was riffing off Woody Guthrie. His writing was moving into areas that dealt with some of the themes that were prominent at the time.

There was no conflict over any aspect of that. Jim and I have always been on an identical page in respect of politics. We grew up in the same place, our parents were friends, and everybody we knew came from a staunchly socialist background. I can't ever remember Jim and I even having any discussions, never mind disagreements, about anything to do with politics. Our views on those things are ingrained and unspoken. By default, we're hardwired to lean to the left. Tories? In Toryglen? Forget it. That's never been in the mix.

But we have never been overtly political. Our ideologies are more to do with what our parents instilled in us. We could always see that there was a lot of hypocrisy within all the main parties. Two colours are far too narrow a spectrum to encompass what we believe in terms of decency and equality.

Although it attracted some controversy, large-scale human-itarian concepts such as the Mandela concert were relatively easy for us to be involved in. Everybody knew that apartheid was seriously wrong. Everybody knows that human rights are incredibly important; the concept is intrinsically nonpoliti-cal: these are your *rights*. Regarding Simple Minds explicitly espousing party-political causes, however, we have always drawn a line. Some people in music can do it well. I love Billy Bragg. He's a great guy and I have huge respect for his integrity and commitment, but Simple Minds couldn't ever do it that way. Within that type of approach, the message has to be really clear and direct, in a language that people can understand. Our music isn't like that.

In time, *Street Fighting Years* came to be described as a political album. There are certainly tracks that grapple with contemporary issues and the title Jim chose perhaps gave the illusion that the album has an overarching theme – but I'm not sure that it does. We built a story around the title. Even songs such as 'Belfast Child', 'This Is Your Land' and the title track are more concerned with addressing an almost nostalgic notion of our values system than espousing any clear political cause.

Kerr/

The period following *Once Upon a Time* was the first time we had any real money. We built our own studio at Dalkenneth House in Perthshire, halfway along the northside of Loch Earn. Residential studios had always worked for us; we had long dreamed of having our own place. We liked the idea of rolling out of bed, going in to work all day, then rolling back into bed.

We considered a few options. Mick was keen on a property in Ayrshire but in time Dalkenneth House became the clear frontrunner. With Mick and Charlie on the west coast and me on the east, the central location was equidistant between the three of us. The studio we built in the grounds was remarkable. It resembled a hexagonal church made with wood, full of light and space.

I was enchanted by Loch Earn. It marked the start of my love affair with the countryside. Growing up in Glasgow, I hadn't been aware of the more bucolic side of Scotland. Whenever we went away for the day when I was young, it was to Ayr or Dunoon. We never visited the green and purple interior. But now I was getting into hiking and hill walking. I would usually stay up there at the weekends when the other guys went home, because I really fell for the landscape. I came to love the solitude and the splendour. I still have a home in the area today.

There is rock and roll in those hills. A hotel in the nearby village of St Fillans is called the Four Seasons; nothing whatsoever to do with the global hospitality chain. Trevor Horn and Steve Lipson stayed there for a period while we were recording. At the time, no one ever bothered mentioning to us the fact that the Beatles had stayed at the hotel in October 1964. I've since dug up pictures of them messing about on the loch. When I found out I said to the owner, who has since sold the hotel, 'Where are the plaques?' Well, there are plaques now.

It was quite a big deal in the local community for Simple Minds to move into the area. From our point of view, to have our own residential studio in the country was fantastic – up to a point. There was an obvious danger in it, which was that it allowed us too much time. I have since learned that a deadline is a useful thing.

Looking back on that period, I can see that Simple Minds were slowing down. The aftershock of *Once Upon a Time* had gone on and on. By the end of the tour in late 1986 we had been going for eight years non-stop, and we were completely shattered. We were starting to get houses. Some of us were getting married and having kids and establishing a life outside of the band for the very first time.

The unceasing work rate we had maintained during the early years of the band had only been possible because there was nothing else in our lives. We didn't need anything else. The band was all we wanted to do.

When you're as utterly focused on a shared creative endeavour as we were, it's like driving a car at top speed. Your foot is constantly pressed down hard on the accelerator. If in time you are lucky enough to have some success, the job of managing and growing that success lifts your foot ever so slightly off the accelerator. If material rewards subsequently come your way, your foot slides further and further off the gas.

Before you know it, your full weight isn't even halfway down on the accelerator. The speed, the intensity, the drive . . . it all drops. And yet, you *have* to slow down and open the windows and let those other things come into your life, otherwise you're going to become a very one-dimensional character. You have to develop as a human. You have to make room for real life.

That is what was going on during at least two of the years between *Once Upon a Time* and *Street Fighting Years*. We opened the window. We looked around. We were trying to establish meaningful lives.

We were working with Trevor as producer and Steve as engineer. I don't think it's unfair to say that many of Trevor's major album successes up to that point had been based on signature breakthrough singles. On closer inspection, there was often little else of substance on the rest of the record because he had spent so much time and money on one or two huge statements. The singles sounded incredible, sure – but what about the next eight tracks?

We suffered a bit from that. We spent too long on the big songs such as 'Belfast Child', the title track and 'This Is Your Land', racking our brains with them. By the time we felt we had got them right, time was running out. As a result, too many other songs got short shrift. I think about 'Take a Step Back'. Put it on today and at the start it sounds great. Three minutes later, *Is it still great?* I don't think we asked that question often enough. The tracks were vibey. That's not enough. We wouldn't have admitted that at the time.

At the same moment that the technology was emerging which allowed us endless options, we hired a producer who was notorious for saying, 'That's great! Why don't we do a blues version? That's great! Why don't we do it with a Motown beat?' There was too much time and too much choice, and we began to second guess ourselves. We called it demo-itis. We would create something off the cuff and everybody would think it was a great idea – *just wait till we get it right!* You spend an age trying to replicate it, but you never can. A certain self-consciousness sets in.

Trevor's obsession at the time was the Fairlight digital synthesiser. It cost about the same as a decent-sized house in London. His wife Jill was a hard-nosed businesswoman who we respected. Before we started work on the album, we were coming to the crunch over the deal for Trevor to produce it. Back then, Jill was getting every band he worked with to pay a huge sum to hire Trevor, then another huge sum to hire his gear, notably the Fairlight, and then *another* huge sum if they ended up recording in his studio. She explained it to us: 'Look, boys, if you want Trevor, you need to have this piece of equipment. It will guarantee you success and Trevor has had to invest in this hugely.' She explained the cost. It was an eye-watering amount.

Jill kept saying, 'You have to think of these as Trevor's tools.' Mick usually didn't say much in these situations, but on this occasion, he piped up with a killer comment. He said, 'This is Trevor's tool? OK. So when you get a joiner to come to your house, does he charge you extra for the hammer?' Jill agreed that her joiner did not. 'So why the fuck are we paying for Trevor's hammer? That's his problem. If he can't make records without it, then he needs to bring it with him.'

We sorted it out in the end. Trevor turned up with his cutting-edge technology as well as some other gear, notably Nepalese temple balls hashish, which we shared. Maybe that's why everything on the record is so bloody slow.

Burchill/

It's a rock and roll cliché.

You have your own studio. You start taking years to make records.

I would travel up to Loch Earn on a Monday morning and come back on a Friday evening. It was a lovely drive. We had built an incredible studio. But the truth is, the entire process of recording has never been comfortable for Simple Minds. We never really enjoyed it. It was always quite difficult, and *Street Fighting Years* was in some ways more difficult than most.

The album was shaped by the fact that we were now our own masters. Being conscious that we had no need to watch the clock had a direct psychological effect on how we worked.

We had a song called 'Middle of the Tracks' which typified what happens when you have your own place and no deadline. It just went on and on. We kept going back to it. We never got it right. Had we been in a commercial studio, we would have moved on from that track. But you carry on because you can carry on.

At the beginning there were no feelings of achievement anxiety, or concerns that we had peaked. In retrospect, it was the last album that we made with Mick and there may have been tensions in that respect towards the end of recording, but not at the beginning. It was a positive time. We were excited to get going. It felt like we had a new adventure coming up.

When we were building the studio, we envisaged recording together as a band. That never happened. By *Street Fighting Years*, the idea of a band aesthetic in the studio was over. It didn't work. In terms of live performance, perhaps, at this time Mel Gaynor and John Giblin were perceived to be members of Simple Minds. But they certainly weren't a big part of the picture when it came to recording. Mel appears on three tracks on *Street Fighting Years*. We would call him in whenever we needed him, which wasn't often. Drum programming had advanced hugely. Technology had facilitated that, and Steve Lipson was particularly good at it. We loved the idea of being freed up. We could alter tracks very quickly without having to go through the traditional and very labour-intensive method of recording live drums.

John Giblin was a fantastic bassist and he wrote the music for 'Let It All Come Down', but he left before the record was finished. We used session musicians on some tracks, but by now it was primarily just Jim, Mick and me in the studio. Mick and I would jam to write the music. We were still experimenting. 'Kick It In' is typical of how Mick and I worked. There are ridiculous time signatures; moments when the track fades out then starts up again; bits that make no sense whatsoever in terms of where the bars fall. We would just throw in weird elements for the hell of it. You can hear them on the track, these chord changes that are not supposed to be there. We played 'Kick It In' live and I still have no idea how we managed it.

At the same time, Celtic influences were coming more to the fore. That strain was always evident in our music. Songs like 'New Gold Dream (81, 82, 83, 84)' and 'Sons and Fascination' had a Celtic sensibility. Now, we were allowing that side to come through more strongly. Trevor encouraged us to enhance it. Perhaps it was the location. We were up in the hills and, after all, we are Scottish and proud of our heritage and our great musical culture. We used to go drinking in the local pub with a couple of gamekeepers who played the bagpipes. We thought, *Right, let's get you on the record!*

The title track is very Celtic, while 'Belfast Child' has whistles, accordion and fiddle. With that song, the traditional melody derived from the famous Irish air, 'She Moved Through the Fair', but when Jim started writing to that tune, it became ours. It was no longer an old folk song. In the process of us stripping it down, some melodies were changed and others removed. It started to evolve into Simple Minds. We had the idea of putting rhythm on it, which we then started jamming over. Jim thought we needed a guitar solo in the middle. *Really?* It was already becoming a big rock beast, with these crashing power chords. Do we need a guitar solo? Apparently, we did. I remember consciously not using a distorted sound for the solo. There are a couple of other instrumental breaks; on one, we asked Lisa Germano to play violin. We ended up with a six-and-a-half-minute epic.

Trevor played a big part in bringing 'Belfast Child' to fruition. He enjoyed Loch Earn. He liked being out in the country. Trevor has a touch of the old hippie about him. Towards the end of the album, Jim and I believe that he started losing interest. Trevor has a different take on it, which itself is indicative of the record. It lacked cohesion. The momentum dissipated. We should have wrapped it up earlier and kept a tighter focus.

It was the first studio album Simple Minds had made in the era of the compact disc. That also, subconsciously, played a part. You could put more music on a CD than a vinyl record. As a result, we didn't have to cut down a song like 'This Is Your Land', which arguably could have done with an edit — in common with quite a few of the other tracks. By default, when writing and recording Simple Minds tended to end up with songs that were too long. In the past we would trim them down. With *Street Fighting Years*, as a consequence of the CD, we didn't have to. Years later, somebody sent Jim and me an acoustic version of 'This Is Your Land' that they had recorded. We listened and realised that it is actually a really good song. Like a lot of tracks on *Street Fighting Years*, we just didn't get it right, in the sense that the end results, as good as they sometimes were, too often did not match up to the promise of the initial ideas that we collectively held in our heads.

Yet it was a successful album, with big songs. 'Belfast Child' gave Simple Minds our first UK number one. I can't recall who would have said, 'That's the single!' It may have been Trevor. It was quite a brave call and one I liked. I was always happy to release something challenging, rather than a more obviously radio-friendly track. Nobody ever really knows what will catch the public imagination. You can't second-guess these things. I didn't particularly care whether 'Belfast Child' bombed or not. We had made a statement, and we were sticking by it. In this case, our prog-folk epic went to number one, which nobody saw coming.

As it turned out, radio stations started discriminating against 'Belfast Child' by not playing the song as often as a hit record would normally be played. They misinterpreted its context as being about the Troubles from a pro-Irish/Republican point of view. It had nothing to do with that. It was about the innocent people caught in the middle. Years later,

I bumped into a well-refreshed Van Morrison at an awards event and he was full of praise for the song, particularly the words.

America didn't want 'Belfast Child'. It was never going to work there. In fact, there was nothing that could have worked in America on the record, and my memory is that we didn't particularly care. We perhaps should have. Having gained a significant foothold in the United States, we might have played things differently and dedicated more time to building on that. But none of that was up for discussion. We were more focused on consolidating what we had built in Europe. The record we released after *Once Upon a Time* was a double live album, which was not a smart strategic move. A&M had asked for another studio album. We said, 'No, Europe needs a live album.' Two years later, our thinking hadn't changed. Nobody was talking about America.

It wasn't arrogance. I don't think we ever once thought, *Well, we've got a captive audience now, so we can do whatever we want.* However, we might well have been thinking, if we were being ruthlessly honest, that it was a gamble to make a record like this. We knew it had the potential to alienate people, but it was the only thing we knew how to do at that moment. We just committed to making the record we wanted to make.

Kerr/

Street Fighting Years is quite a downbeat album. The tempos are too subdued. It obviously didn't dawn on us at the time, because we were heavy on building up the atmosphere in our music, but after four years away we needed to come back with something that burst out of the speakers. And we didn't have it.

Despite the success of 'Belfast Child', I view *Street Fighting Years* as the start of the period when Simple Minds began to lose momentum and profile. We had taken too long between albums. The record was a big hit initially, but the real success of a record is only determined a year later – and it didn't hold up a year later. Or thirty-five years later. We don't play much from that album in our shows. It sounds sleepy; a bit comatose. Why we were like that at the time, what was going on in our lives that made it that way, I can't quite articulate. Despite not writing about it directly, perhaps I didn't wholly succeed in turning away from what was going on in my private life, after all. But we were all feeling it. Too many Nepalese balls, maybe.

I'm glad we took on the challenge to make that kind of record. It was quite gutsy. The album sold millions in some places, in other regions not a thing. From across the Atlantic I could hear the record company executives in America mouthing, *What the hell?* Nobody said that directly to me, but the lack of budget spend, the lack of a US tour and the deafening silence of the telephone not ringing told us all we needed to know after the event.

Street Fighting Years was a disaster in America. The album did nothing there and plans to tour the US in the autumn of 1989 were shelved. I don't blame Bruce for that. It was our record; Bruce didn't make it. But it's fair to say that he had alienated a few people in the States. In Europe, Bruce would spend the night partying with the promotions guy or the record executives. He could talk to them in a very informal way – and it worked. In America, that approach didn't work. The top man from A&M came to visit us in France, and Bruce humiliated him in front of us. Everything Bruce said was right – but that wasn't the point. You didn't do that. The egos of these guys wouldn't allow it. That came back to bite us. Bruce's attempts to generate a US tour fell on unsympathetic ears.

The tour did extremely well in Europe and Australasia, and a couple of promoters got greedy. Off their own backs, they slung in more arena dates at the end of the year. It didn't work out well for them. They wanted to change the deals retrospectively and, unfathomably to us, Bruce suggested that we go along with the proposal. He was being egalitarian: *You know these guys, they're good people! It will all sort itself out in the end* . . . Bruce was a bit of a hippie idealist, but he also had the latest Jaguar and the biggest house I had ever been in. He certainly wasn't motivated extensively by money, but he enjoyed the spoils. *And why not?* He liked a good lunch and a good bottle of wine, and the kinds of restaurants you had to book months in advance. But old jeans and holes in the jumper . . .

Charlie and I were considerably more pragmatic about what happened at the end of the *Street Fighting Years* tour. *Quit dreaming, this is real life, baby.* We didn't owe anyone any favours and we weren't impressed. It didn't mean that Bruce had to leave, but in addition to the fact that a 'juicy' merchandise deal turned out to be nowhere as favourable to Simple Minds as we had previously understood, regrettably it was time to start thinking about making changes. We were keen on an arrangement much more common than not within our industry, where the band's finances are under the tutelage of an accountant independent of management. Bruce took umbrage at that, and it was the beginning of the end.

It was an abrupt change that none of us saw coming. Thankfully, Sandra Dods, who had until recently been part of Bruce's team, stepped in to oversee immediate administrative and accounting duties. On call at all times of day and night for the next two decades while dedicating herself entirely to the business of Simple Minds, to this day we consider Sandra to be the unsung hero within our story.

With Mick also leaving, it was a tumultuous period in terms of the structure around the band. Still, 'Belfast Child' gave Simple Minds a number-one single throughout Europe, and a big hit in Australia. Not too shabby. If you're going to write a protest song calling for change, and in support of one of the greatest political statesmen the world has ever known,

'Mandela Day' fits the bill on every level. Its power lies in the beauty of the tune perfectly matching the symbolism inherent in the lyrics. And the title track is a fucking symphony – in my view, surely one of Simple Minds' finest achievements on record.

And yet *Street Fighting Years* disappoints me. I don't think we got over the finishing line. The marathon killed us.

29
Gods and Monsters

When eating fruit, remember the one who planted
the tree.

– Vietnamese proverb

*Paris, 1989. I am waiting for the man – literally – and having a
nervous breakdown in the process.*

*One of the tracks we have been working on at Loch Earn is called
'This Is Your Land'. In the middle section, for some reason I hear
a Lou Reed voice in my head. So I do my Lou impersonation. Any
excuse. We call it 'The Lou Bit'.*

*Periodically the question arises: what are we going to do with the
Lou Bit? We are running out of time. We need to finish the record.
One day Trevor Horn says, in an almost childlike way: 'Why don't
we just get Lou Reed to sing on it?' I give Trevor an old-fashioned
look. 'Or why don't we get Salvador Dalí on it? There's as much
chance! What are you talking about?'*

*I have listened to Lou Reed my whole life. No Velvet Underground,
no Simple Minds. No Bowie, even. That's how colossal his influence
has been on both me and on the course of modern music.*

*However, I have also read everything there is to read about Lou.
According to a lot of people who should know, he is evil incarnate:
mean, nasty, spoiling for a fight. A twisted character. I have recently
had some minor personal insight in this regard. Unbeknownst to
anyone, I am currently seeing a woman who works for Warner
Brothers. She is doing Lou's press for the New York album. She
calls me every night in tears because Lou is making her life so*

230

utterly miserable. But she and I are undercover. I can't tell anyone. Instead, I say to Trevor, 'I don't think it's going to work. Lou is not that kind of guy. He's not going to sing on a Simple Minds album.'

Charlie *smiles a smile that says,* Nothing ventured, nothing gained.

Trevor makes some calls. Incredibly, we receive word back saying Lou is up for it. He is in Paris doing promotion. We are going to record him there. It is decided, much against my better judgement, that I am going to go to Paris with Heff, the young tape assistant, to meet Lou and do the deal.

Heff and I fly to Paris from Glasgow. The studio is booked for late afternoon. I know that Lou likes good food and enjoys the finer things in life. In my wisdom, I remember a fancy Parisian restaurant that Bruce often raves about. Apparently, Bill Clinton likes to eat there. It's one of those silly places where you have to book six months in advance, but I have a contact in Paris and bag a table.

When we turn up at the studio, I start to have a panic attack as we go down the stairs. I tell Heff, 'You'll have to go in yourself. I can't deal with the magnitude of this.' Heff is bemused. He is so young. He doesn't even know who Lou Reed is. I try to explain what he means to me but also lay out the more salient points regarding his somewhat fearsome reputation.

Having got all that off my chest, I finally make it down the stairs. Lou turns up. It is definitely Lou Reed. Mullet. Leather jacket. Smokes real camp. There is something very dark about his vibe, or perhaps I'm guilty of seeing the persona and not the man. He gives me the limpest of handshakes. 'So . . . what are we doing?' In my head, I imagine he would rather be chained to a radiator than doing this. I say, 'Thanks for coming. It's not going to take long . . .' Oh God. I plough on. 'In terms of later, just to let you know, I've booked a restaurant for us. But of course, if you have other plans . . .' He stares blankly at me. I tell him the name of the restaurant and his demeanour changes completely. 'Wow, you got a table there?! HOW?'

And suddenly the prince of darkness is all sweetness and light.

Kerr/

Once we hit the big league it led to some strange encounters with our childhood heroes. I have often had to pinch myself. Charlie and I will sometimes look at each other and say: *That did happen, didn't it?*

Growing up, David Bowie and Lou Reed were our gods. I bumped into Bowie only once in the flesh. Simple Minds were recording *Real to Real Cacophony* at Rockfield in 1979 and he was also there, working with Iggy Pop on an album called *Soldier*. We all sang backing vocals with him on an Iggy song called 'Play It Safe'. It was fun but fleeting.

Ten years later, while we were making *Street Fighting Years*, there was another interaction. Simple Minds were working in Loch Earn. During this period, Derek Forbes was still very much in our orbit. Although he was no longer involved in the music, in the first few years after he had left Simple Minds, we saw more of Derek than ever. Charlie even lived with him for a time.

Derek did a famously killer David Bowie impersonation. One day the phone rang at the studio. A moment later Dougie, Charlie's guitar tech, came in. 'It's Bowie on the phone.' We were busy. 'Tell "Bowie" I don't have time.' Dougie shrugs. 'Look, just tell Derek to get lost, Dougie, we're in the middle of something.' This went back and forth. Then I realised that Dougie didn't tell jokes. He was the quietest, dourest guy in the world.

It dawned on me: OK. *It's actually David Bowie.*

I went into the hall to take the call. He was just as you would imagine. Very charming. There were a few preliminaries. 'I hear you've got this great place up there. I love that part of the world. Do you rent it out?' 'No, but if you ever want to use it, Dave . . .' 'Good to know, Jim!' I didn't ask whether he remembered that day at Rockfield. I don't think I said, *We named our band after your song.* I hope not. We might have spoken briefly about Robin Clark and her husband, Carlos Alomar. Robin was a big, big part of

Once Upon a Time and Carlos was Bowie's rhythm guitarist for many years.

It turned out Bowie had other things on his mind.

We had the same booking agent at the time. Bowie said, 'I've been offered a tour of Italy. I've been told to call you because the promoter is someone you work with. I hear he's your friend. I've heard lots of stories. What do you think?'

Simple Minds had worked a lot in Italy. We knew the lie of the land. I said, 'He *is* my pal. It's not horse's-heads-in-the-bed stuff, but the bureaucracy down there is crazy. You need to know who to talk to. You need to know who can get the permits. This guy just knows how to get things done.'

'Hmmm . . .'

I said, 'What are you worried about: is it the money?'

Bowie said, 'Yes, it's the money. I don't want to go down there and not get paid. Everyone says it will be fine, but I want to know.'

I said, 'Relax. You'll get paid. He'll give it to you in cash before you even leave the house.'

He finally seemed reassured. It was the most unlikely conversation. In that moment, we were just two guys on a building site: *Did ye get paid? Aye, it was cool.* Two dodgy guys in the car park: *I want to know that I'll get my dough.* It was all about the dosh. Prince played all those after-shows for cash: *I know you've got the cheque, but I need something in my hand . . .* I like the humanness of all that.

Bowie ended up playing Italy on his 'Sound+Vision' tour. A few years later he got married to Iman in Florence. I believe some of the people he had been worried about helped with the arrangements.

Then there was Lou. My God. Landing a cameo from Lou Reed on *Street Fighting Years* was beyond anything Charlie and I could ever have imagined. He was our Picasso. He superseded Bowie for me. He was unbelievably impactful.

When I was still at school, the brother of a friend was quite high up in the management of the Glasgow Apollo. He said he could get me into any gig. Tony Donald and I ended up doing a bit of light roadying. We'd run out to get a sandwich for the bands, or beer and cigarettes.

It meant I was often around to watch soundchecks, and one of the gigs where I was able to do that was Lou Reed. I'd already seen him on the *Berlin* tour. This time he was touring *Sally Can't Dance*. Tony and I couldn't believe it. Lou Reed! We were down at the front of the stage at the Apollo, shuffling about doing nothing very important, when he walked on. Bleach blond. Scrawny. Mirror shades. *Fucked*. He looked like the most debauched person that had ever lived.

Lou approached the microphone. He stared down at these two pasty schoolboys. He pointed directly at us. 'Get those assholes out of my soundcheck.' It may have been the first time I'd ever heard an American accent in real life. It was certainly the first time I'd ever been called an 'asshole' (though not the last). Whatever we had done, Lou wasn't pleased: 'Get these assholes out of here.' We did as we were instructed.

Fast forward more than a decade and Lou was reciting my lyrics in a studio in Paris. I had already put words on the track, but I told him that they were only there as a frame of reference. He could rap whatever he wanted on it. He said, 'I thought the words were *really sweet*.' 'Yeah? I suppose they are! They do fit!' It was a kind thing for him to say. Now, I love those lines: 'Money can't buy me / Money can't buy me / I've got time.' The difference between wealth and being rich: time. I didn't know what I was writing about then, but I do now.

It was only four lines. He did three takes, and we got it. Lou Reed on our track! Afterwards, we went to the fancy restaurant which had so impressed him. It was a long dinner. He was good as gold, but mostly all he wanted to talk about were amplifiers and valves. The different power supplies between France and Spain. In my head, I was screaming, *Give me a break! Talk to me about Andy Warhol.*

Then I watched the great man crumble. It was quite emotional. The Rock and Roll Hall of Fame had only recently been founded. The topic came up during our chat. I said, 'I'm really looking forward to the Velvet Underground being in there.' 'Oh, the Velvet Underground will never be in that.' He started to explain why in a rather self-pitying manner. I stood my ground. I told him the Velvet Underground would be in there one day (and I was right; they were inducted in 1996). Then I asked him why it mattered. After all, he was Lou Fucking Reed.

He said quietly, 'My mom and dad would have liked it.'

After *Street Fighting Years* was released, my relationship with Lou came full circle. The album did very well in Spain, and we played the old Atlético Madrid stadium, the Calderón. Ian Flooks, our agent, called up one day and said, 'You'll never guess who I've got opening for you in Madrid.' 'Who?' 'Lou Reed!' 'You're kidding?' 'No! Lou is opening for you.' I got quite cross. *'Don't say that again.* It's not right.' We forbade anyone on our crew from saying *Lou Reed is opening for Simple Minds*. It felt wrong.

The day came and it was beautiful. Bear in mind Lou at the Glasgow Apollo when I was a kid: 'Get these assholes out of here. I don't want anyone watching my soundcheck.' Cut to Spain. Simple Minds were soundchecking and Lou was standing at the side of the stage with his equipment. All his precious amps and valves. Looking a bit forlorn, like a wee kid waiting to be asked to join in a game of football in the park. I said to Charlie, 'We've got to let Lou on. He needs to soundcheck.' Charlie was having none of it. 'Not now, we've got a problem with Mick's keyboards. We're busy.' Just beautiful. What a turnaround.

Lou Reed wasn't likeable. He was much too caustic and ill-tempered. I have heard that sentiment many times from many different sources: artists, journalists, promoters, industry insiders. Hardly anyone will say that he was a good guy. They will say he liked demeaning people. Playing power games. What can I say? Looking back, he was as sweet as pie to me. He displayed a great generosity of spirit in agreeing to take time out of his promotional schedule to feature on our track. Furthermore, he went out of his way to let me know that he liked the song very much. He requested nothing in return. I will be eternally amazed and grateful to Lou for that, and for the immense influence he exerted over me and innumerable others of my generation. Many years later, in 2013, I happened to be in New York when news of his death came through, and I felt a strong surge of sadness.

To get to meet these people was a privilege. Without them, we would never have started doing what we are still doing today.

It's still a thrill. Charlie and I are still fans. In the summer of 2024, we were playing a festival in France. It was one of those slightly scattershot bills featuring every possible kind of musical style. Alice Cooper was in the midnight spot. On the morning of the show, a beautiful July day was dawning. I was staying on the first floor of the hotel and when I walked on to the balcony, ten feet below me, talking on the phone, was Alice Cooper – looking *exactly like Alice Cooper*.

Immediately, I texted Charlie: *Alice Cooper is below my terrace!*

He texted back within a minute: *I know! I'm in the breakfast room, I can see him outside. How brilliant! How could we ever have imagined when we were fourteen that we'd be having breakfast with Alice Cooper?*

I replied: *And if we'd ever thought when we were fourteen that we were gonna blow the guy off stage tonight when he goes on after us, we would have been carted off to the asylum . . .*

236

Burchill/

I don't usually get starstruck, but I made an exception for Alice Cooper. As kids, we all loved him: Jim, Tony, me, my brother Jamie. *Killer* was one of the first albums I ever owned, if not the first. Jamie and I went to see him when it was still the Alice Cooper group. Punk before punk. Before all the Hallowe'en stuff really took hold. The tunes were great, and the records sounded amazing. We just loved him.

Fast forward half a century. I was having breakfast when I got a text from Jim, who was Alice-spotting on the balcony. I'd already clocked him. He's hard to miss. Shortly afterwards, Alice came over and introduced himself. He said he was a big fan of Scotland. Loved our golf courses. When we had finished chatting, I immediately phoned my brother and said, 'I've just had breakfast with *Alice Cooper*.' We were beside ourselves.

He was great. Still doing it, still invested, still up for it every night. Inspiring. It felt good to know that even as teenagers, we knew the real deal when we saw it.

30
U2 and Us

82, 83, 84, 85 . . .

– Jim Kerr

. . . 86, 87, 88, 89

– Bono

– Simple Minds featuring Bono, 'New Gold Dream (81, 82, 83, 84)', Barrowland Ballroom, Glasgow, January 4, 1985

In the early nineties Charlie and I are spending a lot of time in Dublin.

Over the years, Simple Minds and U2 have developed close bonds of friendship. Our band and crew play regular five-a-side games on the weekend with U2's crew – though the boys themselves tend not to get involved. Football isn't really where their strengths lie.

One weekend I have to be in London and Bono kindly agrees to step in at the five-a-side to make up the numbers.

To be safe, Charlie sticks him in goal.

Later that day, I call Charlie from London to see how the match went. I quickly determine that we lost. Charlie is absolutely raging. Beside himself with indignation.

'Bloody Bono! Couldn't save a fucking prayer.' On and on it goes. I may have already mentioned that Charlie likes to win. Or rather, he hates to lose.

There are no hard feelings. Many, many years later, both bands will still find ways to keep in touch. A text message sent from Dublin

238

to Taormina might land out of the blue at two in the morning. No preamble. 'Ground control to Major Tom, Ground control to Major Tom . . .' The game is to text back the next line without googling.

We don't ever mention the football.

Burchill/

Simple Minds and U2 have known each other for decades. I had first met them at a radio station in Manchester in 1980. Jim was unwell so I was dispatched on promotional duty. If memory serves, Bono and I were reviewing a bunch of new singles on Mark Radcliffe's show. We were all very young. I could barely string a sentence together; Bono was quoting Milton.

By the time U2 released *Under a Blood Red Sky* in 1983, our careers were moving at broadly the same pace. Both bands were climbing the ladder. We would run into each other at some of the same big European festivals. U2 invited Simple Minds to join the bill for their landmark homecoming show in Phoenix Park, Dublin, in August 1983. Unlike Simple Minds, by then they already had quite a foothold in America – and I could tell they weren't going to let the opportunity slip. They made a live concert video for *Under a Blood Red Sky,* and I remember seeing a poster for it on a billboard in London. At that point I could sense that they were going to be a big band. It was obvious. They were so smart and ambitious.

A gradual mutual appreciation formed between our groups. After Phoenix Park, we kept in touch. Jim and Bono talked quite a lot. Bono appeared with Simple Minds in Glasgow during two shows at Barrowland in January 1985. He came on stage to sing 'New Gold Dream (81, 82, 83, 84)' with Jim, and he and his wife Ali stayed over at Jim's parents' house. A little later, we all met up in Dublin and they took us to an Indian restaurant on a hill outside of the city. It was nighttime and it was beautiful.

The bond felt very convivial. During that period, we were moving at a similar pace. Simple Minds by now were also making headway in America. In Europe, we were moving into stadiums. Perhaps inevitably, many critics began making comparisons between the two bands, even though I never felt that our music sounded remotely similar to theirs. There might have been parts that sounded vaguely Celtic, and other elements which filtered through in terms of creating a certain feeling or atmosphere. The Edge and I are in some ways similar guitarists, in the sense that there is nothing gratuitous going on. It's primarily about melody, sound and texture.

I could see broad parallels in terms of the kind of messages we put out. We were both playing big venues. We both had records produced by Steve Lillywhite. We were friends. And critics always love a Blur vs Oasis scenario; in our case, big Scottish band vs big Irish band. But in terms of the actual music, I have always felt that the comparisons between Simple Minds and U2 are wildly off.

After *Street Fighting Years*, Jim and I went to Ireland and Bono invited us to stay at his house in Killiney for the night. We loved the area and decided we were going to rent a place in the neighbourhood to write. Bono had an assistant who he very kindly asked to enquire about what might be available to rent in Killiney. As it turned out, a house neighbouring Bono was available. It was a big place. Seven bedrooms. In time, it became my family home. For now, Jim, Tony Donald and I moved in. The Circus boys. Tony was working as my guitar tech and when we weren't touring he did odds and ends for us.

It was a great spot and a fun time. In the summer of 1990, Jim and I wrote quite a lot of *Real Life* there. During that period there was a lot of social interaction with U2. When I moved in, Bono came round and took me to the five-a-side. Let's draw a veil over that. More happily, Larry Mullen invited Jim and me to his house for a day with all the U2 guys. Larry took us out on his boat, a little Zodiac, across to an island close to the shore in Howth, where he lived. On the way back, we hit a sandbank and clumsily found ourselves stuck there for a considerable amount of time. Had any passing music fan been in the vicinity when we finally arrived safely back at Larry's house, somewhat later than planned, they would no doubt have been surprised to see various members of U2 and Simple Minds soaked and freezing as we squeezed what seemed like half of Dublin Bay from our clothes. It was the night of the 1990 World Cup final between Germany and Argentina. Having warmed up, we all watched it on TV at Larry's and Jim and I stayed most of the night.

We visited their hotel in Dublin, the Clarence, and had a few wild times there. Jim and I were invited on one occasion to a party at Bono's house. Everybody was there, from Jann Wenner, the founder of *Rolling Stone*, to various supermodels. Jim and I spent the entire afternoon in the kitchen talking with Bono's dad, Bob. That was very typical of us. Bob was great. And Jim's dad, Jimmy, got on really well with Bono.

One night, a little later, Edge picked me up and took me to see Seal play the Point. U2 were about to embark on the 'Zoo TV' tour, a hugely elaborate hi-tech live show. Edge asked whether I knew anybody who worked in that area. I'm not sure that I did. The world was changing. The technology was rapidly becoming more and more sophisticated.

There was never any sense of competition between us, and our paths continued to cross over the years. As a band, U2 have done a remarkable job. It is incredibly hard to keep four people together for forty-odd years, and to do it so well. They are four very different personalities, but they work as a unit as well as being really good people, each one of them. There is no attitude, no selfishness, no big egos. They've never been flash; they all have a great sense of humour. They are loyal. You meet their friends and realise these are people they have been close to since they were really young – and *they're* all good people, too. Funny and interesting.

Good guys. Great artists. But footballers? No.

31
And the Band Played On

It is not the strongest of the species that survive, nor the
most intelligent, but the most responsive to change.

– attributed to Charles Darwin

Nineteen ninety-five.

*It is an article of faith in the recording industry: if you don't
treat an album as a big deal before it comes out, then no one else
will. You either front up or flop. That is the theory, at least.*

Simple Minds have made a record called Good News from the
Next World *and Virgin are going to give it the works. Studio time
in Los Angeles. The best musicians money can buy. Big budget
videos. For the sleeve art, it has been decided that we will go to
India. We take with us an entourage that runs into double figures:
wardrobe, hair, film, press, photographers . . .*

*We all fly to India. I lose count of the number of photo sessions
we do. We are up at four in the morning, before it gets too hot and
the light is wrong. You might be forgiven for thinking that we are
shooting a sequel to* Ghandi.

*We spend a fortune, come back to the UK and decide that the
cover artwork is going to be a close-up of a faded piece of paint on
a door. We gaze upon this photograph, heads nodding and brows
furrowed:* 'Yes, yes! I think we've got it!' *It is, in truth, just a bit
of wall. We could have shot it in Toryglen.*

*These are the last great days of rock and roll – for both Simple
Minds and for the record industry. The End Days of the Great
Extravagances are nigh.*

The writing is on the wall in more ways than one.

Kerr/

The nineties started strange and became stranger.

When Mick left, we came full circle in terms of Charlie and I writing together again. Albeit now we were in the basement of a studio in the Netherlands rather than in his bedroom in Toryglen.

On the *Street Fighting Years* tour, Mick had been so much not the Mick that we had known for ten years. He was very uncommunicative. On a personal level, we were actually a little relieved when he didn't show up when we started working on new material in Holland. There's no question, however, that it felt strange, and I don't think we were entirely optimistic. It was a major fracture. You don't lose a talent like Mick MacNeil and not feel it.

These are not conversations Charlie and I ever had. We didn't talk about it directly. In front of each other we didn't blink, because the game was in progress. We got on with it. But by this point we had been going for almost fifteen years and for the first time the volume of my doubting voice was perhaps rivalling the positive one: *What other tricks do you have in you? Might you even be getting a little bored of yourself?*

Street Fighting Years had run out of gas and I was adamant that wouldn't happen again. I wanted a very focused record this time, and that meant very focused songs. I wanted the material up front and I wanted to be harder on it, rather than simply going with the first ten tracks. Although we had just come off a long tour, I was very much in action mode: *We gotta go!* Charlie was fine with that (Mick, clearly, wasn't). We had three weeks in Holland and Charlie came up with 'Real Life', 'See the Lights' and 'Let There Be Love'. The piano was becoming his primary writing instrument and it brought something new to the music. In terms of us continuing as Simple Minds, I thought, *We're going to be all right here.*

Where I didn't feel quite so bullish was going back to the hotel at the end of the night and switching on MTV. *What's this thing called the Stone Roses? What's this thing called Happy Mondays?* I could see the new tribes coming over the hill. There's a great line by Paul Simon: 'Every generation throws its heroes up the pop charts.'

Well, there they were. I thought, *This is going to be tricky.*

It was new territory. There was no manual to which we could refer. There was only the history of popular music, which we knew by heart, and which told us that every shooting star loses altitude eventually. I wasn't quite sure what we were going to do. If ever there was a moment for everyone to pull together, this was it. In our case, the opposite was happening.

Burchill/

At the start of the nineties, it felt as though Jim and I had moved country. We went to Amsterdam and Ireland to write and record, and I got the sense that we were embarking on a great new adventure. Personally, I felt optimistic. It was a new chapter for me and for Simple Minds. I was also very conscious that it was the end of the decade. I could feel the ground shifting.

Although Mick leaving the band was a significant loss, in reality Simple Minds were never going to split up. We never even entertained the idea. Jim and I were going to carry on, because we knew we could still write. After any initial uncertainty, we leaned the opposite way in terms of how we perceived Mick's departure: *Maybe this is a good thing, because it will open up a whole new area for us.* I can see now that this attitude was partly a safety device. Because we were reeling from a seismic shift and trying to get to grips with the ramifications, it was tempting to spin the earthquake into a positive force.

This was all unspoken. Subconscious. The overarching and unarticulated question was: *Where is it going to go now?*

Musically, it was difficult to figure out the answer. In the early nineties, Simple Minds stood back a little because we wanted to see what was going on at the start of a new decade. I listened to a lot of new music – not specifically to guide what we were doing, it wasn't as intentional as that. A friend from Amsterdam sent me dance music during that period. I loved Tim Simenon's Bomb the Bass. There was so much creativity in that field, and it felt aligned to what we did in terms of sequencing and electronics. I was very interested in that. I could see us fitting into that space because we already had those elements in our music.

You had the Happy Mondays and Blur coming through. In America it was the beginnings of grunge. U2, meanwhile, plotted out a whole new approach with *Achtung Baby* and it worked brilliantly. It was a departure for them aesthetically, but there wasn't such a radical shift in their sound. I felt it was almost proto grunge. Everything about the record and the tour was consciously Eurocentric, but to me the sound anticipated what was going to happen very shortly in the States. At the same time, a new breed of producers was in the mix. Flood seemed to be everywhere. I saw U2 working with him and Paul Oakenfold, and later Howie B and Spike Stent.

So much was happening. It was an odd time to try to make sense of where Simple Minds fitted among it all. I didn't have any concerns about having to compete against anything or anyone, and I don't think I ever worried about whether we were going to have continued success. I simply thought, *We've had a great time and we're still here. Let's step back a bit. We'll keep working, keep writing and keep an eye on how the decade is going to shape up.* Jim, on the other hand, was probably much more determined to have a strategy in place for the new decade. By nature, he would have been thinking way ahead. Whereas I just carried on doing what I always did.

We had great fun making *Real Life* with Steve Lipson. Steve played a very creative role with the music. It might sound a little glib, but I don't think we missed Mick all that much. I was writing on the piano and playing a lot more keyboards.

I could never replace Mick, but we had excellent back up with Steve, who was great with keys, and a brilliant Scottish keyboard player called Peter-John Vetesse. Together, we covered a large area. Most keyboard sounds that work well don't necessarily require a high degree of proficiency. If you can play a little, it is possible to get your ideas across.

The idea of being a band in the studio had disappeared with *Street Fighting Years*. The live group and the recording group were by now two different concepts. In some ways, Mel embodied the differences between them. On the one hand, Mel was in Simple Minds longer than Mick and Derek. He was part of the family. When I look back and see photographs from when we were younger, I realise how long we have all known each other. On the other hand, Mel wasn't ever really *in* the band. When we weren't together, we were very much apart. He was in London, and we were in Scotland. Mel took on other projects in between his Simple Minds work. Whenever we were writing and for much of the time when we were recording, Mel wasn't involved. He was only around when we were touring or when we called him in to play on an album.

Mel appeared on *Real Life* but by now a lot of the drum parts were programmed. The bass parts were shared around. It reminded me of the old Willie Nelson joke. He was on a session and the bass player was very late. Willie said, 'Give me the bass. I'll do it.' The drummer said, 'Oh, do you play bass, Willie?' 'Doesn't everyone?' he replied. I played some bass on the album, but I thought we needed to get in a proper bass player and Malcolm Foster was a good musician and a terrific guy. He had toured with us in 1989 after John Giblin left. Malcolm had great energy. He was very funny, always up, buzzing away.

There is a lot of terrific music on *Real Life*. It's a more song-based record than *Street Fighting Years* and some of the tracks are very different to anything we had done before. Even today, 'Banging on the Door' remains a favourite with a lot of fans.

'African Skies' has a beautiful piano melody which Jim sang over. 'Real Life' itself is an epic. We had three hit singles from the album in the UK and around Europe and a top forty hit in the US with 'See the Lights'.

It was a big-selling record, and I felt Simple Minds had moved on. We had developed.

Kerr/

After some of the financial issues around the *Street Fighting Years* tour, we were once bitten, twice shy. Before we toured *Real Life*, a promoter in Germany approached us. 'I'll pay for everything,' he said. 'You, Charlie and Mel will get your money before you even leave the house. It's all on me. I'll take the risk.' At the time we were setting up the dates, the Gulf War was in full swing. Some major artists were cancelling or rescheduling their tours, and here we were being offered a guaranteed return. We practically snapped his hand off.

A year later, Virgin released the first major Simple Minds compilation, *Glittering Prize 81/92*. We got a lot of money for that. The same year, BSkyB used 'Alive and Kicking' to promote the launch of the new English Premier League – we got a lot of money for that, too. It was at that point where I finally thought: *Well, at least we got paid.* I didn't know how Simple Minds was going to fare from here – but I knew the kids were going to be all right and our parents were going to be all right. We would all be OK. That was a full ten years after *New Gold Dream (81, 82, 83, 84)*. I felt a kind of relief. Charlie and I didn't form a band to get rich. We did it to be part of something meaningful. But it would have been pitiful to have had so much success and have generated so much money for everybody else not to have been paid our share.

Simple Minds didn't tour between autumn 1991 and spring 1995, which was a very long time to be off the road in the life of our band. There was a lot of real life being lived by both Charlie and me in that period. Meanwhile, the world moved on. By early 1995, when we released *Good News from the Next World*, the tribes I had seen coming over the hill had settled. A new generation of bands was well-established. Britpop was king. Richard Branson had sold Virgin Records to EMI in 1992. We would go into the record company and people we had known for a decade were no longer there. The individuals who were now in the top positions were all new faces, and they certainly wouldn't get any kudos from helping Simple Minds. They were pushing their own artists.

When we had signed to Virgin, the big deals were Magazine and XTC. By 1995 it was the Spice Girls. That was where we were.

During this period, we also had to work out the new concept of being a duo within Simple Minds. After Mick left, to all intents and purposes Simple Minds became me and Charlie again. It was our baby, even though we still wanted to present the band – and the brand – on stage. Charlie and I have never wanted to be a duo in any shape or form. We started off as a duo within the band in terms of writing songs, but as soon as we were able to open it up and work with our band mates, that's what we did. We were always band guys, and we still are.

Although the songwriting had now come back to being just the two of us, it was imperative to present Simple Minds as a band. On the *Real Life* tour, we still had Mel behind the kit, who fans identified with very much as being Simple Minds' drummer. We had Malcolm Foster on bass, who had toured with us in 1989. Mark Taylor on keyboards. It felt quite unified.

I'm not sure that was so much the case later.

Burchill/

Whenever you bring in a lot of session musicians, it doesn't feel as natural as it should. It was fine in the early days when we might have asked an outside musician to come in to play saxophone or a very specific part. We had Herbie Hancock play synth on 'Hunter and the Hunted', for goodness' sake! But now we were drafting in bass players and drummers. There were session men up and down the very spine of the music.

Good News from the Next World ended up having a very American feel to it, which was not something we intended. We decided to work again with Keith Forsey for the first time since 'Don't You (Forget About Me)'. Keith is fantastic. We had always loved him. He had continued making hit records and we thought he might open us up to more of a pop sensibility; the sacred art of the three-and-a-half-minute radio song. It didn't work out that way, but that was the initial idea.

We started in our studio at Loch Earn. The engineer, Brian, cracked after a few days. In tears, he told us he was homesick and wanted to leave. He had arrived at the airport full of beans: *Great, we're booked in at the Four Seasons!* Little did he know it was the Four Seasons in St Fillans. Not the same thing at all. His quarters were a wooden hut around the back of the hotel. After that bombshell, the weather and the remoteness of the studio really got to him.

Happily, Brian stuck it out and was with us when we moved to Los Angeles to record. To my ears, *Good News from the Next World* sounds far more LA than rural Perthshire. Many of the musicians on the album were very well-known US session players. There are four bassists on the record and three drummers, including Mark Schulman and Vinnie Colaiuta. We were auditioning people in the studio, which was a new experience for me. On the one hand it was great, because these were top-class musicians; Marcus Miller had played bass with Miles Davis and Frank Sinatra. On the other hand, it became a chicken-and-egg scenario. We hired these people because we wanted to generate ideas, but they ended up asking us what the idea was. Mark Schulman did the 1995 tour with us. He was great, but for Simple Minds to have an American in the core band was another big culture shift.

Los Angeles was the epicentre of our activities at the time. We felt we were getting another swing at the States. The vice-chairman of Virgin Records America, Nancy Berry, put in a lot of work with us. *Good News from the Next World* turned out to be the last record we made for Virgin, but the irony is that they probably put more money into that campaign than any of the other ones. The photoshoot in India was just one example. We made big budget videos for two of the singles, 'She's a River' and 'Hypnotised'. We were thinking about taking care of territories that we had neglected in the past. We went to Japan. We went to South Africa.

We were taking a serious shot at it. At the same time, it was starting to feel as though we weren't really a band any more. We were trying to make it *feel* like a band, but it probably wasn't. Still Simple Minds. But not a band.

32
Let There Be Love, Pt 2

The secret of a happy marriage remains a secret.

– Henny Youngman

Spring 1991.

Sliding doors.

Me, Charlie and Steve Lipson are sitting in a studio killing time. On the television, the young British actress Patsy Kensit is being interviewed about her latest film. She is hilarious, which takes me by surprise – though it shouldn't. She is obviously very cute, but she is also smart and sharp, running rings around the interviewer.

I turn to Steve and Charlie. I say, 'If I ever meet her I'm going to ask her out. Guaranteed. She can only say no.'

A few days later we fly to Madrid as part of a European promo tour for Real Life. *When we arrive at the Palace Hotel, I see that some filming is taking place. They are actually working in the corridor where I am staying. Lights, cameras, action – everywhere.*

At first this is mildly diverting. Quite soon it becomes a drag. I have to wait an age before I can get into the elevator. I have a bit of a grumble while doing so.

The next moment I hear a voice: 'Oh! What are you *doing here?'*

I turn around.

It's Patsy Kensit.

Kerr/

Sliding doors. Standing by the lift in a fancy hotel in Madrid, there was Patsy, only a matter of days after I had seen her talking on television. We started chatting.

'Are you playing here? I want to come!'

'Actually, we're not playing, we're here doing some promo. What are you up to?'

She was making a movie called *Blame It on the Bellboy*. Within minutes, she told me that she had been away for several weeks and was by now fairly fed up with it; I later discovered that Patsy was a homebody, which can make life hard when you work in the transient world of acting. I invited her to eat with us that night. It so happened that she finished work late and couldn't, but we had a drink in the bar – and I mean one drink. Charlie was around.

She was everything that I thought she would be from seeing her in that brief TV interview. We talked about music. She was terrific company but seemed lonely. Patsy was in Madrid on her own. No friends, no assistants. She told me that the production was moving to Venice the following week. I said that we were also going to be in Italy that week, continuing promotion for *Real Life*. We exchanged numbers. When our promo tour ended in Milan, I thought, *Maybe I'll go to Venice for a couple of days to see her*. Who doesn't want to go to Venice? And that's how it all happened. Standing at the elevator doors once again.

Quite soon after Venice, Patsy was back in London, where I was staying at the Halcyon Hotel. She came over to visit a few times when I had Yasmin and Natalie with me. The kids loved her. They would ask, *Where's Patsy?! When is she coming to see us again?* She was sparkly and funny with them: *Let's do stuff!* That was a big deal for me. Apart from them all getting along very well, it felt good that the children were no longer seeing me as some lonely guy, as I perhaps had been. In reality, I'm sure they weren't thinking that at all – but that's what *I* was thinking and feeling.

If it was all travelling faster than it should have been, that was simply the pace at which our worlds were moving. Patsy and I met in March 1991, and we were married on 3 January 1992. In retrospect, I can see why people may have regarded it as an incongruous match, but I wasn't aware of that then and I wouldn't have given a damn in any case. When you meet and get to know someone with any kind of media profile, within a very short space of time their public persona becomes meaningless. You simply know them as the human being who is standing in front of you. I had met somebody who very obviously had a lot going for her. Patsy was witty. Exciting. She was young and energised. She was very beautiful.

Chrissie was eight years older than me. Patsy was eight years younger. I had grown up quite a bit. Even so, apart from the glorious feeling of falling in love again, which was hugely exciting, looking back I recognise a common factor in the fact that I got married, twice, relatively quickly. I've heard it said that quite often part of the reason we feel a profound attraction to somebody can be connected to what we think we can do for them. I don't wish to paint myself as the model of gallantry, far from it, but when I met them, both the women in question were in a real bind.

I don't think Patsy loved what she was doing. In the quieter moments, I could tell she wasn't particularly happy in the world she was in. She enjoyed the benefits, but she was uncomfortable with the detritus that came in its wake. It has since come to light what life could be like in those days for a beautiful young actress, away from home, on all those sets, at all those auditions. There were creeps everywhere.

I would go out to America with her sometimes when she was having auditions and meeting scriptwriters and producers. I would tag along to the dinners. It was very interesting for me to see that side of things, because it was a world I didn't know. She was a woman with her own successful career, but at the same time I felt she needed a degree of protection. I wasn't Superman, and I wasn't looking for a cause, but sometimes one of the reasons we get involved with another person is that we feel we can fill in the missing part. It makes you feel good and makes you feel that there's substance to the relationship beyond the romantic side.

From my perspective, to be married twice displayed a keenness to still believe in the core values with which we were brought up. Although Patsy and I lasted only four years, I didn't think I was entering into a stereotypical celebrity marriage where you get hitched on impulse and divorced on a whim. I can absolutely see how from the outside it might look like that, but it wasn't the case.

Out of it all came our son, James. I was in my mid-thirties. Simple Minds was coming to a crossroads. Anything could have happened with the band. Among all the uncertainty, it felt good not to be alone, and to be involved in a family again. Not just a Saturday Dad.

Charlie's life was changing, too. By the time I met Patsy, he had got married and would soon be starting his own family. I can remember the day he met Caroline, his ex-wife. She worked as a receptionist in a hotel in Lausanne where Simple Minds were staying while playing a show nearby on the *Street Fighting Years* tour. Caroline greeted us when we arrived. I think she even took me up to show me to my room.

Charlie liked her. He invited her to dinner, and they kept in touch. She was a beautiful woman, and he was always very happy to see her. The next thing I knew he had gone on holiday, and I got a call telling me that he and Caroline had got married. No best man invite for me! It was all conducted very much within his own private world – and that was fine. It was another insight into the areas that Charlie closes off.

Charlie set up his new family in Ireland. We were already working quite a lot there. We are Scots, but on the side of Glasgow where we were brought up, Ireland is a mystical, mythical place. My first holiday had been over on the boat to Bray. I had uncles from Cork. We were immersed in that culture. Ireland felt a little like a home from home.

It was the time of the Celtic Tiger. It all came to a sad end but for a decade Ireland was on the up and the possibilities were good. There were excellent rehearsal facilities. Charlie is a very sociable person and Dublin is a very sociable place. I bought a house in Killiney. Patsy came over and really liked it. She was tired of London, and we thought Dublin might be a good place for us to set up home. Sadly, by the time I got around to looking seriously at the idea our marriage was already running its course.

Burchill/

When Caroline and I were first married, I was still living in Wemyss Bay on the west coast of Scotland. But not for long. Quite quickly we moved to Dublin and stayed there until the early 2000s. My two sons, Chaz and Chay, were born in the city.

The area Jim and I had stayed in when we were writing *Real Life* was a beautiful area on the coast. Killiney was built by Italians. There are streets called Sorrento Terrace and Vico Road. It looks like the Bay of Naples. I see lots of architecture here in Sicily that is very similar. Caroline and I loved it. We already had the fantastic house that Jim and I had been living and working in, and when it came up for sale, I bought it. The people around us were lovely. We felt we had found our place.

Jim bought a house nearby in Killiney Hill Road. Caroline and I stayed there for quite a while during the time our own house was being redecorated. We were living there when Chaz was born. Jim was in London with Patsy at that time, but he was coming back and forth.

There was a point during this period when artists could benefit from a tax break on their publishing if they moved to Ireland. We ended up not taking advantage of that. We never became tax residents. Perhaps we were the most unworldly musicians on the planet, but we never left the British tax system. We had moved to Ireland simply because we had grown to love the area.

My children were born in Dublin in the mid-nineties, two years apart. On the night Chaz was born, I spotted one other expectant father in the maternity hospital, also waiting for his child to arrive. Liam Neeson wasn't pacing the corridor, but as a first-time father, I certainly was. Culturally, my kids are an unusual blend. Caroline was born in Jamaica. Her father was German and her mother Jamaican; the maternal branch of her family had a big Spanish-Caribbean mix.

I was thirty-five when Chaz arrived, nearly ten years older than Jim when he first became a father. Jim and I weren't constantly around each other during that time, but I knew his kids when they were growing up and Jim knew mine. My eldest son is Charles James Burchill. Jim's son is James Charles Kerr. I'm James's godfather.

It's instructive when your best friend has children and you are often around them. I learned a lot. We talked a little about parenting styles. We talked a *lot* about the paparazzi. Because Jim and Chrissie had been regarded as a showbiz couple, it was inevitable that they would get some degree of hassle at airports and, at times, in London. It was worse when Jim was with Patsy – who I really liked. I had been there the night she and Jim first met in Madrid. Patsy was quite shy. She wasn't brash, she didn't have a huge ego. She was funny and very good company.

I regarded the relationship as quite glamorous; in a strange way, it added another dimension to Simple Minds' popularity at the time. When the children were with them, however, the attention could be a little scary. Jim and I would talk about fatherhood from that point of view: *How do the kids perceive all this? What do you tell them about what is going on, because they don't have the frame of reference to understand it?*

When we got married, Caroline and I were very clear about what I did and what it entailed. It was never a problem – for me, anyway. My life inevitably changed because I became a father, but it didn't particularly affect Simple Minds. We were still working and I wasn't under any pressure not to do so. We wrote and recorded in Amsterdam, Italy, America and Scotland. We toured the world. In that respect, life continued in much the same way as it had for the past fifteen years. I don't know whether it was the same for Jim. The media attention in that marriage was intense. Patsy ticked all the boxes for the press. Jim being completely the opposite kind of character led, I think, to some tensions.

Kerr/

Naturally, Patsy had things to do and places to go in order to support her own career. One of them involved a farcical fellow called Michael Winner, who had taken a shine to her. She kept saying that we had to go to Winner's for dinner.

'Michael Winner? Jesus Christ . . .'

'We've got to. Please say you'll come once.'

Finally, the stalemate came to a head. Arnold Schwarzenegger was visiting London. A big bash was being thrown for Arnie at chez Winner. Patsy was invited and, apparently, I simply had to be there. Perhaps ungallantly, I wasn't having any of it.

She said: 'But Jim, can't you see it's my job to go to places like this?'

I said: 'And can't you see it's my job NOT to?'

She laughed, but there in a nutshell was the dilemma. It was all a long way from *Empires and Dance*.

There were other challenges. Pasty's mother was a truly great woman. They were so close; Pasty's mum was to her what my dad was to me. When her mum fell ill, it was incredibly difficult for Patsy. I think she would say herself that life was never quite the same after that.

Our divorce was finalised in 1996 but it was over before then. I have to hold my hands up. A lot of the time with Patsy, once again, I just wasn't there. I'm not a quitter. I will hang in. Whatever I do, I want to be of service, because nothing feels better to me. That might sound very mechanical when talking about a marriage, but I wanted to serve this thing to which I had pledged. However, when the day came in both my marriages where I realised that I was never going to be able to make these people happy, it made it easier to deal with the fact that they were walking away. Because both Patsy and Chrissie did. There was an element of feeling quite philosophical about it. I thought, *I can't make them happy. I'm hanging in for the sake of hanging in.*

Subsequently, Patsy became involved with Liam Gallagher. Patsy and I had a young son, so I obviously took an interest. I only knew Liam through his public persona and to be honest I feared the worst. *Oh no! OH GOD!* Very quickly I realised that there was nothing to worry about. I would say to James, 'How's Liam?' James would smile. 'He's great! Liam's really great!' As a father, that was all I wanted to hear. I would have been very anxious and distraught had James not liked Liam or said that he wasn't being nice to him. But it was the opposite. They got on very well, and whenever I met Liam we also rubbed along fine. We talked about football, about Glasgow and Manchester. I met his mum, Peggy, who was fantastic.

There was a night very shortly before Liam and Patsy were married in 1997. I was over at the house bringing James home and Liam was there. He asked what I was up to. I was heading over to Holland Park. He said he was going to a pub down the road and did I fancy coming along. Why not? It might well have been the last time I was ever in a pub. We had a drink and talked a little and I sensed some uneasiness about the upcoming nuptials. I don't think I said to him: *RUN!* However, my body language might have suggested

258

something along those lines. Or more likely, *Why so fast? I have learned through experience: take some time.*

There is no better Liam Gallagher than Liam Gallagher. You have to hand it to the guy. He never gave up. At heart, he's the real deal. He loves his band, loves his songs, loves music. I have no idea how his life operates on a day-to-day basis, but we sometimes have a word back and forth, because we have someone who is close to us both. It's ironic, because Patsy and I are no longer really in touch at all.

By the time Liam and Patsy were together I had met my partner, Yumie. Charlie once again played his part.

There came a point in 1995 where it had been established that Patsy and I were not going to continue, during Simple Minds' tour for *Good News from the Next World*. The tour had to be concluded before we got around to the formalities. I was not in a good place. I certainly wasn't looking forward to going home and having to deal with it all. I didn't know this at the time, but Charlie and people close to me were worried. I'd hit a slump. I was just about getting the gigs done. It was hanging heavy on me.

After a show in Paris, I had returned to the hotel and gone to bed. I can't recall Charlie ever calling me after midnight, but on this night he did. He was in the bar downstairs with some people, one of whom was a young Japanese woman, who was there with her friend. He told me she had seen our recent gigs in Japan and would love a photo.

'Come down and give me a hand here. I'm sitting by myself with these people.'

'Come on, Charlie, give me a break! I'm not doing it.'

I put the phone down. He phoned again fifteen minutes later.

'. . . and it's her birthday as well! *Come on!*'

I relented. I went down to the bar and started chatting to a delightful Japanese woman called Yumie. After a while, Charlie headed off to bed. Yumie and I sat talking for the rest of the night and when we said goodbye, we agreed to keep in touch. I really liked her, but the last thing I was looking for was a girlfriend.

A few months later, Yumie was going to Scotland on a trip that she had already booked. I was staying in my place in Loch Earn; not the studio, but a property I had bought up there. I was by myself, rattling around this big house. I felt like the lead character in Iain Banks's great rock and roll novel, *Espedair Street*. The place was a shambles. My circumstances were a cliché of a single man who had been living alone for too long. Everything was falling to bits.

I invited Yumie up to the countryside. She came to the house, took off her coat and transformed into Nanny McPhee. She started organising the place as I started cooking. She told me she had never seen a man cook in her life. We had a great day, and when I took her back to Edinburgh that night, the place was starting to resemble order.

In the thirty years since, Yumie has continued to bring so much order to my life – including with the children, who love her and can't ever remember her not being around, and my mum and dad when they were alive. She is incredibly smart. She speaks several languages. She is very good at putting the brakes on me when I get the impulse to do crazy things.

Along with Charlie, she has become the biggest soulmate, partner and confidante in my life. I absolutely love her, but it's not a conventional relationship. She is based in the south of France and is definitely not for living in Sicily, although she loves coming to Scotland. There have been periods of estrangement. There was a spell where I was almost trying to manoeuvre her *not* to be with me. I didn't want to have any more children. I didn't want to get married again. Those things weren't going to happen. She was younger than me and I felt she should meet somebody who wanted to have all those things. But we have made it work.

You can be guilty of wanting it all. I maintain you don't really know who you are until you are in your forties. Beyond that, in my case, at least, you make peace with yourself. You realise the person that you are never going to be, and the things you are never going to be good at. But you can also say: *You know what? I'm not bad at this! And I know I can do that!* When you get older, you should recognise your strengths and weaknesses, and the things that are never going to change.

Burchill/

My sons may have been born in Ireland and started school there, but they were still quite young when they left. After Caroline and I divorced in the early 2000s, I moved to Rome and she and the children moved to the Caribbean. From there they went to Colorado and then to the Azores of Portugal in the Atlantic. My kids have lived all over the world. Perhaps unsurprisingly, they don't have an accent that could be pinned down as specific to one place, and they don't really identify with anywhere as home. They have British and Irish passports, and I remind them that they are Irish by birth, but there isn't a strong connection. Very sadly, Caroline died in 2024. She was only fifty-five and seemed so much younger.

When I left Ireland, I was trying to patch up my life. Jim and I would touch on the divorce, but when it comes to very personal issues, we tend not to bother each other too much. It's not that we don't care or aren't interested; it's just that in the final analysis there isn't much you can really do to help. In the end, the broader strokes of these things are self-evident, and you are going to have to deal with the fallout yourself. We did talk about the end of my marriage, and I may have asked for a bit of advice because by then he had been through it himself a couple of times. He might have asked, *What happened? What did you do?* But we didn't have long, intimate conversations. Though we are very close, Jim and I don't get overly sentimental. I don't think we're cold, but we don't get wrapped up in our emotions. *Just get on with it!* That comes from our backgrounds. Old school.

When the dust settled on both our marriages, Jim and I ended up with Asian girlfriends. Yumie is Japanese. My partner Win Hong is Dutch, but she has a Chinese father. There is a joke among the Simple Minds crew that the AAA tour pass stands for *Access All Asians*. Recently, there has been a lot of family business that has needed Win Hong's attention in Holland. I go back and forth, but I also need to spend time in Sicily. In the future, the plan is that our life together will be in Taormina.

Kerr/

We didn't talk in any depth about Charlie's divorce. All through that period, he barely said a word to me about it. Usually with best friends sitting around in the wee small hours, these things will come out. But no. When he takes a drink, much the same as when anyone takes a drink, he may be more expansive. But I'm rarely there when Charlie takes a drink.

I vent. I can't hide it: *This thing is driving me completely nuts.* That's not Charlie's style. He is so polite he would feel he was dragging you down by discussing it. Even with me, he would feel that he wouldn't want to be a burden, which is, of course, ridiculous. It is only relatively recently that I think we have been able to talk a little more openly. We have learned that you have to let these feelings come out at some point. It's unhealthy not to have frank discourse when going through difficult situations. More and more now, we will talk about the deeper stuff. Family. Children. We are getting better at it. We're so close, we can't pretend that it's not at the forefront of our minds much of the time.

Looking back, it's strange that I didn't get to know Charlie's wife particularly well. Caroline very rarely came to a gig. I knew his boys when they were young, but I haven't been able to be around them so much in later years. Occasionally they will come to a show or visit Taormina, and it's always great to see them. Chaz is a pilot now. Charlie is very proud of them both, and my kids love Charlie. They know our story. They know how much he means to me, outside of Simple Minds.

Apart from all the other things Charlie and I have in common, we both met Asian women who bailed us out in many ways. What were the chances? Win Hong is great. Everyone loves her. And Charlie and Yumie are great friends.

When we met our partners, both Charlie and I were coming out of a kind of carnage, albeit at different times. Our lives were in pieces: we weren't quite sure where we lived, we had kids in various places, we had parents who were getting older. Both Yumie and Win Hong helped sort out all of that while still allowing us space.

They met us at a later stage in our lives. We weren't naive kids who thought that love could conquer all. They came into a situation where every single thing we do is filtered through the context of Simple Minds. *What does the band do next? What will work best for that?* Simple Minds is what feeds everything, and everybody in our lives has had to understand that. It can sound a little cold and selfish, but experience has taught us that if anything gets in the way of that, we will be antisocial. Also, it puts spaghetti on the table. End of story. We have always looked after a lot of people and you never know what might be around the corner.

With both Win Hong and Yumie, however, it has also been about Charlie and me going into their lives, exploring their cultures and playing a role within their families. Make no mistake, that has been immensely enriching for both of us.

33
The Fall

They flee from me that sometime did me seek.

– Sir Thomas Wyatt, 'They Flee from Me'

By the late nineties, the fire is beginning to go out.

Simple Minds have released a record called Néapolis. *I am going away for the weekend with the kids and I pop into the HMV in Heathrow to buy some CDs. I have heard good things about the new Blur album.*

The man working there recognises me: 'Jim Kerr! How are you doing?'

I tell him I'm doing grand, thanks. He seems sceptical.

'Really? Because your record is not doing well AT ALL! It's doing terribly.'

It is actually funny. He isn't saying it in a nasty way. I detect more a sense of bemused concern: 'What are you going to do? This thing really isn't selling at all!'

The kids look up at me. 'Dad, what is the man saying?'

'He's saying things are going to be just fine, children . . .'

Kerr/

For almost the entirety of the nineties, Simple Minds didn't have a manager. We had personal relationships with various people at Virgin, we had an agent, we had a lawyer. Sandra ran our office in Edinburgh. We had all the parts. What we didn't have, and this is crucially important, was an objective voice to say, *That's good, but is it great?* Or to act as a buffer between us and the industry.

By the point where the nineties were racing towards the new millennium, Simple Minds had parted ways with Virgin and signed to Chrysalis, which was also owned by EMI. The industry was in a flux of mergers and takeovers. Every two years the dynamics were changing, and we didn't have anyone at the coal face to tell us how or where things might be heading. We needed clued-in people to guide us through these changes. We looked around and they weren't there.

Burchill/

The industry had begun to fracture and I'm not sure that we were best placed to deal with it. After Bruce left, we had made a conscious decision to keep everything very tight and in-house. We thought, *How much more experience than us would a manager have?* Which was naive. By then we had enough nous to book tours, but you still have to negotiate deals with agents, labels, promoters. Jim was largely guiding everything, with Sandra in the office doing the deals. It was rough. And worrying. In reality, we were out of our depth.

When it came to making a new record for a new record company, I seem to remember us referencing *Sons and Fascination*. I don't know whether we overtly wanted to make an experimental album, but that's what *Néapolis* turned out to be.

We had asked Brian McGee and Derek Forbes to join us for the initial sessions. It wasn't a question of getting the old gang back together. I don't think we ever thought we would be a band again. We were thinking of their input more in terms of session musicians, because the musical context felt appropriate: *This is more European and experimental. A hint of the old Simple Minds. Let's get Derek in.*

It didn't work out terribly well. Brian was around only for a very short period. He isn't on the record; there aren't a lot of real drums on *Néapolis*. Derek was more involved, but the writing was on the wall from the start. On the first day of us recording with him, Derek turned up four hours late. It was an echo of what had happened in the mid-eighties. We were all hanging about waiting. Jim was beside himself. Derek played on the album and the tour, but at the end of it we moved on with very little discussion.

It was quite fraught, I have to say, making that record. We became frustrated. I felt we were becoming untethered. There are tracks that we laboured over for a long, long time and they just weren't getting any better. A song like 'Lightning' is typical. It could have been great, classically Simple Minds in a 'Waterfront' way. But like so many of the tracks, we didn't quite get it. I was working a lot with computers and Pro Tools, and exploring all the textural options that approach offered. In doing so, I neglected the actual songs. I was unable to recognise that fact while I was in the middle of it, but as a result *Néapolis* fell between the cracks.

Peter Walsh came on board near the end. Pete had produced *New Gold Dream (81, 82, 83, 84)*. He's a brilliant producer and a fantastic guy. However, we weren't recording in a way that allowed Pete to do what he does best. Working with programming and on computers doesn't make for a terribly collaborative process. When you're recording like that and want to give a track a radical facelift, it's not possible to do so in the way it is when you are recording in a more traditional manner, where you can change up the structure or the arrangement and make an impact quite quickly. With programming, change is incremental. You have to do it one piece at a time. Momentum leaches away. Frustrations grow. You lose direction. That all contributed to the malaise.

Kerr/

Not only were we trying to write songs, but Charlie was trying to get to grips with Pro Tools. His endeavour was amazing, he wouldn't give up, but he struggled with the technology.

Rather than bringing in someone who was already skilled in that area, he wanted to learn on the job. The programming would crash. We would lose things. Back to square one. We must have spent a year in that mode. I was tearing my hair out.

I can barely remember Brian being there. I think he came up to Loch Earn a couple of times. We didn't keep anything he did. With Derek, it wasn't like the old days. Charlie and I had written the songs and we asked him to go in and play bass. That wasn't what Derek did; his speciality was jamming. I didn't care who played on the record as long as it sounded great, but it wasn't sounding great. It was actually a bit of a mess. Finally, we brought in Peter Walsh in an attempt to bring some coherence to it all, but it wasn't like *New Gold Dream (81, 82, 83, 84)* where he produced the album from start to finish. It was more akin to a salvage job.

Years later, I was having lunch in a restaurant in Italy. I was in the back room and I could hear music coming from the front area. I couldn't quite make out what it was, but I remember thinking, *That sounds really good.* I went through to listen more closely and realised two things. Firstly, it was *Néapolis*. Secondly, as I stood in the middle of the room between two speakers, it sounded like two different records were playing at the same time. That's how bad the mixing was. The album has its faults, but I still have a special feeling for some of the songs: 'Song for the Tribes'. 'Killing Andy Warhol'. 'Glitterball'. 'War Babies'. We just didn't do them justice.

Derek stuck around for a tour or two. He's a fabulous bass player and great on stage, but it was not a good time for Simple Minds. The *Néapolis* tour was very scrappy. Away from the shows, I didn't really see him. I didn't go to the bar. I had last worked with Derek in 1984. This was 1998. We had all changed. We had different interests. Perhaps his sense of humour wasn't quite our sense of humour any more. It wasn't that he did anything wrong that I can recall, but when it came to the next project, Derek's name just never came up. It might sound cold, but that's the way it was.

Burchill/

Néapolis was the last album where we recorded at Dalkenneth House. Having our own studio had become a burden. As time went on, I found myself alone in this huge place with only a guitar tech. We had ten good years of use from it until the need for studios became almost obsolete. At a certain point, the technology changed everything. So we sold up.

Jim still had a house near Loch Earn. For the next Simple Minds records we started writing and recording there, decamping to CaVa in Glasgow on weekends. For the first time, Jim and I were working extensively with an outside song-writer. In retrospect, we were drifting. Trying to find fresh perspectives.

Kerr/

After *Néapolis*, we wanted to make a more accessible record quite quickly. EMI had given us a lot of money for a couple of albums. The big boss at the time was a Simple Minds fan, even if nobody else in the building was. He was an abrasive Frenchman. Picture Eric Cantona as a powerful music industry executive: 'I want Simple Minds! Get them! Get me "Don't You (Forget About Me)". Give them all the money!'

We said thanks very much, but we were also slightly bemused. Not only was EMI in flux, with various mergers being mooted and then falling through, but the people working there had their own pet projects: Blur. Radiohead. Robbie Williams. It seemed to me that the boss man was trying to foist Simple Minds on to his subordinates, who weren't especially interested.

We were left to our own devices up in Scotland. We were still turning up, still writing, but we needed to bring in new energy, that was very apparent. I probably felt that more so than Charlie. I was thirsting for greater impetus and momentum.

Martin Hanlin and I were still close. After the Silencers had disbanded, he had moved to Austin, Texas, to work with a publishing company owned by Bill Ham, who managed ZZ Top and quite a few other artists. Martin was their young buck, nurturing the up-and-coming songwriters. I went to Austin to see him and while there I met a couple of his contacts, one of whom was Kevin Hunter.

Kevin was from San Francisco, and he had been in a band called Wire Train. It was a very different vibe to Simple Minds, more of a Tom Petty or Bob Dylan feel. As a writer/ producer, Kevin was in increasing demand. At one point he was working in London and Martin suggested that we get together with him. By this time, the studio was gone. We were working out of my house in Loch Earn. Kevin came up and stayed for a few days. He and Charlie got on well and before we knew it we were writing songs. It was a result of osmosis rather than strategising. On one of the best tracks we wrote, 'Space', the lyrics are mostly Kevin's. I didn't have any problem with that. When a good idea was in the air, I was happy to grab it. That was always the case, and it still is.

Kevin was great, and we also brought in Eddie Duffy, Ged Malone and my younger brother Mark to work with us on *Our Secrets Are the Same*. But I don't think Charlie and I knew what a record was any more. Underworld's 'Born Slippy' was our favourite song at the time. Moby had just made a hugely successful record built mostly from samples. Where did Simple Minds fit into all that?

Quite recently, something became clearer to me. Beginning with *Real Life*, we were writing what I still believe were some very good songs, but perhaps they weren't Simple Minds songs. After a while, you're damned if you don't try to change somewhat – and damned if you do. In our desire not to repeat ourselves, we tried to stretch out. In doing so, we perhaps didn't meet certain longstanding expectations around the band – and the brand. We wrote some beautiful music in the nineties but with the experience I have now, putting on my Jimmy Iovine cap, perhaps I should have said: *Great song! But it's not a Simple Minds song . . .*

We had to give something to EMI and what we delivered in 1999 arrived with a kind of unspoken caveat: *This is where we are. What do you think? Is there someone we can bring in who can take this to the next level?* That didn't happen. They hated what they heard, and they had no ideas and no interest in pursuing the record. As a result, I got a little antisocial with the boss when he came up to see us. I'm not very good with bullies. After a while of being belittled I may have tossed a guitar in his general direction and said, 'You fucking play it, then! We need ideas. You seem to know everything, you show us!'

I don't think I was out of order. In a similar way to a struggling sports team needing an inspirational coach, we really did require someone to encourage us and bring in new ideas and positive energy. We could have used an arm around the shoulder; a vote of confidence. What we *didn't* need was a clumsy attempt at kicking us up the arse. As a result, he was lucky not to return to London with his own arse kicked. But it came close.

Caught in the middle of all that turmoil, *Our Secrets Are the Same* sat on the shelf. Before we had reached any certainty on what was going to happen, the album was leaked on Spanish radio, burned on to illicit CDs, and bootlegged all over the internet. In those days, to have a record leak was a death sentence. The album was killed twice before it had even had a chance to be properly heard. Eventually EMI said, 'Just take your record back. Go away.' And because the album was already seen as damaged goods, no other company wanted to take it on.

Compounding everything else that was not working, that was a hammer blow. I felt we were in our own version of Dante's circles of Hell.

At the outer ring was the chaos of the industry at large.

Within that there was the chaos at the label.

At the very epicentre was mine and Charlie's chaos.

We were flatlining.

34
Retreat/Revival

A man is not finished when he is defeated;
he is finished when he quits.

– Epictetus

A new millennium.

*I have come to Taormina to stay with my friend Antonio Chemi.
I am hiding from Simple Minds and perhaps also, a little, from
myself.*

*Next to Antonio's house there is an empty plot of land. Dusty,
rocky, but with the most amazing views. I ask Antonio what is
happening with it. I have a mad notion that maybe I could build a
house there.*

*He tells me that the land belongs to a family who have been
trying to sell it for quite some time – and as it happens, he adds,
there is planning permission to build a small hotel on the plot.*

A lightbulb goes on in my head.

It feels like the first good news I've heard in a very long while.

Kerr/

Before you're reborn, you have to die a little.

In terms of my creative life, I came to Taormina to die and
ended up being reborn.

By the dog days of the late nineties, the gods were no longer
on my side. Until then, everything I had done had worked,
to a greater or lesser degree. Suddenly, nothing seemed to
be working. *I wonder whose fault that is, pal?* I had taken a

272

pounding in the past few years: a waning band, another divorce, a brother who was going through a lot of difficulties. Sometimes you have to take the blows life deals on the chin. If you sustain too many, however, there is a risk of staggering around like a punch-drunk boxer. Contemplating the canvas, I had a lot to think about.

Entering the millennium, Simple Minds had made a record that nobody wanted. Our *Once Upon a Time* fanbase had largely disappeared. The lease was up on our office. We had no manager. Our lawyer was retiring. I tried to rationalise it. I felt that perhaps the universe was trying to tell us something. Charlie didn't necessarily view it the same way. He was in Ireland, renovating his house. He had his boys. He was loved up. I was happy to see him like that, but the communication wasn't great.

Meanwhile, I felt it might be time for me to think about hanging up my hat. The walls were closing in. If there was no management, no publisher, no record company, no agent, then the game was up. They couldn't all be wrong. (*Yet they WERE all wrong!* I saw a poster recently from Live Aid and calculated the number of artists on both bills who are still around and playing arenas today. It's about 3 per cent.)

Twenty years in, Simple Minds were running on fumes. We were in stasis. Blocked. The blood wasn't flowing. I had become so bored with myself. I felt I had said all I had to say, and as a result I was no longer enjoying what I was hearing. On top of that, every review and everything I read about Simple Minds hammered us – and me, in particular. That's all part of the deal, but it had eaten away at my confidence. I probably wasn't much fun to be around. I wasn't dramatic about it, but I felt lost.

In the quieter moments I could contemplate walking away from it all. Nothing has a God-given right to last forever, and Simple Minds had enjoyed a very successful run. We would never have split up. We were never quitters, but I could see how things might fritter away, until eventually we just didn't do it any more. But how do you walk away from yourself? The reason I got up first thing in the morning was to think about a song, a lyric, a show, a strategy. It was an integral part of who I was. *How could I stop being me?*

I would talk to people about how I felt. They would listen patiently and then say, 'You're really strong, Jim. You'll work it out.' *Really?* I could barely breathe, never mind strategise. From time to time, I talked to Iovine. He was always great. To the point. He'd say, 'Everybody went through this. John Lennon. Bob Dylan. Johnny Cash. These are highfalutin names. If it happens to them, what makes you any different?' Chrissie would offer the artist's perspective. She didn't give a damn about the business: *So, are you just gonna give up? This is what we do, and we do it through good times and bad.* A lot of good people stood by us, but others became wary; I sensed a kind of embarrassment. People don't like to see you on the canvas.

Parallel to our own fall was a similarly dizzying fall within the music industry. Suddenly we were hearing about MP3s. Napster. Record companies were being sold or merging. Record stores were closing. Music publications were declining. People we knew in the industry were no longer in position. The landscape we had grown up with was being stripped bare and replaced with something almost unrecognisable. In the year 2000, there was a real danger that the game was up for *everyone.*

Charlie and I could have done with a great A&R. They did exist, but they were thin on the ground at the time. We needed input, we needed new ideas, we needed someone who had a clear view of what was coming around the corner. Would we have listened? Yes, we would have listened. We always listened. I love producers. I love record company guys with a track record who know what they're talking about. Above all, we needed somebody from the outside to believe in us, because my belief had taken a kicking. Even if the greatest A&R guy in the world had grabbed me and said, 'I believe in you, Jim! I'm going to give you a great deal,' there's a good chance I would have said, 'Thank you. But I don't know if I can write a song again.'

Whenever I would launch into a spiel to Charlie, he would hear me out, but in retrospect I realise the unspoken subtext was, *Oh, Jim's just saying that.* It was classic Charlie. Head down and keep on keeping on. At the time I certainly didn't feel that I was merely venting. I believed I was finished.

Hanging around like a bad smell when no one wanted us didn't appeal to me, so I headed for the hills. Other people in similar positions might turn to alcohol or drugs. My escape route was to pitch up under a volcano where no one knew what the hell I was doing. Including me. If I was ever going to fulfil the dream of living in Taormina, there could be no better time than now.

It was another sliding-doors moment.

Touring *Néapolis* in 1998, Simple Minds played Trieste in northern Italy. Dad was there. He had always wanted to visit Trieste. During the gig, I could see some people in the crowd holding a banner: *We're from Sicily! Hello from Taormina!* I had already been to Taormina a couple of times. It's a small town, and my visit clearly hadn't gone unnoticed. I acknowledged the gesture from the stage. These guys had travelled the length of Italy to see us.

Later that night, I was in bed at the hotel but not yet asleep when the phone in my room rang. It was Dad. He was in the bar downstairs with Charlie and some of the crew, as well as the Sicilians I had spotted earlier at the show. They had seen my dad standing outside the hotel wearing a Simple Minds tour jacket, smoking his pipe. When they said hello, he had invited them for a drink.

On the phone, Dad told me that they would love an autograph and a photo. I was tired. I wasn't keen. Following some not-so-gentle paternal persuasion, I agreed to come down to the bar. There I met Antonio and Guiseppe Chemi, two brothers from Taormina, accompanied by their young nephew and their girlfriends. Antonio was a huge Simple Minds fan. He was ten years younger than me and spoke decent English. We got on well, and before we said goodnight he invited me to come and visit him in Taormina.

At the end of the tour, I took him up on this kind offer. I had a fantastic time with him and his family, who owned one of the biggest restaurants in town. I played a few games of five-a-side football with his team. Later, I came back to see them again, and Antonio and I became good friends.

Now, at the point where I was considering my long-term options and the future of Simple Minds, I told Antonio that I planned to come to Taormina for a more immersive stay, at least a couple of months. I had always wanted to learn Italian and I planned to go to language school. Antonio had a large house with a basement, and he invited me to stay with him. I wasn't sure but he was quite insistent, as Sicilians can be. I eventually agreed on two conditions: he let me pay my way, and he didn't play any Simple Minds music while I was staying there. I was coming to Taormina to get some respite from all that. Antonio was reluctant on the first point, though he finally acquiesced. But he was *absolutely* not signing up to the second condition. He said, '*You* might be fed up with Simple Minds, but they're *my* band. I listen to them every day. That's not changing.' I wanted to leave the band behind – at least for the moment, if not forever. It was evidently going to be harder than I thought.

Antonio and his friends played five-a-side football two or three times a week with teams from the other villages and towns. I would turn up to find people had brought along their Simple Minds records. 'No, no! That's not me,' I'd protest. 'I don't do that any more.' Taormina isn't LA. I didn't want to come on like some big-shot rock star. Perhaps I went too far in the opposite direction. People seemed confused: *What does he mean, 'That's not me'?!*

I had come to Sicily for what I thought would be a few months – and gradually everything started making sense again. I had never felt so energised by a place. Physically and spiritually, I began to feel rejuvenated. As the months passed, I started to feel, *Maybe I could just stay here?*

Fate played its part. Charlie and I had been in Ireland at a remarkable time. There had been an exponential boom. Not really knowing where I was going to live, in the early nineties I had bought a couple of properties there. A few years later they were valued at crazy money. A similar thing had happened in London. I bought a couple of things, didn't do anything with them, and four years later they were worth silly amounts. As a result, I was flush. When I saw the land for sale next to Antonio's house, I thought, *Let's see if I can build something here in Taormina.* Out of that came my house and my hotel, Villa Angela. That played a huge part in the changes that underpin my life today.

At that time, Italian dance music was booming and some of the bigger names came from Sicily. A few of these guys started turning up at the door with tunes and ideas. Or they would come to Antonio's restaurant, where I ate almost every day. 'Could you help me with this? Could you sing on this track, or work on it with us?'

I still had no desire to write a song. My stock answer was, 'I don't do that any more.' That lasted a good six months. Finally, I thought I might be appearing somewhat aloof and antisocial. There was one guy I liked, Daniele Tignino. The way he framed it to me was, 'I've got this track but I'm struggling with the English. Could you give me a hand?' And because he was a good guy and he played football with us, I agreed to at least hear what he had.

Daniele played the track to me at the restaurant. It sounded good. Before I knew it, I was sitting down with a pen and a

notepad, writing lyrics. The floodgates opened. Rejuvena-
tion. Excitement. Energy. I had found myself again.

Burchill/

If it was a crisis point for Jim, I didn't fully recognise it. I
knew he had writer's block, and he had definitely expressed
reservations to me about whether Simple Minds was going to
continue. That was a surprise; I didn't think he would ever
have doubts like that. He had always been the rock. Even
then, I thought it was a period that would blow over. And I
was right. His 'retirement' didn't last very long, and I don't
think I took it terribly seriously.

When he built the hotel, I remember thinking that it could
be a significant change, but I couldn't see Jim becoming a
full-time hotelier. He wanted to start a business and perhaps
even set up a franchise, but even if he did express the idea of
devoting more time to that, it was so obvious to me that Jim
was a writer. It's a vocation, not a choice. *That's what you do.*
And actually, there was a whole new life opening up for him
to write about.

Kerr/

Regardless of my fears that I would never write another
song, it turned out that it was only a matter of time before it
started up once more. It was interesting, because the catalyst
for wanting to write again, and believing that I *could* write
again, wasn't Charlie; because we were on hiatus and Charlie
wasn't around. I think, for him, that stung a little.

I started to write in Sicily with Daniele and other DJs and
musicians. We worked up a few tunes and after a time I
brought them to Charlie. He was slightly weirded out. Not
because he was against creativity coming into Simple Minds
from the outside, but I think his first reaction was that he had
let the side down. I know he felt that. I remember saying,
'Charlie, even Prince couldn't write ten great songs on every

album. Who cares?' Well, he cared. Of course he did. Also, he has always looked at music differently to me. I'd bring him something and he would say, 'It's a B, A, D and a G. What's the big deal?' I didn't care what the chords were. If it moved me, I was already seeing cityscapes.

The Italians had got me going. They made a few tunes that I wrote words for. It was *something*. Enough for Simple Minds to go back to work. In fact, we made two albums more or less at once, *Neon Lights* and *Cry*. The first was an album of covers; the second didn't feature a single song that me and Charlie had written together.

We were back from the brink, but we still had a long way to go.

Burchill/

Without expressing it directly to one another, I think Jim and I at that time had recognised that, creatively, we were almost one person. There wasn't much objectivity. That's why we had already started writing with other people.

Now, we went to Naples, where Jim had got to know an electronic band called Planet Funk. He had sung on one of their tracks and suggested I should meet them and maybe we could work together. We went to Sicily, where there were a few people who we worked with on and off at different times. Once again, we were looking to see what we could tap into to generate ideas.

Although it inevitably meant that the group identity wasn't as strong, I viewed working with other people as a positive, because we were conscious that we didn't want to repeat the same old formulas. There are a few interesting moments on *Cry*. There are tracks that I would certainly never have written, but Jim was singing on them so it was still Simple Minds. We allowed ourselves to be open to things being different. In that respect, even if there were songs coming into the mix that I would never have come up with, it didn't mean that we couldn't try to work them into something that would fit on a Simple Minds record. That was the challenge. It wasn't entirely successful. *Cry* was very bitty. It was a case of hammering a bunch of disparate tracks together and seeing if we could make an album – and it sounds like it. Fragmented. The number of names that feature in the songwriting credits is quite revealing.

Before we focused on *Cry*, we spent a few fun and fast days in the studio blowing away the cobwebs. It was Jim's idea to record a number of covers. Working independently at home, I put together arrangements for songs such as the Velvet Underground's 'All Tomorrow's Parties', the Doors' 'Hello, I Love You', Bowie's 'The Man Who Sold the World', and 'Neon Lights' by Kraftwerk. We did 'Homosapien' by Pete Shelley of Buzzcocks. Jim suggested 'Bring on the Dancing Horses', which is a great Echo & the Bunnymen song that at that time I didn't know particularly well.

The Italian guys were involved on Van Morrison's 'Gloria', and Gordy Goudie worked up a great acoustic version of Roxy Music's 'For Your Pleasure'. It was during this period that Jim and I worked with Gordy for the first time. A Scottish musician, writer and producer, Gordy is a proper all-rounder with a great vibe. As well as being involved in several Simple Minds records, he has been part of our live lineup since 2017.

We convened with Gordy in a studio called the Farm just outside Glasgow and started making quite radical versions of the material. It was loose and fun. Spontaneous. The songs we picked chose themselves. There are very few points where me and Jim's tastes diverge; it's almost boring the extent to which we are on the same page. With only a couple of exceptions, we were paying tribute to the music of our youth to get Simple Minds back up and running. That became *Neon Lights*, which came out in October 2001. We didn't regard it as a major Simple Minds release. We didn't really care what other people thought about it as long as we were enjoying it.

That was the spirit of that time. We also thought we might (re)learn something, songwriting wise, by getting into the guts of some great songs.

It wasn't quite a case of buying time, but with both *Neon Lights* and *Cry* it was really about showing not only the world but ourselves that Simple Minds were active again. It wasn't one of the higher points of our career. It was a tricky time and our confidence wasn't high. Jim and I never discussed it much, but we were still trying to figure out where to go and what we were doing.

We were still getting record deals, but the fact that they weren't what they used to be added to the feeling that we were definitely not in the top division any more. It was hard to escape the feeling that the glory days had gone.

Kerr/

Because it felt like it had been so long since we had been in a studio, I asked our new label to add a little extra on top of the (very modest) deal we had signed, in order for us to record a set of covers to get up to speed. The initial idea was that we could use them as B-sides, but that became *Neon Lights*. Simple Minds hadn't released a record since *Néapolis* in 1998, over three years earlier; why not put out a covers album to get things going again? We did it in ten days. It was quite throwaway, but great fun. And crucially, Charlie and I were in the same room again.

By now, I had given up my house in Loch Earn. I felt I was growing too old too quickly in the Highlands. I needed to get some dirt under my fingernails. I went back to Glasgow to see what was happening and who we could work with. One of the musicians we met was Gordy. I had a couple of ideas from working in Sicily and I asked him to come to Taormina to help me Simple Minds-ify these Italian dance records. That was part of impetus to get *Cry* started. Gordy played a crucial role on that album and *Neon Lights*, and has since

281

become something of a talisman for Simple Minds. He has a rock and roll spirit. He really lives it and it's good to have that energy around.

Aside from being exercises in writing, recording and releasing records again, the two albums Simple Minds put out early in the new millennium were about regaining some semblance of competence and confidence. We had been flatlining, but we discovered that there was still a heartbeat fluttering away.

I knew that our long-term future lay primarily in reminding people that Simple Minds were still a great live band. When we went on the road in 2002 with *Cry*, we hadn't toured since 1998. We had played just two shows in almost four years. We were still having to deal with being regarded as yesterday's men and a lack of interest beyond the hardcore fans.

The pressing questions were: *How do we get the engine of this rusty car started again? And if we do get it going, how far and in what direction can we take it?*

Charlie and I had established from the very first show at Satellite City that we could never do Simple Minds by half measures. If we were going to continue, we had to be fully committed. Everything else would have to take second place. It's an incredibly selfish thing that we do. We have to be all-in. That was fine when we were in our early twenties. But we were now in our mid-forties and our status was diminished. We had ceded a lot of ground. Did we have the stomach to be eighth on the bill at a festival? Were we really going to push it in the clubs again?

Even at the lowest ebb, Simple Minds could still draw a crowd. We never dropped down to playing really small venues but still, being booked into a converted cinema in the Gorbals when we had once sold out Ibrox Stadium pinched a bit. On one occasion in Germany, en route to that evening's show in a club, we drove past the arena where ten years earlier we had played multiple nights. You discover a lot about yourself at such moments. Can your pride handle it? Are you up for the challenge? Or would it be easier to sit in the Sicilian sun and enjoy a peaceful life?

By then, it was obvious what our decision was. Retirement would have to wait (and that remains the case). But it took the engine a long, long time to generate sufficient power for Simple Minds to push back up into top gear.

It helped that social media had taken off just as we were starting to say, *Hey! Remember us?* In the late nineties, my nerdy friend Kevin Burleigh had talked about 'social networks' and how they might be a valuable tool for legacy bands like Simple Minds. I had been intrigued, but those were the embryonic days of such notions. Now, Kevin's prophecy was coming to pass. There were a few hundred thousand Simple Minds fans scattered around the world. Even if everyone else seemed to be ignoring us, we could talk to them, and they could talk to each other. None of the newspapers or magazines were interested, but we could all talk to each other. Alive and *clicking*. Promoters were starting to pay attention to these things, rather than record sales or chart positions. Five years earlier, the phone had stopped ringing. Now, people were calling again. Or, more often, emailing.

One of the core traits that has helped Charlie and me survive is a certain stoicism. During this period, my resolve had wavered, but Charlie had remained implacable. He regarded this spell merely as a time of turbulence, at worst. As though we were in a storm that would soon peter out, long before Simple Minds ever did.

By now, I was convinced that he had been right.

Burchill/

By 2005, I felt the uncertainties and equivocations of the past five years had been resolved. We had decided that this is what we do, and we would keep doing it for the rest of our lives.

In the period immediately beforehand, Jim was having doubts and the records were patchy, made piecemeal and in isolation with lots of different people involved at various stages. All those factors had changed by the time we recorded *Black and White 050505*. For me, that was the point where we decided that we weren't content simply to muddle through. We were going to throw everything in and go for it again.

I don't know whether Jim and I had an explicit conversation, but implicitly we had resolved to be more focused about making records, rather than pulling disparate strands together. Listening back, I can hear that idea starting to take shape on *Black and White 050505* and gaining momentum on the next album, *Graffiti Soul*. We had always loved the idea of a concise record. That was once again part of the conversation. *Let's keep it short and cherry pick the best songs.* There are nine tracks on *Black and White 050505*, and we played every single one on the tour. For *Graffiti Soul*, we returned to Rockfield in south Wales, where we had worked on *Real to Real Cacophony* and *Empires and Dance*. Jez Coad, our producer, could also write, and he contributed to a couple of tracks. Jez was a bright guy with fantastic energy, and some of his working practices had an old-school sensibility, which I enjoyed. We even had Mel playing live drums in the studio.

We were still climbing a hill to make those records. The flow wasn't fully there, but there were signs of it coming back. Fans and critics sometimes wonder why bands can't write their best albums again and again. The factors involved are multilayered. You are a different person in a different time. So many elements make it impossible. As you get older, you become more conscious and less instinctive about what you are doing creatively. That is necessary but also dangerous. When you start to analyse what you did in the past and attempt to do something similar again, there is a risk of imitating yourself and descending into parody.

Ultimately, I have learned that the elements that encourage a strong creative flow to return often come from places outside of the mechanics of the music. They are much more about your attitude, your energy levels and the circumstances in your life at any given time. By 2009, when we released *Graffiti Soul*, it felt as though we had re-established a connection with the elements that would enable us to get back to being a truly strong iteration of Simple Minds. The recording process was getting smoother. Everything we were doing was working. Nothing was forced. When it came to the songs, we were taking care of the fundamentals rather than trying to patch things up with bells and whistles.

The days of hit singles may have been long gone – as they were for pretty much every band of our generation – but *Graffiti Soul* gave Simple Minds a top-ten album in the UK for the first time since *Good News from the Next World*.

Our sense of confidence and identity was returning.

Kerr/

So much of songwriting is about using the muscles. When they are working well, you run. Who knows where it might lead?

During this period, I couldn't put the brakes on. In 2010, I released a solo record called *Lostboy! AKA Jim Kerr*. Martin Hanlin was still working in music publishing. Through Martin I met younger songwriters/producers such as Owen Parker and Paul Statham. I would turn up at their little home studios in London and say, 'OK! Let's hear what you've got.'

I also wrote with Iain Cook, who had until recently been in Aerogramme and would soon form Chvrches. My mum was very ill at the time, and I had gone back to live with her in Glasgow. She encouraged me to keep busy. While I was in town, Martin told me about a young musician he knew who lived nearby in Pollokshields. 'He's doing good stuff and he really likes Simple Minds. Why don't you go over and see him?' Within a couple of weeks, Iain and I had written a ream of new material.

In this fashion, I accrued a body of songs in the year when Charlie and I were not so active. We had been working with Simple Minds solidly for two years, but I couldn't stop writing. I wanted to get the songs out.

A lot of good music emerged from that period. As well as the tracks that appeared on *Lostboy!*, some of those songs were adapted and recorded for the next two Simple Minds studio albums, *Big Music* and *Walk Between Worlds*. Best of all, I hooked up with Ged Grimes, who is now the longest-serving Minds bassist. It was all thanks to Yumie, who had previously met Ged and watched him perform with one of her favourite bands, Deacon Blue. 'Hey Jim, get Ged Grimes to tour with you when you promote *Lostboy!* Very classy musician and a true gentleman.' Yumie rarely gets things wrong, and she was spot on when it came to identifying someone I would greatly appreciate collaborating with. Fifteen years later, Ged continues to be one of the main forces behind the resurgence of Simple Minds live and on record.

A Jim Kerr solo album was never going to be any threat to Simple Minds. Perhaps that's why I was a little half-hearted with the promotion. I wasn't quite sure how to pitch it. Hence the strange name.

Burchill/

There was never any feeling that Jim was running off and deserting me. I thought it was a great opportunity for him and, in a sense, just another chapter in our story. And if it were successful, it would reflect well on Simple Minds.

Likewise, I don't think Jim ever felt that it was going to take over Simple Minds, particularly as we were just beginning to really get things moving again.

Jim's dad used to call the album 'Lostbob': 'Hey Charlie, what do you think of that Lostbob stuff?'

35
Past Perfect

We cannot fling ourselves into the blank future;
we can only call up images from the past.
This being so, the important principle follows
that how many images we have largely depends
on how much past we have.

– G. K. Chesterton

Two thousand and eleven.

I am discovering that our new manager Ian Grenfell is relentless in the same way that Jimmy Iovine had been relentless.

At one of our first meetings with Ian, Charlie and I say, 'We want to write new music and we want to write new chapters. We don't want Simple Minds just to be a heritage act.'

Ian listens. He nods. Finally, he says, 'Sure, but you have to go back. You have to give people an excuse to like Simple Minds again. You have to remind them what you were.' Off the cuff, I say, 'How about a show where we play five songs from each of the first five albums?'

His eyes light up:

'Could you do that? WOULD you do that?'

'Yeah, we'll do that.'

I smile. That's got him off our backs, I think. Most likely we'll never hear about the idea again.

Before we know it, Ian comes to us with a prototype of the artwork: 'This has to happen!'

The '5 x 5 Live' project is on.

Burchill/

One hugely significant factor in Simple Minds returning to full strength was Ian Grenfell becoming our manager. We were good friends with John Williams, who had produced the Housemartins and the Proclaimers and handled many BBC radio sessions. We had mentioned to John that we were looking for someone to help us with the management, and John suggested Ian.

At the time, Ian was managing Simply Red (he still does, as well as Suede and the Pretenders). We arranged a dinner and hit it off. It was obvious to us from the get-go that he was trustworthy, highly intelligent and understood all the many aspects of the label side of the business, which is where we particularly wanted help. We could tell that Ian would be a great strategist. He could see the long view.

Ian tells the story that at the time most of his friends said he was crazy to take us on. We only found that out recently. I thought it was hilarious.

Kerr/

We badly needed a manager. By 2009 we had realised that the music industry wasn't dying, but it was splintering off in a variety of new directions and would continue doing so. We needed a current player who understood all that. We had heard Ian was exceptionally smart. I had also heard that he was incredibly choosy. He had a reputation for knocking back so many different artists.

When we met up, I laid out what we were thinking, how committed we were and how we wanted the next few years to look for Simple Minds. I said, 'Let me know when you want to come and see us play.' He said, 'No, I won't let you know. I'm going to come one night to look at things myself.'

After he had been to see a show, Ian came to see me. He said he wanted to take on Simple Minds – *Yes!* – but his analysis was brutal. He said, 'The artwork isn't what it should be.

The merchandising isn't what it should be. The band could be better.' He really went there. His conclusion was simple. 'Simple Minds are world class, but you're not perceived as world class any more. We have to get that perception back. That's the kind of challenge I like.' 'Me too!' *This is great*, I thought. *This is just what we need.* I like it when people come in hard as long as they give honest perspectives and bring new ideas. We needed a collaborator and a strategist. Ian was perfect.

Burchill/

The idea for '5 x 5 Live' came from Jim, but Ian was smart enough to realise that even though the set would feature no *actual* hits, it would be a big hit with our long-term fans. It was a complete shift in focus away from Simple Minds being a band that had been going for more than three decades and released a new record every few years. This was about highlighting a particular part of our story. By the time we did '5 x 5 Live', large portions of our live audience didn't necessarily know the early records, because they had got into Simple Minds at a variety of later stages. We knew we were going to attract a hardcore audience for these shows. We made sure that everybody was well aware what the format was.

It was a fantastic project for me. Getting to revisit those songs using the technology that was now available made it possible to work up versions that were even more powerful than anything we had been able to do in the past. I went in full scale. I programmed lots of the original sounds and we rehearsed hard to make sure nobody went off script. We had to do a lot of work to get Mel *not to be Mel*. Understatement doesn't come naturally to a drummer like Mel, but we had to keep the music contained and make sure no drum fills appeared where they weren't supposed to. Andy Gillespie was playing keyboards. He analysed every song and kept it faithful and concise. That was the remit for everybody: no overplaying. I don't recall any discussion about bringing back the original lineup who recorded those albums. We had been through all that. We had Mel, but no Brian, no Derek, no Mick.

My responsibility was to make sure that it sounded as good as the records. When you play songs live, there is a tendency for them to drift by small increments. Before you know it, you've turned your odd little art song into a billowing rock track. It's very easy for that to happen. We had to make sure these songs didn't drift. Quite a lot of the material had eccentricities and idiosyncrasies that aren't easy to capture. We wanted to preserve them rather than flatten out all the unorthodoxy.

Jim had arguably the most difficult challenge. Not only had his voice changed but he had to try to present a plausible version of the character that appears on the early records. He found a way of doing that authentically, without it being a pastiche of what he did in the past. He worked very hard at identifying with the songs but interpreting them in a contemporary way that didn't jar with the person he now was, thirty years later. An example of where he did that brilliantly was the '5 x 5 Live' version of 'This Fear of Gods'. When the musicians were playing the instrumental sections, Jim was completely static; it was as though he had been frozen. When it was time for him to sing, he was super-animated. He brought an intense theatricality to the song simply through the way he moved.

A quite considerable amount of time needed to have passed before we could contemplate a project like '5 x 5 Live'. There may have been some discourse among fans about wanting Simple Minds to revisit that period, but there was no great demand for it and that certainly wasn't our motivation. The fact that it came out of the blue added to the sense of occasion that grew around the sixteen shows.

I loved every one of them. We didn't have to play 'Don't You

(Forget About Me)' and 'Alive and Kicking'. We performed in relatively intimate theatres, halls and clubs, and it was liberating not to be tied to the hits and the old favourites. I would like to do something similar in the future, though not necessarily with the same material.

We knew '5 x 5 Live' would be a positive step forward if we did it right. And we did. People still talk about it. It shifted a very focused kind of attention back on to Simple Minds. I think we also hoped that it might spin us off in a positive direction when it came to making new music. Which is what happened. When we released our next album, *Big Music*, in 2014, it received the best reviews we'd had for thirty years.

Kerr/

I view the '5 x 5 Live' project as marking the start of the re-evaluation of Simple Minds. Given how pronounced and prolonged the critical panning had been, I never thought we would see the day again where we would be getting good reviews in the *Guardian* and the *Telegraph*. I never thought I would be interviewed on Radio 6 Music. Worse than getting a panning was just being overlooked. Even in Scotland.

You have to give these things time. You have to 'disappear' and then at some point the moment arises when it feels right to start knocking on doors to say, *Remember this?* Ian recognised that the moment had come. That's what '5 x 5 Live' was about, and it galvanised not only our original fan base but also many critics to look at Simple Minds anew.

Musically, it worked exceptionally well. We got the bit between our teeth because they are great records, particularly *Empires and Dance*, *Sons and Fascination* and *New Gold Dream (81, 82, 83, 84)*. For the first time in a long while, we felt reconciled to the very early records. Over time, we had become alienated from them. The songs felt a little like an old suit that no longer fits and now looks vaguely ridiculous. It's like poring over old photographs: you can't bear to be reminded of what you were wearing, or how awful your hair was. It's embarrassing.

But as time passes, you find new meaning and relevance in those snapshots from the distant past. That applied, I think, both to Charlie and me and our fans. We had grown up and older together, and the time was right for us all to inhabit those songs again. I felt an affection and appreciation for them, as well as the idealistic young man singing them. I thought, *I'm going to give that guy a break. If he didn't look that way or sound like that, if he wasn't reading those books and being pretentious, if he didn't care so much and try too hard, then we would never have got here.*

There was a clear obligation to '5 x 5 Live'. We had to deliver the songs exactly as they had been. There could be no half measures or revisionism. This wasn't the time or place for a funky jam version of 'Calling Your Name' – although, come to think of it, that would probably have sounded amazing! We had to act out our parts. Even though we couldn't go back, I had to find the props and the moves to conjure it all up again from the first time around.

Because we weren't just revisiting the songs. We were revisiting a version of ourselves.

36
Charlie Piranha

The greatest remedy for anger is delay.

– Seneca, *On Anger*

November 2015. Thursday night at the O2.

A week night in London can sometimes feel slightly flat in comparison to other cities. This is one such occasion. We are still going down better than most bands, but by our own standards I feel all the engines aren't quite firing as they could or should be. I have a nagging feeling the setlist could be better. That's my department. The doubting voices start running through my head.

When we come off stage before the encore, Charlie confirms my fears. And how. He lays into me about the setlist. It is so unlike him. We both know this isn't the moment to give each other or anyone else in the band or crew a hard time. It means that when I go back on stage to perform for the final three songs, all I can think about is our argument.

After the encore, Charlie and I really go at it in the dressing room. It turns into a screaming match. 'Tell me off if you like, but that wasn't the time to do it. I had another three songs to sing! That was really FUCKING STUPID!!' All our guests are standing outside. It doesn't dawn on us that they can hear every word – and they do indeed hear every word, many of which are of the post-watershed variety.

It culminates in a declaration. 'That's it,' says Charlie. 'I've had it. I've had enough. I'm fucking finished with this.' It is the only time this has ever happened. I say, 'Really?' 'Yeah, I quit!' Top of his voice. To which I respond, 'Great! I'm not quitting. It's all mine!' By now, the people listening outside are in hysterics.

Charlie quickly has a change of heart. 'Nah, I'm not quitting.' I say, 'Yes, you are! Everyone heard you.' It turns into a scene from The Producers. *'You've quit. You're not even allowed in here. I'll get you thrown out in a minute . . .'*

Burchill/

When the original Simple Minds lineup was together, the biggest fights were always between Jim and me. With Mick, Brian and Derek there was no contest. They would bring up mundane topics which weren't relevant to what we were trying to do, and Jim would run rings around them.

Then he and I would get into an argument about the important stuff. We would really have a go. We were secure enough with each other to be able to do that. Apart from having mutual respect and a relationship that went back much further than the others in the band, we both knew that solid points were being made, and we were putting them across relatively articulately. Most of the time, at least.

We were both in agreement about everything that mattered, so we could argue freely on the detail. As we have got older that has continued, albeit nowadays it happens less frequently.

Kerr/

Charlie has a temper. Charlie Piranha.

It doesn't surface very often. If he has a problem or an issue in terms of work, he will let it go, let it go, let it go . . . until, finally, it explodes. And because people know him as being so nice, which he is, they are sometimes a bit shocked: 'Wow! What happened there?'

We have learned it is best not to hold the post-mortem straight after the gig, when emotions are high. The last absolutely seismic fight Charlie and I had was at the O2 in London in 2015. It was one of those days when niggles accumulated.

It was a nightmare getting out there; travelling to the venue, we got snarled up in terrible traffic. Charlie's sons were coming to the show, and they also got stuck in traffic later in the day. Before we went onstage, he was already quite anxious and upset. The issues with the gig and the setlist were simply the spark that lit the fuse.

We've had a few fights like that. Before it all settles down again, it has to become a little infantile. The next day it's:

'Charlie, you choose the setlist tonight.'

'I don't want to choose the setlist.'

'Yup, you're choosing the setlist. I'm having nothing to do with it any more.'

'Well, I'm not doing it.'

'Well, I'm not doing it, either. I don't want to. *Clearly, I'll just get it wrong . . .*'

It's ancient history by half past four the next afternoon. Gone and forgotten. It doesn't linger. It's perfectly acceptable to get it wrong, as long as you can take the heat. You've got to vent, but Simple Minds is the greater cause, and very rarely does it get to the stage where an apology is merited. It has already been well-established that it's not going to happen again.

Burchill/

It was the first time Simple Minds had played the O2. I was particularly vehement because it was obvious that we had blown it with the setlist. It would only have been a song or two, but that's how fine the margins can be.

It is theoretically possible to have a constructive post-mortem after a show, but to come off stage after playing to seventeen thousand people and immediately put the setlist under a microscope and blame your partner for any issues is obviously not the optimal approach. Apart from anything else, other members of the band may have been feeling amazing about the gig; everybody experiences a show differently. Jim pulled me up and he was entitled to do so. He understood the reason I did it is because both of us are constantly trying to make Simple Minds better, but there is a right and wrong way of going about these things. You have to be aware of the timing and the circumstances.

That being said, I think we did change the setlist the following night . . .

Kerr/

Charlie Piranha bared his teeth again over the *Acoustic* album Simple Minds released in late 2016. The project was instigated by our manager, Ian. Until then, Charlie and I had always vowed that Simple Minds would do an acoustic album over our dead bodies. 'Waterfront' unplugged? I don't think so. The 'Bongos on the Beach' aesthetic really wasn't our bag.

Our bluff was called. In April, we were offered a gig in Zermatt, a chichi ski resort in Switzerland. They were desperate to have us play an acoustic set at their annual unplugged festival. We kept saying no and the fee kept going up. Finally, I said we wouldn't do it unless they threw in two huge bars of Toblerone. I thought that would kill it once and for all. In short order, a solemn message was relayed back to us: 'The Toblerones are confirmed.' What could we do? It was a resort halfway up the Matterhorn. We thought, *This is a chance to see if it can work and if it's a disaster no one will really know.*

It went well enough, and we could see how it could be made better, so we decided to press ahead with the *Acoustic* record. In Zermatt we had played without drums, but we felt we would need percussion for the album. Mel would have been too heavy for an acoustic album; the concept didn't play to his strengths. We heard about Cherisse Osei, who was introduced to us initially as a percussionist. When Cherisse came in, I recognised her from several other projects she had been involved with. We realised that she was an amazing drummer who also happened to play great percussion. That was how Cherisse first became involved with Simple Minds. She has now been with us for almost a decade and has proved a dynamite addition to the band.

On the *Acoustic* record, Charlie had to up his game. He was wallflowering a little. On the first day, the musicians and engineers had gone into the studio late morning to set up the studio. I was due to arrive mid-afternoon once things were up and running. I got a call at half-eleven. 'You'd better come down here *NOW*. Charlie has freaked out. It looks like the whole thing is off.' I was laughing my head off.

I went down to find Charlie in a proper strop. 'This is never going to work. It sounds terrible, puny.' Huge rant. Somewhere in the middle of all that, he plugged in his acoustic guitar and played it with all his effects pedals – and a sunburst of celestial sounds came out. The music instantly went from prose to poetry. I said, '*That's* the sound of the record right there. *That is your sound.*' I could see him calming down. He said, 'But this isn't acoustic!' 'Who cares? You're standing there playing an acoustic guitar, but you've still got all your sounds.'

In the end, we cheated a bit with *Acoustic*. We didn't quite do what it says on the tin, but the unplugged approach was just too dry. I would love to revisit some of our newer material using that approach. It's on the list.

We are all capable of having a moment. Sarah Brown is one of the greatest singers ever and yet you have to remind her every night before she goes on how good she is. It's very easy to do, because I believe it. These are fleeting insecurities, but they exist. We all have our strengths and limitations, and when you come face to face with them it can be hard.

Burchill/

Both Jim and I were sceptical of the *Acoustic* idea. It wasn't exactly a novel concept. Many people had attempted unplugged projects, and I thought the majority didn't work very well.

I could envisage us trying to do it and failing miserably. I thought it could be a real disaster.

Ian and Jim convinced me. 'If you hate it, it doesn't have to come out.' That was the compromise. Before we played the show in Zermatt, a variety of opinions were being voiced over what exactly 'unplugged' meant. We ended up doing it without any electronics whatsoever: no click tracks, nothing to keep us in time. I listened back to the recording, and it was obvious to me that that approach wasn't going to work.

On the first day recording the album, I went into the control room to hear the initial playback. It sounded fucking awful; a karaoke version of Simple Minds doing acoustic songs. Cabaret. It was exactly what I had feared might happen.

I went into meltdown mode and told Jim the whole thing was off. It wasn't going to work. Jim was laughing, but he managed to say, 'Look, let's stick with it for a bit.' I agreed to continue only if I could use textures such as delays and chorus pedals. That's what we did, and it worked out. Gordy Goudie has a great natural feel for acoustic guitar and he played a big part in arranging the album. He covered the acoustic side of things and then they sent me in on my own to overdub on each track. In the studio, they started calling it 'Charlie's Magic Carpet'. It was an unorthodox approach but when we put it all together it gave the album a real sense of individuality, rather than being just another acoustic record.

Kerr/

For whatever reason, very occasionally when Charlie and I are writing together we end up on different pages. That can be very frustrating. One of us is hearing something a certain way. The other person is not. A huge part of it is technical. I will get inspired by the same two-chord sequence that, apparently, we used five years ago. I wouldn't know that in a million years and even if I did, I wouldn't care. But Charlie can't get over it. Because he can't get over it, I might get cross and tell him that he isn't trying. And then *he'll* get pissed off.

Usually, our biggest fights aren't about the thing they might seem to be about. One of us will use the wrong word and it's the offence taken at the wrong word that will cause things to blow up. But it's so rare. We have a mutual respect that generally keeps things on an even keel. I have never said to Charlie when he is playing me something new, 'That's crap.' That doesn't ever happen. It's not said because it's not felt, and because I know that time often offers a different perspective. A piece of music that isn't making me feel anything in the moment might speak to me ten or even fifteen years later.

Like so many aspects of what we do, through experience we have learned the benefits of taking a breath and waiting it out.

Burchill/

We never argue about anything outside of music. Even if we're cranky, we always find a way to get along. It's one of the benefits of having a long and close relationship. I can always just sense when Jim hasn't had a good night's sleep, or when he's not in the mood. He has a similarly sensitive antenna when it comes to me. We know when to give each other space.

But when we are working on the music, we can't avoid addressing issues when they arrive and sometimes that can get heated. It's rarely an all-out barney. If there are any disagreements on tour, they invariably arise during the soundcheck. A lot of the time I'm to blame. I can get uptight over why things aren't working. Jim will get involved and there may be a disagreement about how we should resolve it. I might suggest dropping the offending song from the set and that will bring matters to a head. It flares up and dies down quickly. Then we begin to see each other's points of view.

It can be good to let off steam. One of the many great things about us being friends for so long is that Jim and I are in on so many jokes regarding our shared history and relationship. We can reference other situations and ridiculous arguments from the past and make a self-deprecating joke out of a tense scenario.

It never lingers, and it usually ends in laughter.

37

Honest Town

Every day is a journey, and the journey itself is home.

– Matsuo Bashō, *The Narrow Road to the Deep North*

Glasgow city centre.

As soon as I settle into the back seat of the taxi, the driver looks at me long and hard in the rear-view mirror.

'You're Jim Kerr!'

'Yeah.'

He considers this for a while. 'No, you're not . . .'

'OK. I'm not.'

He looks at me a bit longer. 'Aye, but are ye?'

I sigh. 'I don't fucking know any more! I thought I was before I got in here, but now I'm not so sure. You tell me.'

Ah, Glasgow, *I think.* Still as weird as anything we ever saw at the Citz. Still as strange as any Herzog movie. Still mad as all hell.

Kerr/

I have no close family left in Scotland. The Kerrs are almost gone, apart from the periods when I am there. I have old uncles and aunties, but very few. Glasgow is a nostalgic place now. Visits home are partly about processing change and memory, dealing with cemeteries and gravestones. That might sound gloomy. But it doesn't feel that way.

In the winter of 2010, my mum had been ill for several years and it was getting near the end. There had been a whiteout for days and Glasgow was at a standstill. The buses were off the roads. I was staying with Mum and Dad and working with Iain Cook. Mum had been very clear: 'Don't sit around the house. Get out and do something.'

Mum woke up one morning feeling strong. Sometimes very ill people experience a final surge. The city was cloaked in white. Sparkling. The sky was a cold hard blue and the winter sun dazzling. It had given Mum a good feeling and for that, at least, I was thankful.

The weather reports on the radio said that no one should venture outside unless it was absolutely necessary. Mum arrived downstairs. She had already spoken to my dad, and now she said to me, nodding towards the ceiling, '*He* won't take me into town, but I need to get clothes for the Christmas dance at the end of next week . . .' My dad was shouting down the stairs: 'Listen to the radio, you're not going anywhere! Are you off your head?' Mum ignored him and looked at me: '. . . so *you'd* better take me in.' I said, 'Okey-doke. Where are we going?' 'Marks & Spencer.'

It just so happened that our journey into town that morning told the story of her life. She had started out in the Gorbals and worked her way up to the suburbs, and now she and I were travelling back through it all. It was eerily quiet out on the streets, and as she looked out of the window there it was. Her entire life. 'Oh, there's Toryglen! There's Holyrood! Oh, that's where you made your first communion. There's where your dad and I first met. There's where I worked in the factory when I was fifteen.' At one point she turned to me, and she said, 'I love Glasgow. It's an honest town, and they were honest times. I loved the times we lived in.'

I parked in the Candleriggs area. Mum said, 'I want to introduce you to a woman I've known all my life. She sells fruit on Argyle Street. Her boys are huge Simple Minds fans, they've seen you play everywhere, and I used to come here and tell her you were my son. I haven't seen her for years, but

I know she'll be there.' We went to see the woman, who took one look at Mum and instantly understood. She smiled: 'Jim, it's nice to meet you, finally!' Mum smiled, too. I could tell that this meeting had been important for her.

We reached Marks & Spencer and went downstairs into the clothing department. Mum looked at me: 'What can I get?' I laughed. 'Get anything you want!' Her wee face lit up. And then she picked out the clothes that Yumie dressed her in for her funeral. She knew she wasn't going to the Christmas dance. She wanted to get ready.

Shortly afterwards, Mum was leaving the house for what we all knew would be the last time. The ambulance had finally got through to take her to the Beatson, the NHS cancer centre in Glasgow. I had taken her to all these private places and each time she said, 'I don't want to be here. I want to be with the people I know.'

She found the strength to get up, get dressed and come down the stairs. As we were gathering her things together, the doorbell rang. Charlie had been in Holland. There had been a tremendous snowstorm, which had shut the airports. Numerous flights had been cancelled. It had been a case of trains, planes and automobiles for him to get there. But he wanted to say goodbye to my mum. He arrived just as she was going out of the door. She said, 'Oh, Charlie! I can't even make you a cup of tea. I've got to go to the hospital now, but you come in and sit down.' He looked at me and winked. 'No, Irene, I'm coming to the Beatson, too. Jim's getting in the ambulance with you, and I'll follow. I'll see you up there.'

I went in the ambulance with my mum. She was so tired, but she was still chattering away to the paramedic: 'Oh, your ambulance is lovely. It's so clean! How many kids have you got?' When we finally started moving, she lay quietly for a while. Finally, she said, 'It's great to see wee Charlie. It's always great to see his smiling face. Seeing him at the door, it was just like when he used to come up to the flat in Toryglen.'

There was a silence. I let it unfold. After a while, she said, 'Have you boys got any gigs soon?' 'Yeah, we've got a couple in two weeks' time.' There was another silence, and then her shoulders started to shake slightly. I could see that she was laughing. She said, 'Youse two had better go on a diet . . .'

'Honest Town', which Simple Minds recorded on *Big Music*, came out of all of that. Iain Cook had written a beautiful tune, and I was looking for words to match. 'When the light settles down over honest town, you'll see / There's always something between you and me.' It was an act of remembrance for my mum, but it was also for the city that made her, and which she loved so much. An honest town.

In 2019, when Charlie and I started work on what became *Direction of the Heart*, we had just received the news that my dad's situation was the worst it could be. Just as my mum had done, he had instructed me to keep busy. I did as I was told. The first song written for the album was 'Vision Thing'. I was talking about the gifts and the knowledge that Dad had given me: 'You opened up the world . . .'

He lived only five minutes' drive from my house in Glasgow. Because Charlie was so close to my dad, when we were writing there, he and I would often take turns to go and sit with him. Towards the end, Charlie had been away. When he came back to Glasgow, I told him it would be any day now. He wanted to see Dad. I said, 'Just keep hold of the memory of him. Really. He probably won't even know that you're there.' Charlie said, 'No, I want to go and see him.'

We didn't resolve it. We were working on music at my house, and when we ended for the day, I thought Charlie was going back to his hotel. Later that evening, I went to see Dad. He loved the garden, and we had put his bed downstairs in the conservatory so he could gaze out at it. As I arrived, I looked through the house and I could see Charlie sitting next to him, reading. I asked how long he had been here. Three hours, he said. Maybe four. Just being there. Showing up. I still get quite emotional thinking about that. It says so much about Charlie. He saw my dad as my dad, and he loved him, but he also saw him, as we both did, as the last of the generation that he and I had come to respect so much.

Dad went quickly. It was exactly six months from diagnosis to the end. I'm glad it wasn't prolonged. I used to feel guilty when my mum passed away about not being sufficiently mournful. But for both her and my dad, there was a huge sense of relief that it was over, because it was the very worst thing imaginable to see my parents in pain.

I feel so lucky that I had them for so long. They were great people, and we spent so much good time together. They enjoyed sharing Simple Minds with us. They saw things we could never have imagined, things that simply didn't happen to people like us. They were so proud of the crew and everybody that worked with us. They loved the fans. They would remark on the fact that there was never any fighting at our gigs. It was always people having a great time.

In the early days of the band, they weren't thinking in terms of success or failure. They just wanted their boy to be happy. Commitment isn't a word they would have used but they were impressed by the level of endeavour. They supported our dream. I've never forgotten it.

We are products of our parents and our upbringing. More and more, I see my dad in myself on a daily basis. I'll rib someone and just take it for granted that they know it's a joke, but maybe they don't. I'll think, *God, I can't believe I said that! That's exactly the kind of thing he used to say.* And Charlie laughs and laughs, just as he would laugh whenever my dad would do it.

Burchill/

Both Jim and I lost our mothers first. My mum died quite early, in 1994, and after my dad died, I certainly felt that symbolically it marked the end of something. I felt that again when Jimmy died. It wasn't that we lost our connection to Glasgow, but it led to a realisation that Sicily was our place now. It was already becoming more and more like home. Losing our fathers somehow put a seal on it.

My dad went into hospital for three weeks and never came home. I was lucky. I wasn't on tour, and I was able to be there. Later, I saw Jimmy quite often when he was very ill. When I went to the house shortly before he died, it was apparent that he didn't have long to go. It was just me and him and it felt like closure.

After Jimmy died, all four of our parents were gone. It was sad, and of course we still miss them, but I never get the feeling that they're not here, somehow. Their presence is very tangible. Jim and I have talked about the fact that the very last thing your parents teach you is how to leave. After my dad died, it transpired that he had left everything in immaculate order: the clothes he was going to be buried in, a new pair of shoes, good socks, everything dry cleaned. A gentleman to the very end. Perhaps it's a Glasgow thing. It's certainly a working-class thing. The final lesson handed down from the elders in our lives is that it is possible to leave with grace and dignity.

'Honest Town' is not just a beautiful song, it's a beautiful idea. I love that Jim's mother said those things about Glasgow, but it's not just about a city. She was talking about a time in which values were different; Jim smuggled a bit of the old shipyard socialism into that song. Those values were hugely important to our parents, and they remain so to us. We had quite a deep chat recently about a personal issue that was ongoing in Jim's life. We agreed on how important it is to keep values alive. Regardless of how difficult it can make things, you must pay attention to them – because without them, you're adrift.

In that sense, we carry Glasgow with us no matter where we are. It's not lip service. We are very proud of the fact that we come from the city. We identify completely with our personalities and characters being formed there. And as much as Jim and I haven't lived in Glasgow for long periods, we never really left. We still spend a lot of time there. I still find it a very creative place to be.

Recently we were working in Jim's house in the Southside. One morning I decided to walk there from my hotel in the centre. On the way, I passed all the old haunts: where we went to school, where we rehearsed, McGee's old house. So many memories. I noticed a lot of differences, not all good – but in other ways Glasgow doesn't change. The city fathers keep trying to give it a facelift, and it just keeps reverting to what it is and will always be: a mad, strange, beautiful, honest town.

Kerr/

Charlie and I are formed completely from Glasgow granite. That will never change. But the granite has been shaped by so many other experiences and influences, going right back to the time of our first ever hitchhiking trip. The idea of being first Europeans, then internationalists, always held huge appeal to both of us.

Outside of playing shows with Simple Minds, I return to Scotland regularly. After moving to Taormina, I had no intention of having a house in Glasgow again, but when Mum passed away, Yumie pushed for it. She said I should be around for Dad more – which was true. The area where I now have a house is five minutes from where Mum and Dad lived, and a ten-minute drive from Toryglen. A few years ago, I also bought a base near Loch Earn again. I had always regretted selling my house there. I feel a special connection to that area.

I love to be in Scotland in August and September. It's the perfect antidote to being on the road. I love the peace, the poetry, the nature and the history we have. But Sicily is home. We have it so good: the landscape, the culture, the weather, the food. Who wouldn't want to eke out more summer months each year if they can?

I realise now that my choices have been about more than simply chasing the sun. My nephew here in Taormina is Sicilian. My other nephew is a Frenchman. There is a strong Japanese influence in my life. I married an American and an Englishwoman. Mine has been an international existence; Charlie's has been the same. That hunger we had as kids, that curiosity, never died – and it has shaped us.

Yet some core part of us will always be quintessentially Glaswegian. I love the Glasgow spirit, that condensed mix of Irish and Scottish, and everything that comes out of it: the wit and grit and humour. The street-level surrealism. I love the ability to laugh through the tears – and at yourself.

Not so long ago, I was in a rehearsal room doing bits and pieces. It's where all the Glasgow bands go to rehearse, from the up-and-comers to the no-hopers to the well-established. I would pop into the little café and have a cup of coffee with some of the guys there. I was curious. *What's the name of your band? What are you up to?* I loved getting their chat. There was one wee guy in a band. Glasgow's answer to Stevie Van Zandt. He liked the fact that I was interested in him, and by the third day he felt comfortable enough to say to me, 'Hey, Jim? To be honest with you, we're probably not gonna go down that whole stadium road that youse guys went down.' I nodded. 'We had a meeting about it, and we reckon it's not for us.'

I smiled and said: 'You might not have that quandary . . .'

It's a Glasgow thing.

38
A Plague of Lighthouse Keepers

It was the best of times, it was the worst of times.

– Charles Dickens, *A Tale of Two Cities*

I am spending Christmas 2019 with Yumie. One morning, I say to her, 'I've been lucky this year. I usually get a bad cold or flu every winter. Not this time. I hope I can keep that going, with the tour around the corner.'

Her reply is quite strange. 'You should take all the precautions,' she says, rather ominously. 'You should really wear a mask and gloves.'

I turn to her. 'Who do you think I am, Michael Jackson? How ridiculous!'

'There's this thing going on in China at the moment,' she continues. 'People are getting locked up in their houses . . .'

Yumie reads the Asian news every day, and occasionally some of the things she reports back to me seem a little outlandish. I think this newsflash definitely falls into that category.

I smile and put it out of my mind.

Kerr/

What can I say? I called it wrong.

Simple Minds' '40 Years of Hits' tour was due to kick off in Stavanger on 28 February 2020. Every morning during rehearsals, I would look at the news and see it coming. For the first ten days of the tour, we rode our luck. We played two concerts in one day in Copenhagen, because they announced

309

that Denmark was shutting down the next day, when we were due to play our second show. It was as though we were trying to outrun this virus as it swept over the world. But it was impossible.

On 11 March we had to shut up shop, as everyone did. There were tears backstage. Tears for the present and fears for an uncertain future. The hype at the time was that people would never attend concerts again. Venues were going to have to invest millions of pounds in new air conditioning. We could never again go in elevators. It was completely surreal.

My plan was to quickly return to Scotland and then join Yumie, who had gone straight home to France. I was still sorting out my dad's will and I had to organise things in Glasgow and sign some documents. By this time, even the lawyers were closing their offices. I got caught out. The borders closed. I thought, *Well, if I'm going to be trapped, there are worse places to be trapped than Loch Earn.*

I didn't see Charlie all spring or summer. I was up in the hills on my own. He was in Holland. When life started opening up again, I was able to be with Yumie in Nice. It looked like the worst was over. Germany was allowing people to move around, and Charlie and I decided to go to Hamburg to write and record in a studio there, where we knew the engineers. We spent six weeks working in Hamburg before it all started again.

Burchill/

When the 2020 tour was cancelled, I went to Holland with Win Hong. I was there quite a while. When travel was permitted, Jim and I decided we would go to Hamburg and start recording. From there, with the second lockdown imminent, we headed down to Taormina. Jim had said, 'Look, the hotel is empty. We could work there.' What else were we going to do?

We set up the gear at Villa Angela and went to work for most of the rest of the year. It was just the two of us in the hotel.

We commandeered a little room in the middle of the building with panoramic views out to Etna. We could have occupied a much bigger suite, but for some reason we felt better working in this tiny space. After forty-five years, we went back to the bedroom.

We established a routine. I would come in at midday. Jim would arrive at 2 p.m. We worked together until late afternoon, then I might continue for a few hours after that. We did that almost every day. It was very productive.

Kerr/

We had to keep creative. I'd had a double whammy. Not only could the band not tour, but people couldn't travel or go on holiday. When COVID first hit, Villa Angela had shut up straight away and we had to look after all the staff there.

Enter me and Charlie. We set up our gear in a room in the empty hotel. The neighbours knew we were there, and they would send up top-quality food parcels. It felt very strange. Becalmed. There is a great song on *Pawn Hearts*, one of our favourite prog-rock albums, by Van der Graaf Generator. It's called 'A Plague of Lighthouse Keepers'. When the pair of us came to Sicily during the second lockdown, I thought of that song. I had an image of us as two stranded lighthouse keepers, high up in the rocky hills, looking out to sea and over to Etna.

There were many beautiful days, and between working Charlie and I could get outside and walk. Nothing was open apart from one supermarket. We queued up with everyone else for the vaccines. Otherwise, there wasn't a soul around.

Once again, music bailed me out – thanks to Charlie. As we have done so often, we lost ourselves in our work. Disappeared into our own world. Why do we make art? Apart from how it makes us feel, it's the way we make sense of the world and all its madness. Charlie and I were always close, but our bond was compounded in those weeks and months.

311

In the middle of arguably the most profound societal event in our lifetimes, here we were again: just me and him in a room, tinkering away.

It was a contemplative time. We had the chance to sit and think of all that had been and everything that might be coming. Regarding the line from *A Tale of Two Cities*, COVID was a game of two halves. Not for a second to underplay the tragedy of it all and the profoundly traumatising impact it had on so many people, but the pause it enforced on our lives gave many of us a chance not only to be creative, but to think things through.

I was already strolling towards the idea of getting Italian residency. COVID made me run. Up to that point it had been solely my plan. Then Charlie said he was going to do it, too. Not only that, but he wanted to live in Taormina. That came out of the blue. As much as we are both Italophiles, he had always been based around northern Italy and Rome and had a circle of friends there. He really liked Taormina, but it was my patch. At first, I thought Charlie was only coming here to get registered, but it turns out that wasn't the point. The point was that he had fallen for Taormina, and he wanted to stay.

We had to rush to register as Italian residents before the Brexit transition period concluded at the end of December 2020. After that, the bureaucracy would have been ten times knottier. We decided to do it on the Friday and by the Monday it was on. We hadn't even told our partners. As we have done so many times in our lives, the pair of us were running away. It will be another few years yet before we get Italian passports, and the small print is quite complicated, but we are now Italian domiciled.

Charlie didn't come to live in Taormina to be near me – although perhaps he would tell you differently. I just know that I'm glad he's here.

Burchill/

At some point while we were working at Jim's hotel, I thought, *I'm going to buy a house here. This is the perfect place for me.* We had both been toying for years with the idea of living in Italy as permanent residents. In the end, we decided quite impulsively. It was the end of October, and it was going to complicate matters hugely if we did it after December 2020.

We now have residency status, which means we can spend as much time as we like in Italy without having to worry about visas and 180-day limits and all the bureaucracy. We can spend an entire year here. Our entire lives.

Kerr/

Simple Minds finally went back on the road at the end of March 2022, two years after the wheels had stopped rolling. During the pandemic we thought a lot about our crew, and we did what we could to help. The first time we were able to come together, it was a great feeling to see all the men and women who work with us again. To have our team in the same room was a fantastic moment.

And it was great to play, to get this magical force that helps us comprehend the world back up and running. Touring was still very strange to begin with. The surrealness hadn't entirely disappeared. We had bubbles and testing every day. We were doing meet and greets where we couldn't meet anyone. We found ourselves waving at fans from miles away. Photobombing them. It took a while for the enforced absurdity of it all to subside.

I feel we have been making up for lost time ever since. In the period immediately following the pandemic, Simple Minds released our nineteenth studio album, *Direction of the Heart*. We recorded a live version of *New Gold Dream (81, 82, 83, 84)* at Paisley Abbey, which was released as an album and broadcast on Sky Arts. We have issued new standalone tracks such as 'Act of Love' and 'Your Name in Lights'. Joss

Crowley directed an acclaimed Simple Minds documentary, *Everything Is Possible*. We have toured all over the world, including the USA, South America, Europe, Australia and New Zealand. In the summer of 2025, we played Bellahouston Park in Glasgow, the biggest Simple Minds show in almost forty years.

We have barely stopped. The years after COVID have been some of the busiest and most enjoyable in the entire history of the band.

39
The Art of the Setlist

Great things are not done by impulse, but by a series of
small things brought together.

– Vincent van Gogh

Hydro, Glasgow

29 March 2024	30 March 2024
*	*
Waterfront	*Waterfront*
Love Song	*I Travel*
Sons and Fascination	*Premonition*
Sweat in Bullet	*Sweat in Bullet*
This Fear of Gods	*This Fear of Gods*
Let There Be Love	*Let There Be Love*
Solstice Kiss	*She's a River*
Once Upon a Time	*Once Upon a Time*
Glittering Prize	*Glittering Prize*
Promised You a Miracle	*Promised You a Miracle*
New Gold Dream (81, 82, 83, 84)	*New Gold Dream (81, 82, 83, 84)*
Belfast Child	*Belfast Child*
Someone Somewhere in Summertime	*Someone Somewhere in Summertime*
Don't You (Forget About Me)	*Don't You (Forget About Me)*
Encore:	*Encore:*
Book of Brilliant Things	*Book of Brilliant Things*
See the Lights	*See the Lights*
Alive and Kicking	*Alive and Kicking*
Sanctify Yourself	*Sanctify Yourself*

Kerr/

There is never a completely perfect setlist.

Going back to the very first Simple Minds gig, I recognised the importance of getting it right. We needed a big impression at the start and a big impression at the end. I think we pulled that off. In between, however, it's entirely possible we were fumbling around.

Nearly half a century later, I still come up with the setlist each night, but it's always on the understanding that anyone can say, *Are you sure about that? How about this?* I will always listen, whether it's coming from Charlie or the band or the sound and lighting engineers.

Different kinds of gigs call for different formats. If we are playing on a summer evening in a park in Nîmes and there are lots of families in the audience, it's probably not the night for 'Premonition'. They don't really want a song about Pol Pot. If we do play it, the hardcore fans at the front and online might get excited and make it seem a much bigger deal than it is. But in the room, it's most likely not going down so well.

Being out on tour continuously, doing it night after night, year after year, decade after decade, is how you learn how best to put a show together. A good set has to tick a lot of different boxes. The building blocks start with the songs that pay the rent; the ones that the majority of fans would go nuts if we didn't play. *Hey, hey, hey, hey!* But we also want to go back to the early days and show the roots and the origin of the band. We have fans from many different eras. A good set will show the path we have taken: all the big hits, some things people don't expect to hear, perhaps a cover no one would have thought of. Start with a big impact, bring it down, have a dramatic centrepiece mid-set, perhaps a big tearjerker, and then whip it all up at the end.

I think the sets we performed at the Hydro in Glasgow, at the end of March 2024, were almost perfect. We played a handful of quite obscure tracks near the start. I said to the crowd: 'Don't worry, you're going to hear all the big songs.' I felt them relax. 'But first we're going to play the diddy songs.' The comment was tongue in cheek. As we all now know, the 'diddy' songs are actually the great songs.

There will always be the hardcore for whom even fifty songs wouldn't be enough; they would want us to play fifty-five. But a great setlist must almost have the meter of a good movie or play. You can't throw in songs willy-nilly. There is a story being told.

Burchill/

All backstage flare-ups aside, Jim is very good at choosing the setlist. I'll make suggestions here and there, but very rarely. I might suggest switching the order of a song or two. We brought 'Sons and Fascination' into the set in 2024, and I questioned whether we should be playing that song so early in the show. Having just built up momentum, we then went into a relatively obscure track. 'No,' said Jim. 'It works.' Our keyboard player Erik Ljunggren recently input a few ideas regarding the setlist, and Jim explained to him why some of them wouldn't work. It was fascinating because it isn't necessarily obvious. The obvious route is to slip in a hit every three songs, but that doesn't consider the wider ebb and flow of a good set.

There are Simple Minds songs that we feel are twinned. They don't sound like each other, necessarily, but they share a certain sonic sensibility. An example of interchangeable songs are 'The American' and 'Up on the Catwalk', and 'Love Song' and 'I Travel'. We have a few of these couplings. We draw analogies with football teams: *We've got a couple of decent guys in the midfield. Who do you play?* We can vary it from night to night and the pace of the set won't change.

Pacing is a big factor. We will talk about that aspect a lot after a show. A post-mortem would usually be in the form of certain songs getting the blame for a dip and perhaps being

317

moved or even dropped as a result. There is always something to be said about what could have been better.

When I am on stage, I am mainly checking out the audience and I can feel when they aren't connecting with a song. I sometimes have a problem with 'New Gold Dream (81, 82, 83, 84)'. It's a big track for a lot of our fans. The rhythm is so propulsive, yet sometimes when we perform it, I look out and see a mass of people not moving. I think, *Why is that? What are they not getting?* Innumerable times I have gone out front with the sound engineer during soundcheck to hear what's happening in the track, before altering things within it to make it more comprehensible. Some nights it is brilliant. Occasionally, it just doesn't fly.

We are also aware that what constitutes a hit changes from country to country. In Portugal, for example, 'Let There Be Love' gets the same reaction as 'Don't You (Forget About Me)'. Portugal was a slow burn for Simple Minds. It didn't really pick up on us until the nineties.

We put a lot of thought into planning the show. The band, the pacing, the setlist, the drama. We try to make it theatrical and have a sense of a plot running all the way through. Many people who come to our concerts each night are returning fans. People will come up to me and say, 'This is my one-hundred and twentieth Simple Minds show and my fourth on this tour.' I think, *Good, because you will have heard different songs each time.* It gets harder trying to pick songs from the catalogue, because inevitably we have to leave out one that might be someone's favourite.

It's a nice problem to have.

40

Where Are We Now?

The noblest art is the art of making people happy.

– P. T. Barnum

For everyone involved with Simple Minds today, there are only two rules.

1. *Be nice, and therefore appreciative of what we all have here and how we get to live and work.*
2. *Be great. Every time.*

Kerr/

These days the primary reason Simple Minds exists is to play live.

And the primary reason we play live is to make people happy.

In my impetuous, self-righteous youth, I would never have been heard to say that. We wanted to blow people's minds, grab them by the throat and *destroy* them. Certain aspects of that mentality remain useful, but that's not what Simple Minds is about any more. We are in the business of generating human happiness.

Simple Minds today is not the Simple Minds of 1978, or 1981, or 1985, or 2005. That might disappoint some people, albeit mostly those who no longer turn up at our concerts to test their disapproval.

Some long-term fans get frustrated that we haven't reunited with the original lineup for a final victory lap. I understand.

They want their Mount Rushmore back. They want to relive their high-school prom. The evocation of the past that music stirs up is as strong as any photograph. I would love to see the Lisbon Lions play again. I'd love to see the Spiders from Mars. For lots of different reasons, it isn't going to happen. Change is inevitable. Everything in the material world is mercurial. The only constants in life are transition and evolution. People come and they go.

In order to be the band we have wanted to be at different stages of our career, Simple Minds have refused to be frozen in time or tied to any external perceptions of how we should present ourselves. When we started, it was a boy's game. But the boys had to grow up. I felt this particularly when I married Chrissie Hynde. From 1985 onwards, in Simple Minds we have had Robin Clark, Lisa Germano, Catherine Anne Davies, Berenice Scott, Sarah Brown, Cherisse.

It's not for nothing that we work with these people; Sarah is a work of art on her own. I am proud that today's version of Simple Minds is more of an ensemble than five old guys rocking out. As it evolved from being a collective, a gang, to becoming solely Charlie's and my thing, we worked hard to continue presenting Simple Minds as a band. Recently, Ian sent me a proposal for some artwork. I felt bad because the team had worked hard, and I sensed they were pleased with it. But the images were just me and Charlie. We looked like the Kray Twins.

We still want to evoke a group feeling around everything we do; to present the latest version of Simple Minds while still being true to its original essence. Performing many of our early songs with different musicians allows the material to find fresh meaning across subsequent generations. It is something of a conjuring trick, or perhaps an optical illusion, but I believe we have learned to do it well. We might be done with our past, but patently our past is not yet done with us.

Burchill/

Until recently, when it came to recording new Simple Minds music, there was no band. Mostly, there weren't even any other musicians. I played all the music: the guitars, the bass, the keyboards. The drums were programmed.

The earlier albums were different, because we didn't know what we were doing. That's what made them great. We were taking a flyer, working very fast, gambling with attitude. We soaked up every kind of stimuli we could get our hands on, and somehow it came through in the music. I still can't quite explain how that process works. We had no time to think. We just did it.

Losing that kind of spontaneity can be a problem. Once you permit yourself the luxury of time to think, it's possible to procrastinate all day long. Part of me missed the idea of going into the studio for four weeks with a band to make an album. The benefits of that approach are huge, because when you work fast, I'm convinced the ideas are stronger. You might make mistakes, but without the time to ponder, the subconscious usually works much better and throws out fresh and interesting results. And you don't get bored. That's a big factor. After many years of not recording as a band, we have recently tried that approach again.

Our writing process has also changed from the early days. It's not as though I sit down with a guitar and Jim pulls out some lyrics and we go back and forth for hours until we have a song. It doesn't work like that. As we get older, time management is an issue. It is difficult for us both to sit in the same room for eight hours a day. We do so much independently of one another. Once I have got the music to a certain point on my own, Jim comes in – and when that happens, the whole thing transforms dramatically. He will then go away and work on shaping his words and his melodies.

Live, Simple Minds is a different beast entirely. On stage, the power and presence of the band are still crucial. By the

321

third week of a tour, we can all feel it on stage. We are all tuning in and that magic alchemy occurs that can only happen when a group of people make music together.

Kerr/

When we started Simple Minds, there were three things we wanted: to be in a great live band, to take it around the world, and to get a life out of it. That holy trinity still drives us. We *STILL* want to be a great live band. We *STILL* want to take it around the world. We *STILL* dedicate our lives to doing this. In that sense Simple Minds remains a work in progress.

Charlie and I retain a working man's mentality. We came from not much and we have given our whole lives to our vocation, because that's who we are. That's what we do. We've done the miles. We're the real deal. That might not mean much to anyone else, but it means the world to us, and we work hard to protect it.

I understand that our be-great-every-time rule isn't always possible. People get ill or have difficult days. We're only human. But you should *want* to be brilliant every night. When it falls short of that, Charlie, in particular, is merciless. Because at this stage of the game with Simple Minds, he and I are not just showing up for the sake of it. We're saying, *This is what we have done with our lives.* With so much at stake, playing live is a constantly replenishing challenge. We live on our wits every night. It's not enough that the audience love us. We want them to go away thinking it was much better than they thought it could be.

We never forget that we would be nothing without the support of the audience who come to see us, nor that every date on a tour is a special occasion. Concert tickets have become luxury items. People are not only paying a lot of money, but they are also investing their time and their emotions. They bought the ticket eight months in advance and have been looking forward to the concert for a long time.

They have booked hotels and restaurants. Often, they are meeting up with old friends. History is being disinterred and shared. We have a responsibility to give them not just a gig, but a show. There has to be something of the spectacle about it, rather than just five jowly guys wearing black. That has led to the kind of band we now are.

We have to deliver every night. A quality in performers that isn't highlighted often enough is consistency. Of the half-a-dozen times I saw Bowie, on three occasions I had been doing this job long enough to tell that he didn't want to be there. U2 always want to be there. Springsteen always wants to be there. Costello always wants to be there. Eddie Vedder always wants to be there. Ricky Ross always wants to be there. Simple Minds, I can assure you, always want to be there.

In terms of numbers, we are playing to more people than ever before. It doesn't seem too long ago that we were flatlining. I'm thankful that we are still getting a chance to prove ourselves.

If the stage is Simple Minds' natural habitat, where does the album fit into this picture?

When Charlie and I were growing up the album was our holy tablet. The album was how we viewed the world, and how the world saw us. The album was how bands made money. It was all about those twelve sacred inches of vinyl.

The industry has changed beyond measure. Nowadays, the album is a diminished currency. Fewer people listen to them than ever before. An artist can be in the top ten after selling only 5,000 copies. It is a phantom echo of how things once were.

For a band like Simple Minds, there are increasingly scant rewards for saying to the world, *Here are our twelve new songs.* Beyond stimulating the core fan base, the best we can hope for is that a new track will get some radio play or turn up in a TV series or a movie, or that one or two songs might hold their own within the live set. That's the ultimate deciding factor: a great Simple Minds song is one that demands to be played live because it has all the trademarks, the allure and impact of classic Simple Minds. That is a tall order when you have written 250 songs and dozens of hits.

These days, I am drawn to the idea of immediacy, in both the way we record and how we release the results. Charlie and I will always write songs, and Simple Minds will continue to release new music, but I have lost my hunger for being in a recording studio for months on end, listening to a piece of music over and over again.

As Simple Minds approach fifty years at the coalface, more and more often Charlie and I are asked to reflect on the past rather than the future. Looking back doesn't come naturally to either of us. It's hard to be objective about our legacy.

Our band means different things to different people. If I was standing in an elevator – those sliding doors again – and someone asked what kind of group I am in, at any given point over the past half century the answer could be wildly different. We started off as a punk and post-punk band, then became an art-rock band. People have called us electro, stadium rock, a bit prog. Celtic rock. Pop. New romantic. It goes on and on.

Thanks to the imagination and the talent of everyone involved, we could be all those things and more and yet still always be intrinsically Simple Minds. That in itself is quite an achievement: continually to evolve without losing iden-tity. It's not chameleon-like, because a chameleon alters its colours to fit in. We are shapeshifters. We have frequently changed form because we like so many different styles of music, and the genius of the guys was they could play it all. I pay tribute to that.

I don't believe we have ever fitted into any niche or box, any genre or scene. I think of the images on the cover of *Sons and Fascination*. Simple Minds have always been somewhat blurred, in the best sense. Evolving and dissolving.

Burchill/

What is this thing called Simple Minds? I still don't really know. I can't figure out objectively what we do or where we sit in the big picture. I feel our status is fluid. We have been a very successful band over many years, yet I still feel we exist somewhere out on the margins. We have always been quite eccentric. We've never been part of any club. It is probably one reason Jim and I are so close, because we aren't part of a gang. We're not aloof, but by default we're not joiners. We have never had loads of celebrity pals. We never curried favour with the London music press.

If we hear somebody say, 'That sounds like Simple Minds,' Jim and I will respond: 'Which Simple Minds?' I see our story in chapters. Each new period was charged with different emotions, different sounds, different colours. Something we always felt we had to do, and we really committed to it, was change with every album. We made sure that we weren't making the same record over and over again or resting on formulas.

We still crave new colours, but it becomes harder. One problem Jim and I have in our creative relationship is that we essentially think the same way. Two days ago, we went for a walk. I hadn't seen him for a few weeks, and we both said the exact same thing at the exact same time. It's a bit strange. In the context of the band at this point, we need greater objectivity. Jim has been good at fostering that. He has opened the door for other people to get involved in the writing. I agree with that. If he can get inspired by something from the outside and I can then take it away and turn it into something that makes sense in our world, I think that's a great model for us going forward and still being creative.

We have spent a lifetime doing this. We have made mistakes, but I don't think we have ever done anything that we felt wasn't for the right reasons. The results have been good and bad. Much of it was out of our control. My philosophy has always been, *Keep moving.* If you keep going and regularly produce music of good quality, at some point you arrive at a place where what you are becomes somewhat undeniable. Even if our music doesn't appeal, it can't be denied that it takes some kind of talent to stay around for this length of time.

As many other artists have done, including Bob Dylan and Bruce Springsteen, in 2022 we sold the Simple Minds catalogue. Jim and I deliberated long and hard on the pros and cons of selling our publishing and future royalties to BMG. Age was a big factor. Approaching seventy, being offered a lump sum upfront rather than a drip feed over decades warranted serious consideration. Who knows where the industry is going to go? We felt that this was a window that could close very soon, and the long-term certainty it gave us and our families appealed. We took all these things into account and concluded it was the right time.

The albums Simple Minds made from 1990 onwards were a massive factor in the deal. It is satisfying to think that all the work Jim and I did to keep the band going after 1989 paid off. Incidentally, the figures bandied around in public whenever an artist's catalogue is sold are wildly overexaggerated. Whatever we got, however, we got because we have stayed together for so long, released so many records and written so many songs that are still played and valued.

You can't put a price on that.

41

Harvest

The tragedy of old age is not that one is old,
but that one is young.

— Oscar Wilde, *The Picture of Dorian Gray*

Now.

There is a particular road here in Taormina. It is not one we travel down every day. Or even every month.

Today we are driving along it, heading to the airport in Catania as we leave the comforts and certainties and complexities of home to go on tour for the umpteenth time in our lives.

It is such a beautiful vista. Even after twenty-five years, it takes my breath away.

I am suddenly acutely aware that we are not going to see our home again for many months. Charlie is quietly gazing out of the window. I know he is thinking the same.

As I look one last time at the view, I appreciate it so much more. I think, Oh, I wish I'd come down this road last week!

As Taormina vanishes into the distance, it occurs to me that this is an apt metaphor for life itself.

Kerr/

I have an old shack in the hills above Taormina, surrounded by forty olive trees. Most days this week I have been up there, helping to gather the harvest.

It's a beautifully simple process. We lay nets on the ground under each tree, shake the tree hard and then clamber all

327

around it, combing the olives into the net. Once they are gathered, we take them to the press.

My nephew works in Hotel Villa Angela. His house is next to the shack, and he has some trees, too. Between us we will press enough olive oil to see us through the year. I will pass around bottles as gifts. It's a very Sicilian thing to do. Handy for keeping in with the local dignitaries and such.

The harvest is a big deal here. It is a social event and a family affair. Everybody helps. Everyone brings food and, in the afternoon, we break off from work to have a picnic. There are now three generations of Kerrs taking part: me, my nephew and his little boy, who is only two and already a true Sicilian. He loves throwing the olives into the bucket. Charlie was conspicuously missing in action, although I don't doubt he will be first in the queue to sample the results. It may well be his Christmas present.

There is something mystical about the process. A ritual very similar to what we have been doing this week has been enacted in Sicily for thousands of years. To the Greeks and the Romans, the oil was sacred. It gave them light. It gave them sustenance. It gave so much.

It gives me so much, too.

I realised recently that I have spent almost half my adult years based out of Sicily. I like my life here. Dawn is the awakening hour. I need no alarm. I am always eager to greet the day, whatever it might bring. I am fortunate: I have a body that feels invigorated. No major aches or pains to speak of yet, and a mind keen to test itself.

Whatever creative impetus I have is always much more powerful at the beginning of the day, when the coming hours overflow with promise. My mornings consist of between two and three hours reading, everything from low-brow to high literature. I've been reading a book on the life of Harpo Marx called *Harpo Speaks*. Yesterday morning it was a modern history of Ireland. The previous day I dipped back in to *The*

Master and Margarita. What a luxury! Within my reading, thoughts will usually bubble up, and I will break to write something down or make notes.

Later, I'll go walking for at least an hour. The hills in and around Taormina are steep enough to get my lungs firing and my heart thudding as the hotel shuttle buses zoom past. I do it for my general good health, but I'm also doing it to keep in shape for touring. The worst thing imaginable would be to go on stage feeling tired. I have to make the effort, have to keep the energy going.

I don't like to sit in the hotel restaurant like a lord of the manor. I prefer to cook and eat my own simple food. Lentils, beans, tomatoes. Perhaps some fresh fish. The shape of my afternoons depends on what the obligations are. There will be calls and correspondence to deal with. Podcasts. Writing. More reading. I'm not lying on the beach. I may go there to look at the waves for forty-five minutes, but the brain will be whirring. Charlie and I are still learning every day. Still interested, still curious.

I love the Bowie quote: 'Ageing is an extraordinary process where you gradually become the person you always should have been.' By now, I am what I am. As life goes on, I need less. That's the irony. By the time you can afford it all, or most of it, you think, *I don't want much more than the other guy.* Any day is a great day where you wake up healthy and no one you love is ill.

Our society is eternally obsessed with youth and how to retain it. I haven't had any great problem accepting the realities of ageing. I'd love to have been taller, or more handsome, but there is a certain dignity in saying, *This is who I am. I'm fine with it, so you'll just need to be fine with it as well.* I'm holding out for a sponsor's logo for the bald patch.

I have a theory: your fans want you to look *good . . . ish*. They don't want you to look like you've been in the gym for eight hours, because that's not terribly relatable. But they still want a hint of rock and roll swagger, and to know that you are capable of throwing the shapes. It's about energy. Heat. What you radiate. That has been the story of our lives from day one. In my mid-sixties, I feel like the same curious kid I have always been. Supremely positive about what is in front of me, continually caught up in the wonder of being alive.

Given the rewards that have come our way, for the most part Charlie and I live privileged lives rather than opulent ones. We certainly stay in luxurious places on tour and, when time permits, we are not averse to taking all the band and crew out to a top-class restaurant on nights off.

Having already looked after our parents and our children, while also having created a very nice lifestyle for ourselves, we realised some time ago that the most valuable currency is not money but time. We all have a limited stock of that. I hear people say that age is just a number or that it doesn't matter. Maybe so, but *time* matters.

There is only so much left. We have been very selfish in our lives and with the people around us. They know they don't come second, but they do come second in a sense when it comes to time. At a certain point, enough is enough. You are obliged to give the people you love time as well.

All these thoughts raise the question of how we eventually put Simple Minds to bed. Not imminently, but within the long-term plans – and we have always had plans – we have started addressing when and how the curtain falls. We think of Simple Minds as a great story, and a great story deserves a fitting end. A graceful and dignified one. We may not have a say in it. Hopefully, we will. It will all be about seeing how we feel, what the demand is, what the desire is. The level of energy is a huge factor.

I think Charlie will be ready before I am. What I don't want is a situation where I push him to continue for longer than he would really like, simply because he doesn't want to be perceived as letting the side down. That would be unfair to him, and it would be unfair for me not to consider it. I have a different kind of restlessness. The greatest thrill I get in life comes from being in front of an audience and feeling of value in that moment. When that ends, I know I will miss it hugely. However, at a certain point I hope I will think, *I've done it, I did it as well as I could, and I don't want to do it without energy or in a diminished way.*

When I think about the end of the band I inevitably think of where it will leave our friendship. Charlie living in Taormina has changed my view on that. We have found our place here now, and it's getting harder to imagine us being anywhere else. Had we not been living in the same town, our relationship might have become, not less important to each of us, but perhaps more distant. Charlie isn't a great one for email. He hates social media. We both have fulfilling lives outside of the band.

Living in the same place, it is much easier for those lives to include each other. Simple Minds or no Simple Minds, I don't think much will change between us.

Burchill/

The days are flying past. Time is racing on.

I spend almost every day writing or playing music. Creativity keeps us mentally young, and the lifestyle keeps us physically sharp. When you're working within music and touring regularly, by default you feel youthful. Playing guitars and jumping about the stage are essentially child's play.

Jim often says one of the great things about Taormina is that it excels at all the things you loved as a child. Great pizza. Fantastic ice cream. The beach. Zipping around on Vespas. This is a healthy place, but you need to be healthy to live here. It's all hills. I've had niggling problems with my knee and my leg, and within a week of being back here they vanished. The food is great. The light is incredible. Taormina keeps us feeling young, and so do our partners. Being with women in their early fifties, we don't get a chance to dwell on getting old.

We feel young but we are aware that the process of ageing must be acknowledged. These days, Jim and I gravitate towards taking time off without talking about it directly. Tacitly, we block off space in our schedule and know that we're giving ourselves the downtime we need.

Before we went on the road in January 2024, both Jim and I were perhaps slightly lacking in enthusiasm as the date of departure edged closer. Jim's feeling could be summarised as, *Let's get it done. We just need to do it.* I told him I felt much the same way. The previous tour had been so tiring. Post-COVID, the dates had been rearranged, and they were jumbled all over the place. Everybody was great and we got through it, but it was quite hard.

By the time the 2024 tour was ready to start, however, we were energised and up for it. When it comes to the crunch, we always are. It helps that touring has become a lot easier. The buses are very comfortable. The hotels are great. The pacing is good. We have plenty of days off, but not too many that we lose momentum. You have got to appreciate what a fantastic life this is. And always, when we go on stage, we have the payoff that sustains it all.

We have sacrificed a lot in our personal lives to do this job that brings us so much pleasure. We've both had divorces, and our children have probably felt the effects of too much involvement in Simple Minds. But that was the deal in 1978 when we decided to go into this full scale. It's easier now. Jim and I are lucky. Our partners totally understand and, in any case, they come out regularly when we're on tour. And the kids are grown up. They've got their own lives.

To place a fitting full stop on it all would be very satisfying. Jim first mentioned the idea of planning the final chapter of Simple Minds one day when we were out walking. To be honest, it shocked me. Aside from his millennium wobble, it was the first time I'd ever heard Jim talking about *not doing it*. I started crunching the numbers: *When? How long have we got?* After talking in more depth about it, however, I realised that the endgame wasn't anywhere near as imminent or as clear-cut as that. When we started mapping out all the future plans that we have, I said to him, 'You know, we're talking about ten years here! Literally.'

We aren't anywhere close to the end yet, but the idea of how it might look is percolating. That's a positive thing. We definitely don't want Simple Minds to fizzle out into some tawdry parade of bits and pieces. We talk about that a lot.

As for what our post-band lives would look like, I think Jim could spend a lot more time writing, but not specifically for music. He has so many outlets that he could pursue. Likewise, while I would never stop making music, it would be an opportunity for me to work on more abstract ideas. Not necessarily for soundtracks or films but exploring areas where we wouldn't go with Simple Minds.

Whatever happens, Jim and I would continue to collaborate in some form. I'm certain of that. The process the two of us began when we were so young is something I don't see ever ending. I'm always going to be writing music; he is always going to be writing words and melodies; we are always going to be talking about music, books, life, art. At some point we would find a way of putting these things together again, whether in the context of a band or some other way.

I know one thing. When the time does come, I'll be OK with it, and I'll be ready. I try to use the idea as the fuel and the motivation to enjoy every day.

As for the precise nature of the end of our story, I will leave that up to Jim. He's good at that. I know he will do Simple Minds proud.

Outro Music

'Our Secrets Are the Same (Slight Return)'

(Burchill/Kerr)

Burchill/

I'll see Jim later this afternoon.

At the moment we've been talking a lot about a couple of books. He sent me a link to say how great the one he's currently reading is. I replied: 'I know, I read it two years ago!' It's Fintan O'Toole's *We Don't Know Ourselves*, which is about the boom and bust that happened in Ireland while Jim and I were living there. It's fantastic. He's a great writer. Then there's a fascinating book written by the Irish economist David McWilliams, called *Money*.

When we go to lunch in Taormina we talk about books, family, food, football. We go through periods when our chats and phone calls will be mostly about Simple Minds. But in 'off' mode when we're in Sicily, we hardly ever talk about the band when we are socialising. There are so many other subjects to discuss, or a bit of gossip to pick apart. When we walk through the town, we bump into many of our friends, but we rarely socialise with them. Occasionally we will go down to a friend's restaurant, but mostly Jim and I socialise with one another. He comes down to mine. I go up to his. Tragic, really.

My house is a shell at the moment. I overlooked the fact that I would have nowhere to stay when they were working on it. Jim suggested I should look at the apartment he had recently bought, and it was perfect. Two bedrooms. Beautiful views. He said to me, 'It's yours until your house is ready.' This has happened a few times in the past! It got me out of a hole and I'm grateful. It is so kind of him to let me stay in his apartment indefinitely.

Before I started the process of having my house renovated, every Saturday or Sunday Jim would visit. Win Hong would make spring rolls, and we'd watch the game. We still get together for matches. Jim will always say that Celtic could be winning 4–0 in the eighty-ninth minute and I'll still be going crazy if they make a bad pass. He's just as bad. I've seen him throwing oranges at the television.

Even on tour, Jim and I sit together on the bus, and we'll talk away for a few hours on the journey. Then he will go to the back for a sleep. On the day of a show, we will often go for lunch or a walk. We haven't done it recently, because we've been travelling back and forth, but in Taormina we used to go walking every morning together up into the hills. We did that for months. We talked about everything under the Sicilian sun and had a lot of laughs.

Jim may have a different take on it, but my feeling is that we will be here until we are old, old men. And even if for some reason we aren't as physically close to each other, I would never go long periods without seeing him. We are stuck with each other.

I'm still a fan.

After we had recorded some shows on the 2024 tour for the *Live in the City of Diamonds* album, I went through the tapes to ensure that everything was fine before it was mixed. I was struck by just how good Jim's vocals were. He was considering re-singing a handful of things, because when you're on stage jumping around you sometimes lose a bit, vocally. I called him: 'Jim, you don't need to touch this. We should leave it exactly as this.' His vocals on the album are brilliant, as they are every night. I tell him he is getting better and better, and I believe it.

I have always viewed Jim's writing as a series of different phases. *New Gold Dream (81, 82, 83, 84)* is very optimistic, imagistic and colourful, capturing a young man and a young band with the whole wide world in front of them. Towards the end of the eighties and into the nineties the writing became more reflective and more personal. Recently, it has become much more focused. Jim has written and narrated a prize-winning BBC Radio 4 documentary on Jim Morrison. He has penned forewords for books. He posts thoughtful mini essays on social media.

I have started to realise the extent to which all his writing really reflects the kind of person he is. No matter the stage of our career, one of the most telling features running through his lyrics is an incredible unselfishness. His writing has very rarely been about him or his problems. It has never been self-indulgent. It has never been nihilistic or petty. It is still filled with wonder and positivity, optimism and curiosity at the world.

Jim's true character shines through in his words.

Kerr/

I went round to Charlie's new apartment the other night to watch the match.

Celtic got absolutely hammered but, somehow, we managed to come away with a draw. Anyone peering through the window would have seen two grown men reduced to Beavis and Butthead. Screaming at the television – at different times, of course, because after a while one of us would need to have a rest. We were taking it in shifts to have a combined heart attack. I like to think that we are two educated people with quite sophisticated tastes, but there we were, shouting at a TV screen in a small room in Sicily.

Who else is going to put up with us at this stage of the game?

On those nights, it still feels like going over to Charlie's house when we lived in the flats – except I'm still not used to seeing him wear slippers.

What is the essence of Charlie Burchill?

If it was yesterday afternoon, I would have pointed to the huge bowl of salsa he had made. It was a new talent on me: 'How long have you been practising that?' He likes to cook. He always has the best food in the fridge. We're both that way. (He always has the best wine, too, but I don't care about that.) An order of fresh ingredients had just arrived for him at the hotel. Charlie has it delivered from an Asian supermarket in Holland.

When Charlie and I are spending time together socially, we switch off from Simple Minds. It would be an insult to the importance of the band to start chatting about a new song or a tour at half-time. And there are usually other people with us, so it would be bad manners to talk business.

He has a great house in Taormina that he's completely gutting. I had recently bought another apartment, with the thought that friends or family might use it when they're visiting. It's a nice place, but no one had lived in it for years. I had to convince Charlie to move in. Characteristically, he was so reluctant to impose, but he seems happy there. He has started calling me 'The Landlord'. He sent me a message the other night. He's not really one for sending messages, but he had taken a couple of photos: *This place is great!* The guitars and keyboards were already set up, the screens and the laptops. He's very neat, Charlie. Everything is where it should be. Wherever he is staying, the ammunition is always there, ready to come alive at any minute. No matter how much noise he makes, the neighbours will fall in love with him, because they always do.

When I go to see him in the evenings there is always a feeling in the room that he has been busy. I like that. I'm much the same. It is remarkable how close our tastes are in so many respects. Admittedly, Charlie has his guitar heroes, people I wouldn't listen to like Jeff Beck and Jimmy Page; I've never been a Led Zeppelin fan, although I recognise that they were amazing. But that's about all we differ on. We have both ended up having Asian partners. Occasionally, we still have a prog-rock weekend. If he gets hooked on a book, he'll send it to me. Even our taste in home furnishings is similar. We are almost worryingly aligned. In the end, it really does make life easier.

To me, he is simply Charlie, essentially the same person I got to know when we started walking to school together over fifty years ago. First and foremost, he's a gentleman. He is so conscious of everybody's needs, no matter who they are. He has never swerved from that. Aside from when he becomes Charlie Piranha, which usually is born of frustration with the music, he is a delight to be around.

Beyond everything he has brought to my life and to Simple Minds, Charlie has always been great fun. He still is.

Ultimately, he'll either get me bumped off or I'll get him first.

Acknowledgements

The 'art of collaboration' is a practice we have pursued throughout our entire lives. Whether playing street games with childhood friends or conspiring to form a world-famous rock band, in innumerable forms it has brought the most joy and accompanying reward. Heartfelt thanks to Graeme Thomson for agreeing to collaborate with us on the telling of our story to date.

Thanks also to Ian Grenfell, Gemma Reilly-Hammond, Matthew Hamilton, Andreas Campomar and Holly Blood.

– Charlie Burchill & Jim Kerr, July 2025

Picture Credits

Section 1

P7 top (Steve Rapport/Hulton/Getty Images)

P8 bottom left (Trinity Mirror/Mirrorpix/Alamy Stock Photo)

Section 2

P9 top (Ebet Roberts/Redferns/Getty Images)

P9 middle (Ebet Roberts/Redferns/Getty Images)

P11 top (Trinity Mirror/Mirrorpix/Alamy Stock Photo)

P11 middle (Pete Still/Redferns/Getty Images)

P11 bottom (Georges De Keerle/Getty Images)

P12 top (Trinity Mirror/Mirrorpix/Alamy Stock Photo)

P12 bottom (Mick Hutson/Redferns/Getty Images)

P13 top (Rob Verhorst/Redferns/Getty Images)

P14 bottom (Simon Emmett)

P15 middle left (Marius Dobilas/Alamy Stock Photo)